COURSE CORRECTION

A Map for the Distracted University

Course Correction examines what the twenty-first-century university needs to do in order to recover its focus as a protected place for unfettered commitment to knowledge, not just as a space for creating employment or economic prosperity. The university's business, Paul W. Gooch writes, is to generate and critique knowledge claims and to transmit and certify the acquisition of knowledge. In order to achieve this, a university must have a reputation for integrity and trustworthiness, and this in turn requires a diligent and respectful level of autonomy from the state, religion, and other powerful influences. It also requires embracing the challenges of academic freedom and the effective governance of an academic community.

Course Correction raises three important questions about the twenty-first-century university. In discussing the dominant attention to student experience, the book asks, "Is it now all about students?" Second, in questioning "What knowledge should undergraduates gain?" it provides a critique of undergraduate experience, advocating a Socratic approach to education as interrogative conversation. Finally, by asking "What and where are well-placed universities?" the book makes the case against placeless education offered in the digital world, in favour of education that takes account of its place in time and space.

PAUL W. GOOCH is president emeritus and professor of philosophy at Victoria University in the University of Toronto.

UTP insights

UTP Insights is an innovative collection of brief books offering accessible introductions to the ideas that shape our world. Each volume in the series focuses on a contemporary issue, offering a fresh perspective anchored in scholarship. Spanning a broad range of disciplines in the social sciences and humanities, the books in the UTP Insights series contribute to public discourse and debate and provide a valuable resource for instructors and students.

Books in the Series

- Paul W. Gooch, *Course Correction: A Map for the Distracted University*
- Paul T. Phillips, *Truth, Morality, and Meaning in History*
- Stanley R. Barrett, *The Lamb and the Tiger: From Peacekeepers to Peacewarriors in Canada*
- Peter MacKinnon, *University Commons Divided: Exploring Debate and Dissent on Campus*
- Raisa B. Deber, *Treating Health Care: How the System Works and How It Could Work Better*
- Jim Freedman, *A Conviction in Question: The First Trial at the International Criminal Court*
- Christina D. Rosan and Hamil Pearsall, *Growing a Sustainable City? The Question of Urban Agriculture*
- John Joe Schlichtman, Jason Patch, and Marc Lamont Hill, *Gentrifier*
- Robert Chernomas and Ian Hudson, *Economics in the Twenty-First Century: A Critical Perspective*
- Stephen M. Saideman, *Adapting in the Dust: Lessons Learned from Canada's War in Afghanistan*
- Michael R. Marrus, *Lessons of the Holocaust*
- Roland Paris and Taylor Owen (eds.), *The World Won't Wait: Why Canada Needs to Rethink Its International Policies*
- Bessma Momani, *Arab Dawn: Arab Youth and the Demographic Dividend They Will Bring*
- William Watson, *The Inequality Trap: Fighting Capitalism Instead of Poverty*
- Phil Ryan, *After the New Atheist Debate*
- Paul Evans, *Engaging China: Myth, Aspiration, and Strategy in Canadian Policy from Trudeau to Harper*

COURSE CORRECTION

A Map for the Distracted University

Paul W. Gooch

UNIVERSITY OF TORONTO PRESS
Toronto Buffalo London

© University of Toronto Press 2019
Toronto Buffalo London
utorontopress.com
Printed in Canada

ISBN 978-1-4875-0490-8 (cloth)   ISBN 978-1-4875-2356-5 (paper)

∞ Printed on acid-free, 100% post-consumer recycled paper with
vegetable-based inks.

Library and Archives Canada Cataloguing in Publication

Gooch, Paul W., author
Course correction : a map for the distracted university / Paul W. Gooch.

(UTP insights)
Includes bibliographical references and index.
ISBN 978-1-4875-0490-8 (cloth). – ISBN 978-1-4875-2356-5 (paper)

1. Education, Higher – Aims and objectives.   2. Education,
Higher – Philosophy.   I. Title.   II. Series: UTP insights

LB2322.2.G66 2019   378.001   C2018-906207-X

University of Toronto Press acknowledges the financial assistance to its
publishing program of the Canada Council for the Arts and the Ontario Arts
Council, an agency of the Government of Ontario.

 Canada Council
for the Arts

Conseil des Arts
du Canada

 ONTARIO ARTS COUNCIL
CONSEIL DES ARTS DE L'ONTARIO
an Ontario government agency
un organisme du gouvernement de l'Ontario

Funded by the
Government
of Canada

Financé par le
gouvernement
du Canada

 Canadä

MIX
Paper from
responsible sources
FSC FSC® C016245
www.fsc.org

For all those from whom I've learned,
my colleagues,
my students,
my family:
in gratitude

Contents

Preface

Perhaps, like me, you remember the first time you visited a university with the thought that you might study there. I was near the end of high school, on a road trip through parts of the province of Quebec. As we drove through one town a small university came into view, the summer sun on its buildings, promising the prospect of an undergraduate education that might be had at some fabled Oxbridge college. Prominent were the Gothic chapel and the adjoining hall with academic offices. Classrooms and laboratories, residence halls, and the library completed the main quadrangle. A few months later I sent in my application, applying as well to the university in my home city. When comparable offers came for admission to the large urban university and to this little collegiate place, I chose the small. Partly I wanted to leave home for my university years; but the collegiate architecture also played its part in my decision. I wanted to live and study in a place that looked and felt like a university. I didn't realize then that I'd spend my whole life in universities. I moved from study at the small collegiate undergraduate place to graduate work at the large urban university, then taught at a newly established college on the outskirts of the city before moving back to the urban campus of the largest university in the country, ending up at a smaller federated university.

Over the course of my academic career, there have been large changes in the look and life of universities – not just in their size and number, but also in what's expected of them, with attendant changes that can affect the core of the institution. The university hopes to remain true to its calling, while having to listen to competing and countermanding voices that distract, threaten, and sometimes entice in other directions. I'll say more about these distractions in the Introduction, but let me prepare the way for what follows by offering a short account of what I'm up to.

When you're distracted, something unimportant (or worse, harmful) has captured your attention. You're thrown off course. To regain focus, you need to remember what's central to your enterprise and very existence. What's been happening with the university over the past four or five decades has sometimes clouded that focus, so I want to recall the university to its fundamental vocation. That means exploring the nature and functions of the university, along with the requisite values and commitments for doing well what it is supposed to do. I'm interested in explaining how the university should go about its business, the reasons it acts the way it does, and the sense of place in which it should operate. And I'll examine some of the twenty-first-century challenges to the university's identity, life, and work. I'll say a little more shortly about the approach I take in this book, but first let me point out what I don't do.

You won't find much of a historical perspective here. I don't explain how universities got to be, or how they have developed over the centuries, or what they have contributed to society. Other people have done that well. Nor is there a broad global perspective, comparing what universities are like in Europe with North American institutions, or with universities in China or India or the global South or Africa. For a time in my administrative career I belonged to an international association of university presidents, and there's much to be done in this area. But I don't do it. Instead my experience is largely, though not narrowly, Canadian. I do, however, draw on material from the United Kingdom, the United States, and Europe. We're fortunate in the quality of the Canadian university system, but although good practice has been a valuable teacher, we are not immune to our own illuminating distractions.

Several eloquent voices have been raised in defence of liberal education, as universities struggle to meet the expectations of society and students for more technical training. Although I do comment on the kind of knowledge that should form an under-graduate education, the main focus of the book is more generally about the university and knowledge – not just the knowledge that might make up the content of a liberal education.

Other advocates for universities have written about funding, often making government the object of their concern. They argue persuasively about the benefits of supporting universities, and engage in critiques about the lack of understanding of the academy among politicians. There is much to what they say, but it doesn't turn up often in this book.

Those looking for brand-new ideas about universities will be disappointed if they keep reading past this Preface. I don't think I ever use the word "disruptive" (I just mentioned it here, but didn't use it). In periods of accelerated social and technological change, things get broken apart, and that can be cause for excitement and celebration in the hope that something fresh and new will emerge. But one has to be a peculiar sort of prophet to predict what new thing will work and what won't – prophets typically discern the seeds of disaster rather than of hope. I mention as an example without comment the optimism about efficiency and efficacy that initially surrounded massively open online courses. I have no pro-phetic qualifications, and do not set out a vision for the university of the future that should or will emerge from the present.

What, then, is this book? It's an attempt at *explanation*. To explain is to describe, but also to provide reasons for, the way something is or the kind of thing it is. If we don't fully appreciate the why, we can end up messing about with something, misunderstanding or devaluing it. Explanation demands attentiveness and patience. It isn't served by snap judgments, platitudes, or witty comments. The book arises out of the conviction that the university does need explanation these days. Or, rather, we need to understand again what the university is – what it's for, how it works, and why it works the way it does. And in a world so altered by technology, we need to figure the place of the university, both in geographical and in human terms.

But "*the*" university? Shouldn't one really speak of universities in the plural instead of using the grand singular? After all, they come in so many different shapes and sizes, under significantly different kinds of governments, and with widely different educational missions. Well, sometimes I do use the plural, for substantive as well as stylistic reasons. But my interest is indeed an institution called the university. What I want to explain is that institution – what all things that are properly called by that name have, or should have, as distinguishing features. Even if it's not fashionable to assume that objects have fixed essences, the university is a human construct, created by society, and we can indeed ask whether a particular institution shares sufficiently in the features that mark off a university from other institutions.

In one way, then, asking the question I raise is like asking a question about comparative anatomy. There are many different-looking bodies of primates and members of *homo sapiens*. But they have in common brains, spinal columns, eyes, hearts, and so on. We can describe how their organs function and what they are for, and come up with an account of the basic features of a primate body. It's not quite the same, however, with universities: we aren't trying to classify objects in the world, but societal organizations. So, by thinking of the intended purposes for and the functioning of these institutions, we should be able to arrive at a decent description of their defining features. How we decide exactly what those features are is not a matter of authoritative stipulation. The decision arises from deliberation among those who are interested, knowledgeable, and committed to good reasoning. In other words, an entity can't simply declare, properly, that it is a "university" just because it wants the label. Nor can a political or religious authority properly dub something it creates a "university" if it doesn't have the features a university should have. Conversely, changing or denying the name doesn't erase the features of a properly constructed university. Of course, words can be pressed unwittingly into the purpose that their users want to accomplish; many entities call themselves universities without any warrant at all. You can find on Wikipedia a long, long list of such places under "unaccredited institutions."

Another way of stating the aim of this book, then, is to offer an account of what makes an institution a proper university, undistracted by the demands of myriad voices. It's an offering, not a pronouncement, and the issues it raises are open to debate by those with an interest in universities – politicians, policy makers, parents, board members, faculty, administrators, students, and, again, that fabled general public. The kind of deliberation invited here is an instance of what has come to be known as public philosophy. Public philosophy can be characterized in two ways, either as concerned with a particular set of questions or as a way of doing some thinking. The set of questions has to do with issues of public significance because they affect everyone or because they have been overlooked by those who decide what's important. To do public philosophy as a way of thinking is to engage in discussion and debate in order to clarify positions, understand objections, and advance good thinking. That way of thinking is, broadly speaking, *philosophizing*, even if it's not done by people with degrees in philosophy. In fact, professional philosophers can find their work improved by such interactions.[1]

That the nature and function of the university has great public significance needs no further argument, I take it, for anyone who has read this far. To describe and justify the functions of the university, then, requires clarity of thought and argument – the kind of philosophizing that may be carried on by anyone with the patience and attention to follow and assess an explanation.

This book is an invitation to that exercise.

Two additional matters before I end this Preface. First is a recognition that, just as there are assumptions about what one should expect from a university, so there are assumptions about the motives and experience of those who write about universities. Everyone thinks and writes in a particular context. Who is this author, and what are his commitments? The short answer is that this author has spent almost fifty years in the university in various roles – lecturer, professor through the usual ranks, chair, director, dean, vice-provost, president – and, of course, eight years before that as undergraduate and graduate student. If you want to know more about the contexts that have informed the thinking in this book, you can amuse yourself with the Epilogue.

The second is another recognition: of the invaluable contribution so many talented and committed colleagues have made to the experience that has shaped this book. It would be impossible to name them without inadvertently missing some, so I must make do with pointers to clusters of colleagues. Most recently, there are my senior administrative colleagues at Victoria University in Toronto, who exemplified not just the effectiveness, but also the deep personal satisfaction of collaborating as a team. Before that, there were the sterling team at the University of Toronto in the presidential and vice-presidential offices from 1994 to 2000, and the deans in the School of Graduate Studies during my terms there from 1988 to 1994. But those are just my immediate colleagues. From my students, I have learned much about their experience; from alumni, their affection and generous support for their alma mater; from Board members, their commitment and trust; from Canadian universities and their presidents, the selfless dedication, often without adequate thanks, to the scholarship and teaching so essential to a good and caring society.[2]

University administration, though not at all a solitary vocation, is often a lonely one because of the many confidences one must carry and the final responsibility for decisions that affect many people. It's done well with intelligent, wise, empathetic, and understanding support. It's done even better when that support is a partner who cares about both the institution and the administrator. Where I might have done better myself, it wasn't for lack of such support, and for this I thank, and thank again, my wife, Pauline Thompson.

Writing, though not necessarily lonely, is solitary, but it too needs proper support and circumstances. I'm grateful to Clare Hall, University of Cambridge, for a visiting fellowship in the first half of 2017, and to Victoria University for supporting my research leave.

Some of the ideas advanced here have benefited from earlier exposure and comment, for which I am grateful: material on Socratic education at Dartmouth College, on public philosophy and the university at Trent University, on place and universities at Bishop's University, on autonomy at Massey College, and on academic freedom at Clare Hall. The particular opportunities of the urban university have been discussed with colleagues at the University of Toronto's Jackman Humanities Institute. I benefited from discussing with Victoria College students many of the broad themes in the book in a section on Universities in the College's

Ideas for the World program. At the University of Toronto Press, Len Husband graciously welcomed and supported the book. Two readers for the Press, and its Manuscript Review Committee, offered encouragement and sane advice. If the readers' comments weren't always consistent, that's one point of peer review: to provoke reconsideration in the light of informed comment, and to revise, restate, or affirm accordingly. The book is better for their advice. It's also better for the acute eye of copy editor Barry Norris. Warm thanks to all.

As for the rest of my colleagues and acquaintances, should anyone caught up in this sweeping acknowledgment of my indebtedness chance to read these words, accept my heartfelt thanks for the part, large or small, you played in shaping my life in the university. Where I have said things you can't agree with, feel free to attribute my wrongheadedness to the influence of some other colleague. Take credit for what's right: I didn't make this up by myself.

COURSE CORRECTION

A Map for the Distracted University

Introduction

The twenty-first-century university is distracted by a cacophony of voices. Some are strident, some plaintive; they come in polite murmurings, subtle insinuations. The voices belong to those with power and purse, to ordinary citizens and parents, and also to members within their own communities. These sounds echo in the ears of administrators and governing boards. Even when the brashest voices are not heeded, the attention they demand makes it difficult to listen properly to what's important.

It would be too dramatic to see the university as an Odysseus struggling against constraining ropes, enchanted by the Siren sounds that promise prosperity but end in disaster. The institution itself has been around for over ten centuries; it has navigated rocks and shoals and escaped monsters. But the sailing has been seldom smooth. If not enticing Siren voices, there are often other distractions to throw the university off course: swift currents, rocks and shoals, or the drift that comes from inattention. There are concerning signs of more diversions and disturbances these days. Especially when change is rapid, it's necessary to have steady, vigilant eyes focused on the goals that define the institution and guide its continuing journey.

The university of the twenty-first century is distracted not only by competing voices, but also by large societal currents that sweep it along willy-nilly. Surely among these are the advancing waves of enrolment as participation rates have increased dramatically in many countries. The rate of population growth has been outstripped by student growth. A search for figures will confirm that undergraduate numbers in Canada have doubled since 1980; the same is true of college graduates in the United States, while in the United Kingdom undergraduate numbers have tripled.[1] This expansion undoubtedly will continue because of the widespread belief that an undergraduate degree is socially desirable and necessary for a decent job. That expectation, in turn, colours the way the university thinks of its mission and purpose. If someone wants you to behave in certain ways, and you need to keep their interest in order to function, then doing something to meet their expectations does have its own logic. So the university listens to the hopeful voices of parents and students, looking for "relevant" education that will make them job-worthy upon graduation.

It's not just families that speak this way. Government has a legitimate responsibility for creating and improving the conditions for a society with meaningful life and work, including a strong economy. If an undergraduate degree is seen as the ticket to a good job, then government will ask for the relevant indicators of success. And universities listen, posting on their websites the employment rates of their graduates as a significant measure of a successful education.

For many faculty members, such concerns have little relevance to the life of scholarship and teaching they signed up for. In fact, they worry that the university has become a corporate entity, rather than a community of scholars. The language of corporatization isn't very precise, but talk of "the corporate university" isn't about an in-house university for employee training like Disney University – which isn't a university at all, given the conditions I'm about to set out in this book.[2] Rather, it's claimed, "corporatization" is a disease that infects the very life of the university. In the corporate university, according to the Slow Professor Manifesto, "power is transferred from faculty to managers, economic justifications dominate, and the familiar 'bottom line' eclipses pedagogical and intellectual concerns."[3]

An egregious example of this brand of institution, some might argue, is Liberty University in Lynchburg, Virginia. On its website, declaring it a Christian university, is the promise that it "will equip you to enter a competitive job market" – but it's not that goal so much as its business orientation that makes it "corporate." According to the *New York Times Magazine*, Liberty University is the second-largest provider of online education in the United States, with up to 95,000 students paying for credits.[4] Its call centre houses recruiters in three hundred cubicles who are expected to sign up eight new students a day; a division of about sixty carries out recruiting from the military. Although non-profit, the latest available audited statements, for 2013, show spending of $260 million on instruction, academic support, and student services against income of $749 million in tuition and fees. Hence the "business orientation," because Liberty U seeks to make an economic profit from education despite its legal non-profit status. Its revenues assist the development of its campus, including a $3 million shooting range and a $7 million "Snowflex Centre" with year-round skiing.[5]

Although the corporate ambitions of universities in Canada and most other countries have not reached the heights of Liberty U, faculty members do express frustration with what they experience as managerial attitudes and bureaucratic requirements that erode the collegiality desired in the pursuit of knowledge. That frustration explains, perhaps, the welcome reception accorded the popular 2016 book, *The Slow Professor: Challenging the Culture of Speed in the Academy*. Its voice is one of lament about the inability of faculty to take the time for reflection, for personal interactions, and for the pleasures of pedagogy.

Undoubtedly, reasons other than "corporatization" lie behind the frustrated voices of faculty. A highly competitive system, in which hiring, advancement, and research funding depend largely on publications, requires academics at all ranks to devote most of their waking hours to activities that will advance their careers. Where that advancement is validated by outputs such as numbers of articles or citations or supervisions, rather than assessment of quality, it's easy to feel "managed" instead of valued. Even quality assessment exercises can become bureaucratic: quality audits of universities can generate hundreds of pages of documents and hundreds of hours of faculty and administrative time.[6] The highly desirable virtues of accountability and transparency in the conduct of the university's work have generated in their own way some of the vices of bureaucracy.

Collegiality is further eroded by some of the virtues of new technologies. With online library access, it's not necessary for many scholars to leave their home office to do their research and writing; with email communication, they don't have to sit in their office to answer student inquiries. So departmental offices sit empty for many hours of the month, or get shared by the occasional lecturers who come in to teach a couple of times a week. Conducting business by email looks more efficient than face-to-face meetings. But unless the issue is straightforward and non-controversial, not only does the quality of discussion suffer; time is eaten up with iterations and threads stretched out over long periods at unwelcome hours. In this world, collegiality is expressed, it seems, mainly at end-of-term parties to bid farewell to retirees.

New technologies, especially the Internet and social media, create other large and powerful waves that continue to hit the university. Technology entices, but it also brings problems trailing in its wake. Universities look for technological solutions to the challenge of teaching large numbers of students, and to online education to increase enrolment and tuition revenue. Students find greater flexibility in virtual education: instead of going to university, they may now hold the university at their fingertips. But where change is so radical, we may well ask what a Liberty-like experience has to do with a liberal education.

Throw into this sea of change the pronounced increase, among undergraduates, in problems loosely grouped as issues of mental health. Insecurity and stress are connected, according to some observers, with the way social media presents the self. Self-cutting and suicide are found among the brightest and most accomplished. Whatever the causes, the unprecedented mushrooming of counselling services require resources that are necessary distractions from the university's fundamental purposes of teaching and research – necessary, because these anxieties enervate the desire to learn. If a proper education is to take root, student voices, sometimes only murmuring their confusion and insecurities, must be heard.

Of course, not all student voices whisper anxieties; some are loud, even raucous. They are highly distracting when it comes to protests about speakers with unpopular and offensive views. The incidents in recent years have mounted, mainly in the United States but also in Canada.[7] Although a university's policy on free speech might indeed permit a controversial event, the attendant distractions, including costs and logistics, can have chilling effects.[8] Not all student confrontations are about free speech; the curriculum has come under scrutiny as well. For instance, Reed College announced "major changes to its signature humanities course ... months after student protesters charged that the course was too white, too male and too Eurocentric."[9] What's taught to undergraduates has always been a fertile source of debate, especially among colleagues who suffer from either too many, or too few, students in their disciplines. Debate has sharpened, however, with the pointed jabs of someone like Jordan Peterson, social psychologist turned media guru, who has attacked the "postmodernism" that he sees infecting large parts of the university: "It's come to dominate all of the humanities – which are dead as far as I can tell – and a huge proportion of the social sciences ... We've been publicly funding extremely radical, postmodern leftist thinkers who are hellbent on demolishing the fundamental substructure of Western civilization."[10] From a very different place comes the voice of the American novelist and intellectual Marilynne Robinson, who writes: "To be painfully candid, I consider part of what is offered to students as intellectual discourse, at least in the humanities and social sciences, to be a sort of higher twaddle ... [I]t is deeply harmful in that it wastes time and teaches students to think and write badly, to master as they can the terms and assumptions of twaddle." It is more than time, she concludes, "for our splendid universities to take a long look at themselves."[11] When such comments spring from such astoundingly unalike critics, the right response surely must be self-reflection, not just defence. Who, though, is listening? If the university is allowed to drift away from humanistic learning – that is, learning that takes account of what it is to be fully human – what will be the eventual consequences for society? There are, fortunately, a few voices raised in concern, but one hopes for more evidence of their having been heeded.[12]

Any catalogue of distracting voices must, unhappily, include the protests of those who teach – not necessarily about what is taught, but about their conditions of employment. The entire system has, in large measure, brought labour unrest upon itself, even if unwittingly. To speak of Canada, faculty unions have exercised their legal ability to strike, usually to the detriment of students; but universities have created understandable dissatisfaction by turning over a significant percentage of teaching to contract and contingent staff. There can be no greater distraction from the purposes of the university than the suspension of its knowledge functions. No one can feel anything but regret for a place such as York University in Toronto, where a strike continues into its tenth week as I write, adding to about 250 days of strikes in the past two decades. More generally, and in many other places, relationships between faculty groups and university administrations often turn adversarial. If collegial governance is impossible, perhaps – as some propose – a new model is required.[13]

Return briefly to the role of the state in university affairs. Although Canadian universities have a great deal of autonomy, especially in the conduct of their academic affairs, the university is a civic institution and must conduct itself in accordance with the law. However, whether government action is an intrusion into the proper sphere of the university or a warranted intervention is not easily determined. A prolonged strike may require resolution by legislation.[14] When universities are financially irresponsible, their practices may be questioned. But how is responsibility to be determined? The Alberta minister of advanced education publicly criticized the president of the University of Alberta for "lining his own pockets while he's cutting money being spent on classrooms and students," according to a report in the *Edmonton Journal* on 19 March 2018. Four weeks later, the provincial government set salary caps for senior administrators in Alberta's higher education institutions.[15] Sometimes the state places boulders with warning signs along the university's charted course, to be ignored at peril, and sometimes political swirling waters create new submerged shoals. Whatever the danger, universities must keep from being distracted.

At the risk of adding too much to the list of disturbances, let me finish with one more set of distractions: the voices of donors. Money speaks: it can beguile but also threaten. It's difficult to choose just one example of the undue influence of donors on academic programs, but an almost random perusal of higher education news produced a story from the United States about a revelation from George Mason University, near Washington, DC, that some gift agreements from the Charles Koch Foundation between 2003 and 2011 had provisions for donor participation in the selection and evaluation of faculty members, including the withdrawal of funds if the provost and the selection committee could not agree.[16] Closer to home, donors to the University of Alberta were outraged by the decision to grant an honorary degree to environmentalist David Suzuki, an outspoken critic of fossil fuels. A Calgary law firm cancelled its remaining commitment to donate $100,000 to the university's law school. Within the university, the deans of engineering and business openly criticized the choice despite the president's unambiguous defence of the decision.[17] Although controversy over honorary degrees is not new,[18] the uproar from critics damages the reputation of universities in some quarters, and is surely yet one more painful distraction.

That, however, is enough for now. If you need more evidence of the myriad distractions that beset the university of the early twenty-first century, you might simply keep reading the news – especially the media that attract popular attention. I'll assume the point is made. But what next?

In setting out my aim for this book in the Preface, I observed that, if we are to appreciate the proper vocation of the university in the midst of these myriad distracting voices, we have to spend time thinking about its essential functions and the conditions under which its functions can be effectively carried out. What follows in the succeeding chapters, then, takes on these distractions, not case by case, but by recalling the institution to its central purposes.

In Chapter One I assert that the defining functions of the university have to do with knowledge. That's not surprising – if asked, you'd probably agree that any form of education is about getting to know. But this is a very general claim, and we should ask just what is the relation of the university to knowledge and knowledge claims – especially when society's expectations, and the hopes of students, seem to be about social and personal issues that are more economic than epistemic.

If, as I argue, the university should be valued for its preservation, production, critique, and authentication of claims to knowledge, then it must have a reputation for integrity. Without demonstrable integrity, there can be no confidence in the quality of the degrees the institution awards or the research it conducts. That's the burden of Chapter Two.

What, though, are the conditions on which a reputation for integrity rests? There are at least three. We'd be suspicious of an institution that turned out to be a spout for the ideas and plots of a particular government, corporation, or religious or ideological party. We would not trust an organization's claims to freedom of inquiry if it censored the expressions of members who don't adhere to the party line. Nor, third, would we have confidence in an institution that, while professing the right principles of intellectual integrity, was unable to administer itself in accordance with those values. In Chapter Three, then, I address the precarious nature of university autonomy. Although pipers play the tunes they're paid for, it's a subversion of the very nature of the university to generate and bless only ideas their patrons desire. We are fortunate in Canada that legislation recognizes the autonomy of university bodies – boards or senates – in setting academic standards and policies. Democratic governments, however, face complex challenges. Liberal democracies are sensitive to abuses of political power, and their governments are correspondingly sensitive to public opinion. If government believes that society wants affordable university places for undergraduates, it will find ways to regulate enrolment and manage tuition levels. Sometimes the state should use the authority by which it has created autonomous universities to intervene for the sake of the public good – for instance, when a strike has a significant effect upon students' education or when there is financial irresponsibility. But the university must be always vigilant: its autonomy can be weakened by small erosions, not just by major perturbations. That vigilance must be self-directed, too, against internal decisions that cause the university to drift away from its true course. The gift tied up with strings might be too much of a favourite thing for a needy department. Donors must be cultivated with understanding as well as with care.

Boards are responsible for safeguarding university autonomy, and one of the most important means by which they do this is by conferring academic freedom upon the members of the institution. Where the ability to pursue knowledge and to challenge knowledge claims is hampered by fear of reprisal, confidence in the integrity of researchers and teachers is challenged. Yet academic freedom is easily misunderstood and misrepresented – and also easily invoked inappropriately. In Chapter Four, then, I take on the task of explaining the messy necessity of academic freedom. The necessity has to do with fundamental freedoms of enquiry, belief, and expression, but the messiness lies in the challenge of determining the limit of such freedom. We think about who has it, what it protects and what it doesn't, and its relationship to freedom of expression both on the campus and outside its protected space. I end the chapter with a discussion of freedom of conscience and academic freedom in religiously oriented institutions.

The conditions of autonomy and academic freedom must be grounded in appropriate policies and practices within universities. It's the function of governance to oversee the development of these policies and to ensure that they are observed, reviewed, and revised. Governance, broadly speaking, holds the administration accountable, and is entrusted with the long-term flourishing of the institution. It appoints the president and approves the delegation of powers. So far, so good. Universities, however, are unusual in their structures of authority, rendering decision making complicated. Relationships between presidents and board chairs in Canada haven't always been smooth, and although responsibility for friction needs to be more widely distributed, it's crucial for the players to understand how the university works. Thus, in Chapter Five, after setting out the basic administrative structures of most universities, I ask for an understanding of what I call the "academic form of life." In its knowledge functions, the university relies, not on hierarchical authority, but on the authority of peers. The determination of academic matters is to be made on the basis of peer assessment. Peer review isn't infallible, and has its own messiness, but it's the best we've got, and the alternatives are unpalatable if an institution is to be a university. A related value is collegiality, sadly eroded by the forces and voices we've just been thinking about – so damaged, in the view of some, that governance should be rethought. Accordingly, in this chapter, I point to the problems for effective accountability when there is far too much information in the name of transparency, and I conclude with some comments on the respective roles of the president and the board chair.

In the remaining chapters, I raise three major questions that all universities now face in these early decades of the twenty-first century. Perhaps the most notable shift over the past fifty or so years has been what we might call the turn towards students. Students have always been there, of course, but the focus of the university has shifted in their direction. So, while I began with the claim that the university is all about knowledge, we now find ourselves asking whether these days it isn't all about students. In Chapter Six I give a brief account of the ways in which the university has reoriented its attention and services to students and their "experience," and argue that, although this has been by and large a positive change, it is not an unqualified good. It has created a social burden for the university, for one thing, adding to institutional complexity. And it can pose its own challenges to the integrity of student experience, particularly when "student life" issues get addressed by administrators, while the life of the mind is the concern of academics, with neither group talking much to the other.

The life of the mind? That leads to the question I pose in Chapter Seven: what knowledge should undergraduates gain? Much of the language these days about university education is filled with concepts such as skills, competencies, critical thinking, engaged learning, learning outcomes, and assessment. It's often assumed that everyone knows what these words mean, but they occasion a great deal of discussion.[19] It's the same with "liberal education," which usually involves debate about the place of humanities courses in the university's many programs. The turn to students has placed welcome emphasis upon how students learn and upon curricular content. Amid the voices repeating these concepts – some of which are distracting, it must be said – we ought to attend to an insistent question: what are the fundamental habits of mind and expression that mark what Northrop Frye called the "educated imagination"? If an undergraduate education doesn't inculcate these habits, the university is failing in its knowledge functions. Claiming that education is best understood as interrogative conversation, I invite deliberation, not on curricular development, but on the kind of minds that should emerge from any course of study. In short, the university's raison d'être is knowledge, and its graduates should have learned how to come to know.

One more question for the final chapter: what are "well-placed" universities? It's the notion of place that is interrogated here, with the claim that "placeless" education – that is, virtual education that happens anywhere there is an Internet connection and a screen – ignores the fundamental embodiment of human beings. Although technology has its purposes, and online learning can be helpful in certain contexts, interrogative education is deeply personal. Taking account of the human condition in time and location, in Chapter Eight I argue that universities do best when they cultivate relationships among their members across time and when the knowledge they cultivate is rooted in their particular locations.

You might suspect from this account of what follows in the book that, although I've referred to distractions that tug, push, or entice the university from its proper and true course, I am not offering strategies for handling obstreperous students, fending off external interference, calming angry faculty voices, building new forms of governance, or passing out packages of panaceas. Your suspicion is right. There are two main reasons for this, along with the obvious one having to do with my own limitations and preferences. The first is that we must resist the temptation to make do with the temporary and expedient. Universities must face twenty-first-century challenges with values and commitments that have borne the weight of time. They must remain undistracted, focused on the conditions that enhance the generation, assessment, preservation, and transmission of knowledge. If we don't understand and debate those conditions, we are in danger of continuing to drift even if we manage to bail out enough water to keep afloat for a while longer. When different communities connected to the university have incompatible expectations for the institution, agreement on contentious issues can be reached only by compromise, without lasting commitment to institutional values. Let there then be sustained and informed deliberation on the themes raised in this book – and deliberation across those different communities. So, although faculty members might be curious about academic freedom in Chapter Four and undergraduate teaching in Chapter Seven, and student services staff might turn to Chapter Six to see what I say about "student life," both groups should be talking with each other as well as among themselves. The governance issues in Chapters Three and Five raise questions for external board members and alumni, but these groups might do well to read elsewhere, and join the wider conversation. One would hope, too, that it would be difficult for students to graduate without having reflected, somehow, on the purposes of the university and the aims of their education. So, although readers might be drawn to some sections more than others, the assertions in the third, fourth, and fifth chapters do follow from the first two chapters, and the questions I raise in the last three chapters build on those assertions.

There's a second reason for the book's lack of specific counsel on contested issues. Advice can descend to the specific, where the complexities of the problem can be untangled a little, and that means knowing something about the players, their contentions, their experience, and their hopes. Although I dare to speak about "the university" in these pages, institutions have their own histories and character, as I acknowledge in Chapter Eight. In the midst of crises or the messy confusion of competing voices, it's only human to crave answers and directions. It's particularly human to attend to the commanding presence, the clarion call, the all-seeing expert. To err, alas, is also human. Even good advice can be too general; principles, after all, require judgment in their application to circumstances. Again, then, what is called for is deliberation that takes account of particularities.

The word deliberation crops up over three dozen times in this book, so let me close with a comment about that activity. We take decisions in a variety of ways – sometimes out of habit or on authority or precedent, sometimes because we've been enticed or browbeaten, or because we're lazy. When we deliberate, we ponder, weigh in the mind, consider carefully. That's when we need to call upon underlying principles, commitments, and values. Given our limitations, however, we ought to *deliberate together*. That opens us up to objections and qualifications – to other perspectives. It exposes our differences, and gives us opportunity to reconsider, offer reasons, and arrive at resolutions. Of all human institutions, the university ought to be the place for collegial deliberation.

I know, that's too idealistic: my platonist predilections get the better of me. But what's the alternative? If there is no conversation in search of common understanding and purpose, then of all the distracting voices the loudest and most persistent will prevail. Even without the crises of hidden rocks and shoals, there will be drift. Thankfully, there are constellations by which to chart the course of the university's enduring search for knowledge. Look up.

PART I

Five Assertions

chapter one

It's All about Knowledge, Period

It's about Knowledge

Let's begin at the beginning. What's the point of universities? Why does a society want them? Why do students go to them? Do those who work in universities share the same views as those outside?

No one answer works for these questions. If you ask what is the point of, say, having children, you will be given several different motives, often held by the same person. It's the same with universities. But a very common reply will be that society needs young people who have learned some skills that will contribute to society and that perhaps will increase their chance to earn enough to live a satisfying life. Parents and politicians, as well as students, might agree on this reason. Students certainly are looking for better careers as the outcome of attending university; and *better* means better-*paying* careers. Politicians understand that, too, believing that universities make a worthwhile contribution to economic growth. Parents appreciate the economic argument, but, especially if they themselves didn't have a chance at a university education, they hope their children will be able to have not just more money, but better lives, more rewarding careers. Motives like these are found as well among those who actually live in universities. They might believe that whatever goes on inside their institutions will help the economy and provide the means of social mobility; they themselves might be enjoying such benefits because of their participation in higher education.

Nevertheless, even when an activity has a set of accompanying benefits, it doesn't follow that the activity is justified or explained only by those benefits. There might be a more fundamental reason to support the activity, making those benefits possible. For example, having children might provide a kind of insurance for old age: they can look after you in your dotage, and they bring certain tax advantages. When the children are older, they can do chores or perhaps take over the family business. Yet parents, by and large, don't have children simply for the sake of such benefits; they want family for family's sake, for all the precarious but incalculable joys that belonging together bring.

It is the same with universities. There is a fundamental reason for their existence that makes possible those other personal, social, and economic benefits. There's a reason for the university in literate societies, and it's the same reason for working in the institution. That reason and purpose is simply stated: *the university is about knowledge.* Or, to put it slightly differently, it's *about knowing.* (*Knowledge* is the product; *knowing* is the process that yields up the product.) Those who carry out the university's business do it for the sake of knowledge; those who study in it do it for the sake of knowing. Just as human beings have families for family's sake (we are social creatures who need to value and be valued by one another), so human beings seek knowledge for the sake of knowing (we are curious creatures built to find things out).[1] The additional benefits that often look like answers to "why have universities? why go to one?" are available because of knowledge. *It's about knowledge.* If we are going to understand what a university is, how it works, and why it is the way it is, we must start and end with knowledge. There is, of course, much more to say between the beginning and the end.

Right off we should acknowledge that much of the language around universities is a little more elevated, having to do with truth and truth seeking. A quick Internet search will throw up the names of many universities whose mottos refer to Truth, though that word isn't as common in the ubiquitous mission or values statements that institutions feel obliged to provide.[2] Be that as it may, faculty members do use the language of *truth seeking* in describing their efforts. In so doing, they are distinguishing the object of their inquiry from mere opinions, received beliefs, hunches, guesses, prejudices, and all sorts of bad thinking. The human condition is a state of what we might call epistemic patchworks: some bits get sewn into the fabric of our belief-consciousness without much inspection, some are discards that we shouldn't have accepted, and some are made of new material not yet tested. Where the fabric is comfortable or looks pretty, we are reluctant to have it picked at. Truth seeking is the endeavour to inspect with care the fabric of beliefs, figuring out its origin and its reliability.

I have used the word "elevated" to characterize the language of Truth in university mottos. That's because, for the past half century or so, our postmodern world has been wary of grand claims to have discovered and captured the Truth about anything. We've become painfully aware of the hubris of thinking that any one mind or one culture has managed to sew up the ragged ends of beliefs into an immutable, everlasting garment. Unfortunately this appropriate epistemic humility has tended sometimes to degenerate into a pervasive scepticism that seems to claim that any bit of belief-fabric is as good as any other scrap as long as the owner likes it. We (or at least some of us) have recently arrived at the *terminus ad absurdum* of this degeneration: past the point of Truthiness to the era of Post-Truth. Fortunately voices have been raised to call out the nonsense of post-truth, factoids, and alternative facts. For beyond truth there is only anti-truth: deceptions and lies. There is no knowledge in that land – only the ambitions of the powerful, who manage and manipulate the beliefs of others. The powerful need not be larger than life; there are the petty powerful, the slick, the painfully sincere, anxious to win our trust.

To be properly human, we need to come back to the land of knowledge. If we can't finally say that we've explored the whole land and found at last the whole cloth of treasured truth, we must always strive to throw away the bits that are faded, threadbare, poorly manufactured, and incapable of serving good purposes. Truth seeking is not just noble and grand; it is essential to our very personhood. I use here the language of knowing and seeking knowledge only because it emphasizes the continual quest, rather than the final accomplishment. But, of course, knowledge and truth are intimately connected. If we discover that something isn't true after all, we revise our language to confess that we only *thought* we knew it. Philosophers discuss the relationships among knowledge, true beliefs, warranted or justified beliefs, and so on;[3] it's enough here to agree that the preoccupation of the university with truth can be discussed in the vocabulary of knowing and seeking to know. That vocabulary has the added advantage of being employable in more relational and practical contexts, as in not just knowing that something is the case, but also in knowing someone and in knowing how to do something. Universities, I argue, are taken up with knowledge in its various manifestations.

One last piece of vocabulary, before working through the ways in which knowledge is at the very heart of the university's functioning: the notion of *knowledge claims*. By a knowledge claim, I simply mean the profession of *a conviction that something is the case.* I use "knowledge" fairly loosely here, since those who are pressed about a particular knowledge claim might have to back-track and confess that, well, they *think* it's so. Knowledge claims, in my usage, are those convictions we assume we're entitled to hold and profess as being the case. They can be dogmatic or tentative, reflective or automatic, and about anything at all. They're what we say or assume about the epistemic patchwork that makes up our cognitive consciousness. And they are what universities work on.

The Knowledge Functions of the University

It's time, then, to attempt to say more about the work universities do. The functions of the university have to do, broadly, with the *generation* and *assessment* of knowledge claims. That's very general, though. We can be more specific by looking at several knowledge functions that can be found in the university. We'll find that these functions are interwoven, rather than distinct strands, but for the sake of gaining an appreciation of the work of the university we can separate them out.

(1) The first is the *discovery of new knowledge*. That's what university research is about. It's not grade-school "research" in which students discover for themselves what someone else already knows; it's the search for answers yet unknown or unsubstantiated by others. The importance of this function is obvious, even if we haven't articulated good reasons this research should be done in *universities*: anyone who has benefited from advances in medicine, engineering, or technology can understand why research is good for society. We still need to ask about the social importance of research in other disciplines, but for now we should realize that new knowledge is also discovered in the study of literature or history or philosophy. Archival research, of course, uncovers what could be otherwise lost to memory, but new *interpretations* of familiar texts and ideas also add to the store of human knowledge. Some writers, regarding research as the finding out of new material, prefer to call this interpretative activity *scholarship*, rather than research. That leads me to the next point.

(2) We might well want to say that interpretations and theories are not so much discovered as created. This is the second, closely related, function of universities: the *creation* of new knowledge. Creation is the work of mind and imagination, bringing into being what was not there before, rather than discovering what was there, unrecognized, all along. To line up neatly discovery (research) with the sciences and creation (scholarship) with the arts and humanities would be wrong, however. Science often employs imagination, and proceeds by creating explanatory models; literature can help us discover things about ourselves that were there all along. But do poets, artists, composers actually create knowledge? Do the arts fit into my description of the functions of the university? Given a broad appreciation of kinds and ways of knowing, yes. Many of the arts do create *understanding* of aspects of the human condition, even if that understanding cannot be articulated fully in propositions. So I would argue for placing them in the knowledge-creation functions of the university.

(3) It could be argued that the most fundamental knowledge function of a university is the *critique* of existing knowledge claims. After all, research is motivated by dissatisfaction with the current

state of understanding and by curiosity to search for answers to questions that continue to dog, disturb, or intrigue the mind. Interpretative scholarship implicitly – and usually explicitly – claims to have assessed the scholarly literature on a topic and found it insufficiently convincing. If the language of assessment plays more gently in the ear than the notion of critique, so be it, but the assessment universities carry out is *critical* assessment: the weighing of evidence to reach a judgment about the truth or adequacy or explanatory potency of a claim. A very large part of the life of a faculty member is spent in assessing, not only what's been growing or languishing in one's field of expertise, but also the performance of students. Students themselves should be learning how to assess material critically, as we will see in the discussion of undergraduate education in Chapter Seven.

(4) In order for the members of a university to assess, correct, or revise existing knowledge claims, those claims and the material on which they are based must be available to them. Although university-level research requires more than just finding out what has already been thought and written on a topic, it's still entirely necessary to have *access* to this material. Universities have always had the function of *preserving* knowledge for the use of faculty and students. The obvious physical location of preserved knowledge is the library, which, in collegiate architecture, had pride of place along with the chapel. Ascribing the preservation of knowledge as the library's domain is, however, insufficient in two ways. First, libraries these days do far more than act as guardians of received knowledge; they are actively engaged in instruction in *information literacy* – helping students to discern what sources are available and what are reliable. That is an exercise in critical assessment – the formation of judgment that is essential to reliable scholarship and research. Second, universities preserve knowledge through the publications of their faculty members, even if they don't get purchased by the institution's library. It's a fundamental principle of all university research that it be made publicly accessible, save for a time limited publication ban approved by, say, a dean to protect legitimate interests.[4] To value the preservation of knowledge is to acknowledge the importance of the past, about which I shall have more to say, again in Chapter Seven.

(5) We have seen, in some of the above remarks, that knowledge is not the private possession of those who discover, create, or preserve it. It has to be passed on, especially because, as I confessed earlier, it's difficult to be certain that one has grasped the truth. Making one's claims available is thus an invitation to deliberation, refinement, and correction. The *transmission* of knowledge, however, is broader than this. This function is expressed in classroom and lab; it is the *teaching* function of the university. We will see later that "transmission" is too weak a term for what must transpire in successful pedagogic interactions, but it will do for now. Even though I've just said that the critique of knowledge claims is fundamental to the university, the pragmatic response will be that knowledge transmission takes precedence because the financial resources of the university depend (in many jurisdictions) on student numbers, tuition, and government grants. Universities wouldn't, and couldn't, exist without their commitment to transmitting knowledge.

(6) I haven't yet said anything about the obvious, and socially desirable, role a university plays: it awards degrees. Its authority to do so is usually conferred by the state – in Canada by Royal charter or provincial legislation. Put simply, this is the function of *certifying the achievement of knowledge*. Further, the forms of this certification are *university degrees*, of which there is a well-established hierarchy. After four (or sometimes three) years of successful postsecondary study, a student becomes a bachelor of arts or science or commerce (or, these days, some other field of knowledge). Further study leads to the degree of master; and even more study, to becoming a doctor. (It's not hard to see how the name of a degree at the level of master reflects mastery of a subject or why we call "doctor" someone who is able to teach that subject; "bachelor," however, remains enigmatic. The Wikipedia article on the subject proposes an etymology that the Oxford English Dictionary regards as spurious – a good example of the need for critical assessment of sources.) All that said, the appetite for credentials in the form of degrees has grown ravenous, evidenced not only by the mushrooming of university enrolments, but also by the proliferation of new degrees, especially at the professional master's level. An educational institution that doesn't grant degrees doesn't make it

onto the list of universities. Although something might be called a college without degree-granting authority, the trend in Canada has been to rename colleges as universities (or "university colleges") to differentiate those that certify knowledge by the awarding of degrees.

(7) Let me explain a seventh possible function of a university. The knowledge functions I describe here are carried on largely within the walls of the university – we'll see in Chapter Three, in discussing autonomy, why the university has been known as the Ivory Tower. It goes without saying, though, that subjects of the knowledge generated and assessed are ubiquitous, not confined to the campus. The products of research and scholarship often make a difference to how we live and think, so universities may be said to be in the business of *applying* knowledge for the sake of public and personal well-being. Faculties such as engineering, education, medicine, social work, music, pharmacy, and the like typically get called "professional" because their graduates enter their relevant professions. A highly simplified view would be that these students have learned "know-how": the application of critical knowledge to the "real world." They have put to use the knowledge that others have generated through research and scholarship. What lends support to this simplified idea is that there are some stand-alone institutions dedicated to professional education – music conservatories or engineering schools, for instance. If their work can be carved off from the fundamental task of generating knowledge, then perhaps the application of knowledge is not a central function of the university. But that is indeed too simple. Professional programs must be built upon the best knowledge available, knowledge that is generated by research and critically appraised. Further, when knowledge claims are applied to particular situations and problems, they might be found inadequate in some respects. Applied research can feed back into the discoveries of so-called pure research, aiding in the process of critical assessment.

Given this dynamic among generating, applying, and assessing knowledge, I conclude that this seventh function is indeed proper to a university. Are we able to say, however, which of these functions are absolutely essential for an institution to be called a university? Can some of them be contracted out, so to speak?

A Distinguishing Knowledge Function?

Here's what emerges from our discussion so far. Without degree-granting authority, an institution can't be classified as a university in our part of the world. Several of the functions we've considered can be discharged by entities that are not universities. Discovery and creation of knowledge don't require universities – think tanks, for example, can do research on specific problems. Knowledge can be preserved outside university structures – there are stand-alone libraries that don't offer academic programs and degrees. The transmission of knowledge is carried out in elementary and secondary schools. And, as we saw, independent institutes can educate in practical and professional knowledge. All these activities require some elements of the critical assessment of relevant knowledge claims.

It might seem, then, that the *certification of knowledge* in the form of degrees is the distinguishing feature of universities. But that, of course, cannot take place without other crucial knowledge functions of the institution. Of those, the preservation of knowledge could conceivably be farmed out: as long as the members of a particular university have access to the store of knowledge in a library system somewhere, they can carry out their business. I'd add, though, that their faculty members should still be contributing to the store of knowledge by publishing their ideas in books, articles, forms of artistic creation, and the like. Some universities offer a particular range of degrees that don't require much in the way of the *application* of knowledge – liberal arts colleges don't have professional schools and comprehensive universities don't need to have the full range of professional programs.

The core we're left with, then, includes those functions intimately connected to the awarding of degrees. They are the generation of knowledge in discovery and creation, the critical assessment of knowledge, and the transmission of knowledge that leads to degree certification. These functions are indeed woven tightly together. Although we have picked the strands apart to identify them, we don't have a university unless they are all present in the intellectual and social fabric of an institution. We haven't raised the issue of whether there needs as well to be physical fabric – buildings and places; that must wait till the last chapter of this book.

Is It Really *Just* about Knowledge?

Is the university just about knowledge, then? Well, yes and no. But the no is irrelevant. As I noted at the start, universities are valued for all sorts of reasons. When alumni look back on their university years, they often reminisce about the antics they got up to and the friendships they made. The university experience provides special opportunities for social bonding with others, often from very different social and cultural places, with whom one discovers unexpected affinities. Marriages are made on campus, even if weddings nowadays are delayed beyond graduate school. So universities are about socializing, friendship forming, and the discovery of life partners. But in this they are not unique. And this value is not really connected to their knowledge functions – clubs and summer camps, churches, synagogues, and mosques fulfil the same functions. We don't need universities for this purpose.

Many of the other reasons for universities turn out to depend on their work in generating and assessing knowledge, even if they don't appear to do so at first. The knowledge students gain gives them entry to occupations and professions, and is an important factor in social mobility and in creating the conditions for a better life. To put it succinctly: the perceived benefits of universities for the economy and for a healthy, culturally vibrant, democratically strong society would not be realized without the knowledge functions of the university. It's about coming to know, assessing what's thought to be known, helping others to know through preserving, transmitting, applying, and certifying what's known, and continuing to engage in the business of knowing. It really is all about knowledge.

Since this is the case, the university must fulfil its knowledge functions well. There are certain conditions necessary for success, without which the university will falter and fail to be true to its fundamental reason for being. To these conditions I now turn in the next four chapters.

chapter two

Reputation Requires Integrity

What is required in order for a university to fulfil its several knowledge functions in a satisfactory way? There are many conditions of
success. They're tedious to list, however, and I won't spend time
on the most obvious necessities: a set of accomplished faculty
members, reasonably prepared students, and dedicated staff and
administrators. Money, of course. Policies that assist the smooth
functioning of the institution. Access to the resources that make
learning possible. If you want more on the list, visit the website of
Universities Canada to check out the criteria for membership in
this national organization.[1] Here, though, I'll focus on two broad
areas: the *public presence* of the university, and the *relationships of
power and authority* that assist or hinder a university in its functions
with respect to knowledge. The first of these has to do with how
the university is perceived in society – its reputation and trustworthiness. The second set of conditions arises when considering how
the university conducts its work in relationship to external bodies
and influences. Although the legal authority to grant degrees is
conferred by the state, the social value of a degree from a particular
university is a different matter, having to do with its perceived academic authority. How that authority is derived depends, in part,
on the relation of the university to other centres of power in society.

There is a very impressive architectural example of these relationships in Helsinki, Finland. In the centre of the city sits Senate Square, constructed in the first part of the nineteenth century
on a plan by Johan Ehrenström. The Berlin architect Carl Ludvig

Engel, who had a large part in constructing St Petersburg, laid out neoclassical buildings facing each other around the square. On the south, near the sea, were merchant houses; to the east, the state government; to the west, the university; on the highest point to the north, the Lutheran cathedral. Business, government, church, and university enclose the town square, expressing architecturally the conversation and commerce between and among the parties. Imagination can easily construct expectations brought to the university by the other parties. Whether in Helsinki or in any city with universities, the parties will look across the square at each other, anticipating some benefit or other.

Indeed these expectations seem heightened in recent years. Business looks for graduates who are ready for work; government wants not just accountability for tax dollars, but also programs that serve societal interests. If religion's role is diminished in some places, expectations around the university's responsibility for student belief and behaviour have increased. For its part the university looks increasingly to non-governmental sources of income, including donations and tuition revenue. How should these relationships be structured so that the knowledge functions of the university can flourish? This is a fundamental question, often answered piecemeal around particular issues or submerged by pressing needs for resources. These urgencies can be distracting. But unless we get this right, we are in danger of weakening the very identity and purpose of the university in the twenty-first century.

I'll begin in this chapter with public perception and the importance of trust and reputation, both of which are dependent upon the integrity of the institution. I'll then move on in succeeding chapters to more complicated issues of institutional autonomy, academic and other freedoms, and the principles of decision making in university governance. Just as it is important to appreciate the distinguishing features of the knowledge functions of the university, so it is important to recognize that issues of autonomy, free investigation and expression, and governance require special consideration in universities. Universities are situated in the public square, but if they are to succeed in generating, assessing, and certifying knowledge, they must occupy a social space not quite like that of other institutions. Or so I intend to argue in the rest of this book.

Public Perception: Reputation

There's a well-known quip about campus politics and university life. Why, goes the question, are academic politics so nasty? The answer: because the stakes are so small. There is no agreement about the origin of this piece of wit. It's associated with Henry Kissinger, but a professor of political science in the 1970s, Wallace Sayer of Columbia University, is often credited. Although you can find other possible sources of like sentiment by a little Internet searching, anyone who has lived the academic life recognizes the signs of misdirected passion in the service of trivial distinctions.

University administrators spend a good deal of time in dinner conversation with those they hope to impress, and for the sake of small talk I once repeated this quip to a pleasant stranger seated next to me at an event for some cause or other. My companion thought for a moment, then asked: "Just what are the stakes in the academic life?" It was a perceptive question, to which I answered as best as I could at the moment: "Well, it must be one's reputation. Members of the academy can't make direct judgments about the scholarship of most of their colleagues, especially in other disciplines. So we rely on what others think about status and reputation in the field." My dinner guest could not have been impressed by this lame attempt to make conversation, but was too polite to point out the obvious truth: reputation is no small or insignificant matter.

Perhaps I answered too hastily. Although the cutting review and damning reference do attack reputation, some fights are just petty territorial markings. Nevertheless, when it comes to universities themselves – as distinct from the self-esteem of particular scholars – reputation is indeed crucial. Were it not so, there would be no university rankings, no league tables, and money for "branding" and image creation would be spent elsewhere. In an increasingly competitive market in which revenue is generated by enrolment, a university has to distinguish itself by offering advantages claimed to be particular to the institution. Such marketing is difficult for more than one reason.

The main difficulty is that universities are all in the same business, by and large. They can be distinguished by program: not every institution has professional schools, and few offer a large array of doctoral programs. As a rule, however, universities depend on significant undergraduate enrolment for revenue, and the broad character of undergraduate education doesn't vary widely across higher education systems. Where everyone is selling the same product, distinctiveness is the challenge. So some schools emphasize additional benefits such as sports, residences, meal plans, financial aid, and a whole range of student services that we'll need to think about in Chapter Six, on students. Almost every institution invokes some kind of ranking in which it has distinguished itself, especially research-intensive universities that promise superior undergraduate education – to be countered by small colleges that stress the personal interaction they can offer. A visit to the "Future Students" web page of any university you can think of will impress you with the promises held out, along with photographs of young people in the best of spirits and health, usually engaged in some sport or group activity. It's hard to sell an image of the perplexed brow trying to figure out the meaning of a poem, if not of life itself.

An equally difficult problem in marketing lies in the nature of the product being sold. A university education is a good sought by a significant percentage of the world's population – some reports suggest that a third of the student-age global population was going to university in 2012, and the figure must be higher now. But what kind of good? The literature distinguishes between public and private goods – between the advantages to society of an educated population for employment, innovation, health, and so on, and the advantages to the individual in terms of career, status, quality of life, and like goods. So the story is a simple one: the higher the university participation rate in any society, the more of these goods. That's why it is in the interest of government, business, and families to encourage participation in a decent postsecondary education system.

Committing to an undergraduate degree program, however, isn't like buying a restaurant meal or some other consumable good. If I don't like the service at a new restaurant, I won't return even if the menu, with its multiple enthusiastic thesaurus-generated adjectives, looked promising. Next time I will patronize a different provider of the pleasures of dining. Signing on for a degree is an entirely different matter. For one thing, the time commitment, even for the first year, is significant in itself and in terms of foregone opportunity, including income. For another, in many jurisdictions the price is high enough to incur long-term debt. And then there's the nature of the good purchased: it's hard to tell whether the service is just fine when you've never had this particular experience before. It's not as though you've tried several universities for a few courses before you settled on this one as the provider of your ultimate credential. If your university isn't "working for you," you can drop out or attempt to transfer, but there are few other recourses. Given the nature of the good sought, then, reputation is pretty well what you've got to go on in making your choice of university. For the providers, the stakes are high enough to merit unprecedented attention to brand identity and customer loyalty – new concepts in the once-sheltered world of the academy.

I've strayed, I fear, into the language domain of marketing and commerce, in which transactions are constructed in terms of economics and contracts. That's an impoverished, and reductionist, way of regarding the university's functions in transmitting the knowledge it generates and preserves. We need to dig more deeply into the grounds for reputation, and to broaden its scope to include reputation for the reliability of the university's knowledge claims, not just for the quality of student experience. (The sad reality is that students choose their university for reasons other than reputed academic excellence: friends and photographs are better known, and more determinative, than faculty.) What's involved in the very notion of reputation for a university?

Public Confidence: Trust

Most basically, a good reputation depends on trust that its object has good intentions and is reliable in carrying them out. At the interpersonal level, trust is the stance of one person towards another in which the trusted subject is expected to be honest and truthful, to keep implicit and explicit promises, and to be reliable and consistent over time, all in the context of what's beneficial and good for the parties and their relationship. (That's why "Trust him to be late again" is an ironical use of the word.) Trust is nurtured and exercised in families and in friendships. An essential feature of trust is its ability to sustain a relationship when one party does not have access to relevant information about the other or when intentions are opaque or unavailable. Lack of trust is manifested in suspicion, in prying, in quiet attempts at independent verification of claims. Not to be trusted causes ruptures in relationships or prevents their formation in the first place.

Philosophers have written about trust as a stance between persons, but they seem to have left it largely to social scientists to deal with what it is to trust an institution. Or perhaps it is more accurate to say that many sociological studies focus not so much on trust itself as on repairing lost trust, since societal health – and thriving business – is eroded by lack of confidence in institutions and organizations. Recent polls reveal a widespread pattern of levels of trust across many nations, placing highest confidence in the military and very low trust in government and politicians.[2]

The manifestations of loss of trust in institutions include suspicion, but to the list we should add disengagement, cynicism, alienation, and even hostility. In the case of universities, trust operates in more than one sphere. In order to fulfil its knowledge functions, the university must enjoy public trust: there must be broad support for the quality and social importance of the education it provides and for the reliability of the knowledge claims its members produce and transmit for the ultimate benefit of society. When popular journalists deride faculty members for alleged preoccupation with their own research and compensation at the expense of first-year students, trust in the institution suffers. When commentators ridicule the titles of funded research grants, confidence in the significance of the humanities or social sciences diminishes.

Trust is also required in the sphere of the university's internal workings. The past half-century has witnessed cycles of student involvement and disengagement – when student leaders feel alienated from the administration, they express their lack of trust in political action. Some observers of more recent university politics see growing alienation among faculty members, especially in organized faculty labour's mistrust of academic administrators as managers serving other interests, rather than as colleagues committed to education and research. I reflect on these issues in Chapter Five, on university governance. For now it's enough to recognize that the erosion of trust damages reputation, and to ask next about the foundation of trust: integrity.

Integrity and Public Trust

The concept of integrity requires a context to fill out its meaning, although we can say that trustworthiness goes along with it. The root meaning of integrity has to do with wholeness, and when applied to moral character, integrity depends upon the ideas of completeness, soundness, and sincerity. When something is corrupted or corroded, it loses its integrity. The corrupted have their moral sense eaten away. The insincere cannot be relied on – they mislead, make unwarranted claims or false promises. A person of integrity, however, can be trusted to act on principle, rather than bend circumstances to self-advantage.

It's similar with institutions: the integrity of an organization or profession is founded upon our ability to trust its claims and practices. Members of the medical or legal profession lack integrity if they are inattentive to those in their care, do not have the requisite competence, are shoddy with financial or other records, or place their own interests above those of the patient or client. They betray their profession, and one wouldn't want to be treated or represented by them.

Integrity is even more fundamental to democratic institutions such as a free press and an independent judiciary. Here the root idea involves *not being intruded upon* so as to destroy wholeness. Interference by government or by those with particular power and influence would destroy that integrity. We couldn't rely on courts for justice in our own case where there is another thumb on the Scales of Justice; we couldn't trust the press if censors cut out information. I'll say more about the necessary autonomy and independence of these institutions in the next chapter, but for now let's think about the particular context for integrity that is the university.

The proposition is straightforward: for the university, *academic integrity* is a crucial foundation of trust. Without that integrity, reputation is hollow, and trust in the deliverances of research and the quality of degrees is unwarranted. What, then, is academic integrity? Resolve and the ability to resist external pressure to bend the institution to another's will, no doubt. Success in supporting members to fulfil the knowledge functions, including competent administration, that define a university, certainly. And observance of appropriate policies and procedures, since failure to do so would undermine the foundations of institutional life and erode confidence in the university's work. Academic integrity requires vigilance about external intrusion and internal shoddiness and misbehaviour.

But that's all quite general. Can one say more about how academic integrity is manifested and insured? Indeed, but it's sometimes more instructive to come to a positive understanding by providing negative examples. It's fairly easy to point out where academic integrity has been violated.

Start with research. Any suspicion that the results of research have been skewed or suppressed by influences external to the inquiry itself casts a large shadow over academic integrity. Even when a researcher has been careful to observe the accepted standards of inquiry, the involvement of a funding source with an interest in the outcome will cast that shadow. That's why codes of ethics in research require disclosure of potential conflicts of interest. But there are many ways in which research practices can go wrong, including sloppiness or deliberate misrepresentation by the researcher, making the knowledge claims generated unreliable.[3] The most egregious would be suppressing or fabricating evidence that doesn't support a predetermined or unwelcome claim – that would subvert the whole enterprise of research and scholarship.[4] Given that the generation and discovery of knowledge is at the heart of the university, this aspect of academic integrity is crucial.

And so is integrity with respect to the educational function of the university. Students must understand clearly the forms of misbehaviour that constitute academic misconduct, and fair and appropriate penalties must be applied for the sake of the integrity of the degree and its societal value. According to some reports, plagiarism among undergraduates is a pervasive issue, especially with the amount of material readily available on the Internet. And there are other forms of cheating, including collusion, using unauthorized aids, assisting another to commit an offence, and even bribery.[5] The reputation of an institution believed to be lax about cheating will suffer, as will the perceived value of its degrees.

It's not only students, however, who need to embrace academic integrity. Faculty members enjoy freedom in teaching, but that freedom comes with attendant responsibilities. They must keep current with their subject, present material accurately, develop appropriate assignments and examinations, and assess performance fairly. Even when failure to teach responsibly does not constitute a formal breach of an academic conduct code, it nevertheless nibbles at academic integrity and the trustworthiness of the university. There could be good reasons for including some less-demanding classes in a degree program, but a system in which all students achieve the same recognition regardless of their level of interest or ability would subvert the meaning of the grade. Given the long tradition of the faculty member's sovereignty within the classroom, grading practices aren't easily managed in the academy,[6] and sometimes it's a challenge for an institution to get it right. The degree is cheapened when standards are loose; if they are too strict, morale and enrolment suffer. Standards, then, are indicators of academic integrity, implicated in a range of decisions from admission through degree requirements and graduation rates.

I will mention, but not deal with, other aspects of institutional integrity such as financial probity, procedural justice, and accountability and transparency, which are also necessary for trustworthiness, and discuss some of this in Chapter Five on governance and decision making. But here I want to keep the focus on academic integrity and its conditions.

As I noted a few paragraphs back, there are both external and internal challenges to integrity. The most important safeguard against the erosion of integrity on the inside surely must be a set of clear policies and procedures, developed and applied conscientiously and fairly. Policy making takes place in the sphere of governance, and policy application is the work of administration. When I consider decision making in the university later, a discussion of accountability and transparency will be particularly relevant to institutional integrity.

Sound policies, of course, are necessary to meet external challenges as well. For a university to be trusted to fulfil its knowledge functions responsibly, it must not be influenced – or appear to be influenced – by considerations that are extraneous or inimical to the pursuit and transmission of knowledge. That means independence from vested interests – including personal, corporate, governmental, ecclesial, and social – that seek to trump the impartial and honest pursuit of the university's mission. For the institutions and organizations grouped around a Helsinki-like public square – and for the people in the square itself – to have confidence in the academic integrity of the university, they must be assured that no external influence or interest is able to trump the university's own commitment to, and practice of, the pursuit of knowledge and its related functions.

Neither corporate interests nor personal ones must intrude into the development, staffing, and administration of academic research and teaching programs; those programs must be authorized by due academic process in accordance with the university's knowledge functions. Wealthy merchants should not give their money to the university in return for favours for their children or their particular interests; neither government nor church should question the academic legitimacy of this particular program or that particular professor. Only if there is a shield of integrity around the university will those in the square – and those around the square – be able to trust the university's knowledge claims and its certification of knowledge in the awarding of degrees.

There's a paradox in trust that applies to the university and society. As we saw with personal relationships, to trust the other means to suspend judgment in the face of lack of knowledge, to give the other freedom to be, and to respect the privacy and integrity of the other, rather than to interrogate each motive and examine each action. Even though trust depends upon honesty and openness in the relationship, that kind of intrusion would be the denial of trust. So it is with the university. The shield of the university's integrity requires a deliberate decision on the part of those around the public square, and the citizenry itself, to believe that what goes on behind the shield is reliable and trustworthy. It means granting the university autonomy and respecting its academic freedom. Why should a society do this, and why does academic integrity require this special institutional status? Isn't the age of the Ivory Tower long past? Doesn't academic freedom mean jobs for life, even protecting an incompetence that itself erodes academic integrity?

To these questions I turn in the next two chapters on the precarious nature of autonomy and the messiness of academic freedom, and then end the first part of the book with a chapter on the peculiar decision making that goes on in universities.

chapter three

Autonomy Is Precarious but Necessary

I have argued so far that the university, in order to perform its knowledge functions successfully, must have a deserved reputation for academic integrity. It must enjoy the trust, especially of its members, and the respect of the society in which it is situated – these days an increasingly global society. Further, there are conditions for earning this respect, among which is a certain independence from power and authority with vested interests in what the university investigates, in who performs the university's work, and in who benefits from its activities. My next task, then, is to examine this independence as it is expressed and safeguarded in the autonomy of the university. In the following chapter I'll look at academic freedom as a distinct and necessary value. But paying tribute to autonomy and academic freedom isn't enough. A university must be administered and governed by policies and practices that give living expression to those principles; in Chapter Five, then, I'll consider how decisions are made within universities. Here, however, let's about think how the image of the Ivory Tower has changed: what the current interest in student engagement and the societal benefits of the university has done to the notion of the university as a protected place. I will need to explore the idea of university autonomy in its relation to academic freedom, and to ponder potential challenges to autonomy from government and other interests, including donors. And I'll conclude with some observations on how to defend this fundamental value.

Ivory and Glass, Tower and Mall

Perhaps the most graphic – and nowadays unflattering – image of the vaunted independence of the university is in the label "Ivory Tower," an image as problematic as it is memorable. Its problems are twofold. First is the material of construction: ivory was always rare and precious, not the sort of material to be used in the quantities required to build a tower. Of course, the reference is only metaphorical, signifying an imaginary place of great value. But especially today, when the ivory trade has endangered the survival of species with tusks, not even piano keys are made of ivory.[1] What might have been, for earlier centuries, a metaphor of value has become an embarrassment and a token of forbidden luxury and privilege. Worse is the second problem: the very idea of a tower. Towers are defensive and self-enclosed, protecting their inhabitants from the interactions and vicissitudes of quotidian life. They have narrow windows or openings, not for an expansive view of the world, but to spot and fend off enemies. Surrounding moats ensure entry only to the approved. To think of the university as a tower, then, creates further distance between the observer and the objects kept securely within – inaccessible except to the privileged.

That's why to use Ivory Tower these days is to deflate through irony or sarcasm the university's other-worldly self-importance. In fact universities themselves are at pains to disown the metaphor. But the phrase was not always ironic or dismissive. Steven Shapin traces with great care and detail the history of the expression from its earliest use in religious contexts, signifying rare and costly purity and beauty,[2] through its revaluation in the nineteenth century to refer to a necessary condition of artistic endeavour. Only in the twentieth century was it applied to universities, mainly in the United States, as the disciplines important to war efforts – mainly science and engineering – exited from the tower to engage with "real world" problems.[3] Shapin argues that the term has now become entirely pejorative, betraying an attitude towards knowledge that validates only that which improves the material conditions of society, and has no room for the distancing required for private reflection and contemplative critique.[4]

I'd like to explore further the notion of distancing as related to autonomy, but first let's recall the manifold interactions that have always taken place between the academy and the wider society. Theses are most obvious in the professional faculties. Medicine and the health sciences, law, engineering, education – and more recently, management, social work, and now information studies – are deeply connected to the "real world." Their graduates contribute directly to the order and well-being of society. Indeed, were they stuck in the tower, the rest of the city and countryside would be in very bad shape. Some of their faculty do work in offices and laboratories in the basement, as it were, but what they learn and pass on to their students and the rest of the world has perceived value, for the most part, for the way we live our lives and conduct our business.

The immediate utility of other disciplines, however, is harder to discern. If one believes that the "liberal arts" and the "pure" sciences are pursued for their own sake, then they might be regarded as games only a few people enjoy. But, the conversation continues, these games are not spectator sports, and they don't generate revenue at the turnstile. In a free society we could let philosophers and physicists work away inside the tower, just as we let people play Scrabble or video games in their homes. But society shouldn't pay for personal pleasures, however innocent or refined. Let the knowledge-for-the-sake-of-knowledge folk pay their own way with the help of anyone who wants to play with them. And such thinking ends with the suspicion that these games, at least as they are typically played, don't belong in public institutions. Their symbolic location is deservedly the ironically named Ivory Tower.

The belief underlying this attitude is that universities are set up to benefit society – a perfectly good assumption that needs little argument. In the case of the "practical" subjects researched and taught at universities, there is good evidence, as we've just seen. They have measurable effect, whether through improvements to daily life occasioned by technology or through the training of a skilled workforce that delivers desired services. For the pure arts and sciences, however, measurement is much more difficult. So universities have had to argue, not about the social significance of universities per se, but about *what constitutes benefit*. That means taking the long view, rather than looking at what's immediately present to sight; it means making judgments about value, rather than relying on the promise of numerical certainties. (I'll come back to the importance of the long view in Chapter Five on decision making, and to the heresy of its opposite, presentism, in Chapter Seven on undergraduate education.) Even then, the long-term justification for arts and sciences that universities often provide turns out to be economic – about the money. A typical argument is about the "education premium" in life wages, even given the cost of a degree and foregone earnings.[5] With higher wages come higher contributions to tax revenues (at least in some countries – in Canada, for instance, university graduates pay more than twice the income tax of those without a degree). Graduates' unemployment rates are significantly lower and their general health is better, so their health care costs are lower. Although some of the statistics vary by field of study and occupation, in general the economies of societies fare better, over time, because of universities.

With such arguments, advocates hope to dissuade critics that even the liberal arts and pure sciences aren't mere games for the privileged – they actually do make a difference to societal well-being. In fact, if one attends to evidence, rather than to impressions and worn rhetoric, the myth of the Ivory Tower is exploded, as even these practitioners interact with society on many levels.[6] The old divide between gown and town might have pointed to class distinctions and the unwelcome behaviour of undergraduates, but it's a dead dichotomy that should be buried along with the Ivory Tower metaphor.

Having disowned their identity as places removed from the distractions of quotidian life, universities now seek to emphasize their accessibility and relevance. That means a new vocabulary, the more succinct the better. Hence the current watchword: engagement. It turns out to be linked to the current watchword of society and government in particular: employability.

Engagement

That a watchword is current doesn't mean it's bad. Engagement is surely a welcome notion, in a double sense. Its opposite is a kind of passivity in learning, the sort of education that can be had at minimal effort by meeting basic requirements. Students in large urban universities often suffer from anonymity in large classes; the majority of them must spend long hours in commute and yet more hours in low-paid jobs to meet their costs. They are often disengaged from the life of the campus as a place of intellectual and social interactions. That kind of educational experience is impoverished,[7] and universities are striving to assess and improve engagement through such tools as the National Survey of Student Engagement (NSSE), completed by 5.5 million students since 2000.[8] Universities can assess the perceived level of academic challenge experienced by their students, their interactions with diverse peers and with faculty, and the support offered by the campus; they can also benchmark results year over year and against peer institutions.

This is engagement within the life of the institution, but there's a second mode of engagement: with the community and the world outside the walls, so to speak. In recent years, departments and faculties have been encouraged to structure the curriculum to include engagement with the community through service learning, internships, co-op schemes, field placements, and the like. Indeed three of the six "high-impact" practices targeted in NSSE surveys involve this extramural engagement in which a course includes a community-related project or students gain educational experience in other settings, including study abroad.

There are compelling reasons for universities to connect with the wider world beyond the desire to raze the image of the Ivory Tower and demonstrate "relevance." Chief among them is the intellectual challenge of understanding and evaluating the "real world." That world is so complex, intriguing, and misunderstood that it yields more than sufficient material for sustained reflection. Academic disciplines are renewed and enriched by this connection; without it, it's hard to think of urban geography or bioethics or social history or global health studies or, well, the wide culture of a society influenced by the study of literature or of the creative and performing arts. And that's just those pure arts and science areas. Much of the research in the contemporary

university, especially engineering and medical, requires partnerships with industry and commerce.

But students have another and different reason for valuing
engagement: they believe it increases their chances of finding a
job. They are joined in this belief by parents and by government.
If your resumé includes involvement in campus activities you will
be considered a leader; if you've had an internship, you can get a
letter of recommendation. The second watchword of the day, then,
is employability.

Employability

Just as universities have good reason to value engagement, so government has good reason to care about the employability of university graduates. The links between employment, the economy, and
quality of life don't need elaboration, neither do the links between
education, innovation, and job creation. Government would fail in
its duties if it didn't pay attention to these things. And since universities continue to be dependent upon government for funding,
they also are attending to their success in moving students through
the system into the job market. It's one fairly obvious, if somewhat
rough, way of demonstrating their social utility.

In many jurisdictions, then, universities report publicly the percentage of students who complete their programs within a prescribed
timeframe and the percentage of graduates employed full or part
time after, say, two or four years in positions related to their course
of study. This is the case in Ontario, where the universities provide
all sorts of metrics that permit comparisons across the system.[9] In
the United Kingdom, the newly introduced Teaching Excellence
Framework uses similar metrics as a proxy for teaching excellence as
it grapples with what counts as evidence of quality. One of its stated
aims is to "provide clear information to help employers recruit students with better and known skills."[10] Across Canada, ministries
with responsibility for higher education are often linked with skills
and employment, a situation not at all unique to this country.[11]

Again it's important to stress that government, parents, and
students themselves have a legitimate interest in careers and

employment. Students should be better at their chosen vocations because of their education. Some will have developed expertise in their programs that equips them for professional practice. Others will have formed habits of investigation, assessment, and expression that will carry them across several different careers. Engagement within and beyond the university will be important in their employment. But it is worth thinking about how employability and engagement are building a very different structure for the university. The implications for the metaphor of the Ivory Tower are profound, if not always articulated.

Put starkly, the moat is gone, whatever drawbridge might have been operating is now permanently down, and the round, cannonball-deflecting tower has been reconstructed as a glass edifice – a mall purveying various goods that is open for business to a public looking to buy its wares. The transparent glass not only lets in light; it also permits those outside to watch and assess what's going on inside.[12] The availability of access and information is in direct contradiction to the shuttered, self-enclosed tower image. But it also loses something of great importance: the sense of protected space, where the crucial business of reflection at critical distance can be carried out. Demolishing the tower to reconstruct the university in public space carries with it the danger of ignoring a defining and necessary condition of the very being of the university: its autonomy. It's time to spell out the meaning of this essential value.

University Autonomy

I'll consider the particular space of the university in Chapter Eight. For now, it's enough to acknowledge the difference between private and public space. The private sphere is protected not just by social convention in the world we inhabit, but, more important, by law. Public space may be regulated by various rules (no dogs off leash), but it's open to anyone who obeys the rules. The presumption about private space, however, is the opposite: no one has access without permission, and there must be good reasons in law should the authorities decide to trespass its boundaries.

What sort of space does the university occupy? For many universities, property is granted in legislative acts and, although almost all universities in Canada are public, their property is private. They are able, therefore, to invoke laws that pertain to all private property. At the same time, universities occupy a legal and societal space that is *autonomous*: that, after all, is the point of the *tower* metaphor, regardless of its material of construction. Autonomy protects the institution against uninvited and inappropriate intrusion. As with academic freedom, autonomy marks off the university as a place of knowing – a place protected for unfettered inquiry and expression.

Although the definition of academic freedom has been the subject of extensive debate – and will take up our attention in the next chapter – university autonomy does not appear to have attracted the same amount of detailed study. Dictionary definitions point to self-governance: the ability to make decisions, rules, or laws free of external influence. That's far too general for our purposes. The language of freedom always needs context, and autonomy with respect to the university requires further elaboration.

Recall from Chapter One that, in order to be credible and trustworthy, the knowledge functions of the university must be carried out free from undue or unwarranted interference from external bodies or individuals. What's *unwarranted* is, of course, the crux of the issue. But let's agree that there are some fundamental decisions to be made in the exercise of knowledge functions: who gets to teach whom and what; who gets to determine what knowledge claims are to be investigated and how; who receives what credentials for what achievements. This is the sphere of the core academic functions of a university, where autonomy is crucial if the institution is to enjoy the confidence of society. Such decisions, however, have to be made by duly constituted institutional authority and in accordance with approved policy. Questions of autonomy must also include, then, considerations of governance. And since decisions can't be implemented without appropriate resources, the ability of the university to make its own financial decisions must be included in our discussion as well.

One can see why the European University Association, one of the few organizations to study the issue, includes four categories in its criteria for university autonomy: institutional (largely about governance), financial (decisions about fees, borrowing, and property), staffing (hiring and dismissal), and academic (admissions, programs, quality assurance). The association further refines its criteria into thirty-eight measures, and it ranks universities in twenty-nine European jurisdictions according to these indicators.[13]

University autonomy is closely related to, but should be distinguished from, academic freedom. For our purposes here and as I discuss in the following chapter, the values of academic freedom can be located in the research, publication, and teaching especially of individuals within the institution. Autonomy, however, pertains to the institution itself and its place in society, in relation to other centres of power and influence. Of course, these two values are closely related. If an external authority forbids a university to teach a particular course, the institution's autonomy is compromised, but so is the academic freedom of the department and instructor. One way to relate these two values, then, is to think of the exercise of autonomy as the institution's ability to protect the academic freedom of its members. It's the function of the tower to safeguard the valued activities that are carried out within it.

Formal and Practical Autonomy

It's helpful, I think, to recognize that the actual day-to-day life of a university might or might not reflect its legal position in society. Legislation might grant it a formal autonomy that isn't always neatly practised – the result, perhaps, of informal pressures from government or other authorities: the quiet phone call or the expression of disapproval taken as a veiled threat. One doesn't have to stray too far from home, or in time, to discover instances of suspected influence. In the earlier twentieth-century history of my own institution a distinguished but outspoken scholar was forced to make a public apology; in March 2017 the press carried stories of a faculty member's resignation from a Canadian university following political criticism of an article.[14] Or a university might find that its autonomy has been eroded by its own actions in currying the favour of some benefactor. Like individual human beings, institutions don't always live out the freedoms they espouse.

The converse is also true: an institution without formal autonomy nevertheless might enjoy a significant amount of freedom. A state or religious founding body might leave out statements of autonomy in its enabling legislation, and have a strong hand in appointments to the board, yet it might grant the board freedom in practice to make decisions on academic values and priorities alone. The degree of autonomy actually enjoyed by any university must be decided, not on what's written down, but on how it is able to behave in practice on the sorts of measures I've mentioned. The institutional freedom of autonomy and its corresponding responsibilities are exercised in decisions about the academic functions of the institution; I'll spend more time on this issue when discussing questions of governance in Chapter Five. For now let's think about autonomy in relationship to two forms of external influence: government and donors who provide funds for programs and projects of interest.

Government and Universities

The history of the relation between universities and their founding authorities – the state or, in some cases, the church – is appropriately characterized in the language of mutual dependence and mutual suspicion. Societies and universities need each other; but when independence is a condition of a relationship, the parties don't always trust each other. It's hard not to pass judgment on how freedom is exercised, and hard not to think that you're misunderstood when you're criticized.

In this section, I briefly set out the formal autonomy that is characteristic of Canadian universities, then consider whether that independence is in any way compromised in Ontario. A report on a 2017 debate in the British House of Lords provides an interesting comparison with Canada.

Autonomy in Canada

In the Canadian university system – or systems, since education is a provincial matter – there is a noteworthy degree of formal autonomy. The system is almost entirely public, with universities gaining their degree-granting authority from the state. They are created by provincial acts, though some have Royal charters; and spheres of autonomy are enshrined in legislation, providing some formal independence from government interference. It wasn't always so.[15] The Report of the 1906 Royal Commission on the University of Toronto claimed that the difficulties of the university were largely due to the "exceptional and unsatisfactory method by which the powers of the Crown in relation to the University have been exercised." The commission recommended a system of governance whereby the state, having appointed a board of trustees or governors, would delegate authority to the board; further, academic matters would be in the hands of academic staff, rather than those of the board.

The governance of Canadian universities has, by and large, followed this model. The state exercises its power to create degree-granting institutions, but in the case of public universities cedes authority to a board that oversees finance and property and appoints the president, and to a senate body that oversees admissions, programs, and academic policy. For example, in the 1978 amendments to the University of Toronto Act, the governing council appoints the president and is given authority for appointments, admission, programs of study, examinations, and the award of degrees, property, and financial matters. The lieutenant governor in council appoints only a third of the members of the governing council (16 of 50), but in principle a quorum could be met without any of them. Although there is no mention of autonomy in the act, the delegation of these powers creates independence from direct government involvement.

Since, as noted, education is under provincial jurisdiction in Canada, the relationship of the state to a university's governing board is constructed slightly differently in different provinces. At the Université de Montréal, the lieutenant governor of Quebec appoints a third of the university council on the advice of the minister of education. The act governing Dalhousie University in Nova Scotia gives government fewer than half the board appointments on the recommendation of the university. In Alberta, however, under the Post-secondary Learning Act (2004) covering all postsecondary institutions, the government appoints all members of boards, it can examine and inspect the financial or administrative condition of any board, and can appoint an administrator to assume the powers and duties of the board and the president. Academic matters remain under the control of a general faculty council.

Despite such differences, Canadian universities enjoy in practice a good deal of freedom from overt interference; according to a highly knowledgeable expert on university governance, they "probably have as much or more autonomy than any other public universities on earth."[16] As for other jurisdictions, data from the European Universities Association are useful as a snapshot at a point in time for the countries that report on its measures. But things change, sometimes subtly, as in the case of Ontario, and sometimes rapidly, as we will see with the British experience.

Government Interests and Influence

A significant and central responsibility of government is the education of its citizens, since an educated society is essential for the robust functioning of a democratic state. So there can be no dissent from the claim that government has an interest in the well-being of its universities and in the flourishing of their knowledge functions. Wisely, democratic governments have understood that institutional autonomy is a necessary condition for the successful functioning of the university. Nevertheless, although formal autonomy might be acknowledged, government is able to exercise influence on the operations of universities in several ways. Even if autonomy is not directly challenged, the ability of a university to manage its own affairs can be compromised, especially in financial matters. No one will seriously argue that government should permit universities to mismanage their financial affairs in the name of autonomy.[17] Nor should it meet all requests for funding from universities, although there are good arguments for the long-term social benefits of adequate funding and about the disproportionate budget support for health care. Apart from government grants, university budgets are funded mainly from tuition fees and to a lesser extent from donations, including endowment income. According to some reports, tuition in several jurisdictions now accounts for about half the cost of an undergraduate degree for domestic students.[18] Whatever the exact percentage for any institution, the level of tuition fees is significant; without that source of income, a university could not fulfil its functions. It's important that legislation permits university boards to set levels of tuition, but are universities actually able to exercise this freedom? Despite their formal autonomy, the reality is otherwise: the province sets the most significant fees for the universities in its jurisdiction. In Ontario, for example, a university may be free to increase tuition beyond the announced amount, but the additional sum would be deducted from the government grant – a "freedom" not worth having. The effect of this control on the university's finances is direct, and an erosion of board autonomy. Likewise with government-directed expansion programs, where funding is targeted to particular areas. Universities find it difficult to resist additional money, even when the government's agenda of the day is not aligned with their own program and research priorities.

Government Interests and Influence: Ontario

An institution trying to balance autonomy and accountability sometimes faces difficult choices when government actions slide across the thin line between reasonable accountability and meddling with the business proper to the university. Without arriving at judicious and measured conclusions about some recent government actions close to my own institutional life, let me point to half a dozen cases in which, some might argue, the line was impinged upon. I shan't discuss these actions in any detail, for the point is to illustrate, rather than to adjudicate, some of the ways in which government expresses its authority with respect to the administration of universities.

(1) In June 2006 the Ontario Freedom of Information and Protection of Privacy Act was extended to Ontario universities even though they had their own access-to-information policies. This gave the Privacy Commission authority to direct universities to release documentation to any member of the public regardless of the nature of the request.[19]

(2) Four years later the Broader Public Sector Accountability Act, 2010 treated universities, along with municipalities and colleges – although the government habitually refers to "publicly assisted universities" – as public institutions. Part IV of the act gives the government the authority to determine what allowable expenses can be claimed from university revenues. Alcohol became contentious, but why? It was not because of alcohol abuse or concern for health – were those the motives, the ban should have been on paying for desserts, since sugar is thought a major contributor to ill health. Expense accounts are publicly accessible, so it was not about transparency or accountability. Nor was it because government pays most of the expenses of the university; it doesn't. Instead the reason must have had to do with appearances, political in the wider sense if not slightly puritanical, at least from a European perspective. This was a tiny move across the line to control decisions that had been made within the walls of the university.[20]

(3) Also in 2010 the Ontario government passed a compensation restraint bill for the broader public sector, but in universities targeting only non-unionized employee groups. This was not popular across the sector. Later the Broader Public Sector Executive Compensation Act, 2014 restricted restraints to senior administrators, limiting salary increases for presidents, vice-presidents, and senior executives, even though founding legislation cedes salary decisions to university boards.[21] Again, transparency cannot be the issue, with the public disclosure of public sector salaries over $100,000 – the so-called sunshine list.

(4) In 2012 the auditor general of Ontario undertook an audit of teaching evaluation at three Ontario universities. A team entered each university, looked at evaluation results, and interviewed administrators, faculty, and students. The concern was whether universities were doing a decent job in educating, especially for

the workforce. The report commented not just on how teaching is evaluated, but also on tenure and promotion policies, workload, and employment rates postgraduation.[22] Four years later the auditor general presented a follow-up report on the implementation of the report's five recommendations, almost all of which were "in progress" rather than completed.[23]

(5) The fifth case occurred in 2012 as well, when a zealous minister of the Crown decided that university education would be much more efficient if the undergraduate degree was only three years in length, not four; if a third of the courses were delivered online; and if the university year was three semesters, including the summer, not two.[24] Without the power to enact any of these ill-conceived ideas, no minister could actually override the due processes of university governance, but the very announcement of such thoughts was rightly regarded as an intrusion of government into areas where it had no business (or indeed competence) to intervene.[25]

(6) Universities have well-developed appeal processes. It's common for them to have an ombudsman office and for that office to make public reports. It seems not enough, however, for them to be publicly accountable for the way policies are implemented. In January 2016 the Ontario government extended the mandate of the provincial ombudsman to cover universities.[26] The ombudsman's website states that, with respect to universities, the office can recommend changes to improve bureaucracy, governance, accountability, and transparency. In a nod to the status of universities, the legislation says that academic freedom will be "considered," which, of course, falls short of its being respected and observed.[27] This is yet one more instance of government's assumptions about universities, which are often regarded simply as part of the public sector, like municipalities and community colleges, with very little explicit recognition of the independence and autonomy required by their founding legislation. Accountability and transparency are insufficient: government now is willing to subject to detailed scrutiny any university policy or process that anyone wishes to challenge, and to investigate, assess, and comment on how the university does its business.

The tower, although glass in the name of transparency, has been opened to auditors and ombudsmen, the agents of political authority, who are able to wander into its rooms taking down notes about its behaviour. This is an unusual exercise of authority that is difficult to interpret as anything other than a lack of trust in the ability of universities to manage their own affairs in accordance with the principles of autonomy and accountability.[28]

These examples present salient cases for reflection on the proper spheres of government authority and university autonomy. If some seem trivial, that's because one can easily make an argument about the use of funds regarded as public, and I don't think dissent from the substance of regulations is worth the bother. But the real question is about responsibility and authority: who gets to make those decisions, and why. And isn't it troubling when government decrees and regulations override legislation deliberately delegating authority to university boards and senates? Unless there is open debate on these issues, universities will not have a firm place from which to preserve the independence that is crucial – let us say it once again – *crucial* to the effective fulfilment of their knowledge functions. Yet there has been no public dissent about government intrusion, no newspaper editorials or statements from the universities. Nor in many cases of recent legislation has there been any acknowledgment on the part of government that universities have their own autonomous place in the broader public sector.

Government Interests and Influence: The United Kingdom

If universities and their boards in Ontario have been relatively silent on issues of autonomy, that is fortunately not the case everywhere. A very different instance of unease about the government-university relationship took place in early 2017 in the United Kingdom. The government, wishing to implement some necessary revisions to the legislation governing higher education, introduced a draft bill on higher education and research that made its way to the House of Lords. There it received detailed scrutiny by members who had a great deal of experience in university research, teaching, and administration.[29] A major concern in the Lords was the bill's failure to define a university and the lack of reference to university autonomy.

Accordingly Lord Stevenson of Balmacara introduced an amendment setting out five marks and functions of a university, the first of which is: "UK universities are autonomous institutions and must uphold the principles of academic freedom and freedom of speech."[30] In introducing the amendment, Lord Stevenson explained: "They are at their best when they are autonomous, independent institutions which have the freedom to develop a range of missions and practices, while at the same time being public institutions, serving the knowledge economy and the knowledge society as well as being tools of economic progress and social mobility. They use the precious safe harbour of academic freedom to seek truth wherever it is to be found and publish it for all to see and discuss. They transmit and project values of openness, tolerance, inquiry and a respect for diversity that are the key to civilisation in an increasingly globalised world." Baroness Deech added, in the debate, "[t]he autonomy of higher education is not only valuable to the universities and their surroundings; it is the hallmark of a democratic and civilised, progressive society."[31]

The amendment passed 248 to 221, in a rare defeat for the government. While debate continued, the minister of state accepted that university autonomy is a bedrock, and was reported to support an amendment that would place on the sector regulator "a requirement to have regard to institutional autonomy in everything that it does. This is a significant shift, and one that signals the strength of our commitment to the autonomy of [Her Majesty's] Institutions." He went on to say: "As universities are rightly autonomous institutions they must continue to be free to determine how best to meet the needs of their students, employers and support wider society. It should not be for government to define a university's characteristics and impose wide-ranging obligations in statute."[32]

It's not inevitable, then, that the legitimate and important interest of government in universities should intrude upon institutional autonomy. Universities need articulate defenders of their freedoms, especially when they are ill-understood or eroded out of benign ignorance. Fortunately, despite those voices of criticism sometimes raised, universities have many supporters, especially among their alumni. We need to turn next to questions about the level of influence that might be exercised by the friends of the university, rather than by government.

The University and Its Donors

As I have noted, government financial support for public universities has fallen across Canada and in many parts of the world, requiring increased tuition levels and contributions from the private sector: corporations, foundations, and alumni. If those who pay the piper are interested in calling the tune, we might expect increasing concern on the part of donors for how the university spends its money. For their part, students decide where they will put their tuition dollars – at what university and for what program. They are increasingly aware of the large contribution they make to operating costs. Deans react to student demand by shifting resources from less popular subjects to oversubscribed areas. When budgets are structured so that a division's income must cover its expenses, tuition dollars become even more crucial. If students can influence university decisions, what about donors? Do they pose a challenge to university autonomy? Perhaps no particular decision on reallocation is dramatic, but drift might well occur over time, and the mission might be skewed because of dependence upon private money.

The question needs asking, even if the answer is not always clear or easy to determine. To understand how undue influence could develop, let's reflect on the typical interests of donors. In my experience, three broad areas of appeal have been successful. First, for many alumni with modest levels of "capacity" (as the professionals put it), student support in the form of scholarships and bursaries has direct appeal: the gift goes to a particular student in recognition of need or accomplishment – a student who can write a thank-you note about the meaning of the award. Second, donors with greater resources have often been interested in capital projects, and there has been no lack of these with university expansion or renovation. Third, more recently, endowments have been raised for programs, often focused on a chair or professorship, where salary and benefits are funded from private money.

In fundraising it's not just the project that must be appealing, but also the form of recognition the donor is offered. Occasionally someone wishes to remain anonymous, but that is highly unusual in the university fundraising business. It's not hard to recognize donors of scholarships by naming the award for them (or for someone of their choosing), a practice that often adds a personal dimension to the recipient's experience. Buildings can bear the name of their patrons; indeed, it would be an interesting study to examine the shift in the names of university buildings over the past many decades, from those honouring scholars and educators to those celebrating generous philanthropists. Likewise with schools or faculties, programs, chairs and professorships: in the past two or three decades, the number of named chairs or professorships at the University of Toronto, for instance, has mushroomed, and in areas where one might not have expected donor interest – in the Vic One undergraduate program, for example, there are eight professorships, with some teaching responsibility for first-year students.

One more factor has been significant in attracting private support in some institutions: matching funds. In the 1990s the University of Toronto attracted significant money through matching schemes, including a double match from provincial funds for student bursaries. Of course, it's a rare institution these days that has unrestricted resources that can be made available for matches, and donor expectations have had to be adjusted to that reality.

Universities have to compete diligently, especially with health care, for charitable dollars. They need, then, to make the donor experience attractive and the rewards meaningful. That means that the temptation to compromise ever so slightly to meet a donor's own interest is never far away, especially when financial constraints add urgency to the need for success in fundraising. Without telling tales about actual cases, let me signal some potential dangers in fundraising that could erode university autonomy.

It should be taken as given that the fundamental rule of fund-raising is that the university seeks private support dictated not by donor preference, but only for projects that advance its own mission, determined by due process within the institution and developed in an academic plan. That rule should deal with donors who for personal reasons believe that some neglected field of study dear to them should be introduced at their alma mater regardless of faculty competence, library and other resources, or student interest. Nevertheless, even when an area is congruent with the university's academic plan, there remain the dangers I have in mind.

The first is the challenge of unintended or unexpected budgetary consequences. A donor might offer support for something that, though not inimical to the university's aspirations, nevertheless is not a high priority, but the gift might not cover all expenses and even incur ongoing costs. It takes a strong will to improve, or even decline, an offer that would redirect base funding from higher priorities to augment a project not fully funded by a gift. Capital projects often involve cost overruns; endowments for named chairs might not yield returns that match inflation.

At least, with this first challenge, one can do some cost analysis. It's much harder to predict the future of a field of study – we're all rather hopeless, in fact, at guessing demand and discipline development over time. So every university that's been around for a few decades can tell stories of scholarships for students in specialist subjects that have morphed into minor areas of study or been combined with other disciplines. Indeed, the only reliable prediction about areas of study is that some of them will dwindle, fade, or die, or be reborn in barely recognizable form. Accepting scholarships or creating chairs that are restricted to narrowly defined disciplines or programs can be imprudent business these days. Although it does not directly impinge upon university autonomy to have, say, scholarship funds no longer capable of use because they are tied to specific areas of diminished relevance, still there is an indirect effect: financial support has to be found for developing areas, and there is no money in the bank. Fortunately this is a challenge that can be addressed. No gift should be accepted without an explicit donor agreement referring to relevant institutional policies on academic freedom, recognition, reporting, and the like. Donor agreements should have a clause in which the donor, recognizing that university priorities may change over time, agrees that the gift may be redirected to a similar purpose that respects the fundamental intent to support students or programs. (There should also be a commitment to inform the donor or representatives if possible, but the university should retain the ability to make the shift.) For scholarships it would also be helpful for the agreement to include words such as "this award is given *with first preference*" to students in the subject dear to the donor.

A third type of challenge arises when a donor has definite ideas about the purpose and use of the gift, especially a large and transformative one. The donor's desire to be involved in the academic plan, in hiring, and in assessing performance is not unfamiliar, nor is it an unexpected expression of interest in the institution's good stewardship of the donor's generosity. Nevertheless the university must protect its autonomy for the sake of academic freedom. Decision making belongs to duly established processes governed by academic expertise. The university also must protect its reputation, so even if a donor might not in fact influence decisions, no opportunity should be provided that suggests an apparent conflict of interest or invites suspicion. It's good practice to have written guidelines on advisory committees so that donors and other interested parties can be assured of the appropriateness of their role; they want to help, and they will be grateful for clarity about their involvement.[33]

Let me bring this section to a close with three further comments about fundraising. The first is that, in the interplay between appearance and reality, appearance seems to be winning more often in these times of instant and uncontrollable "messaging." Donor agreements are often complex, making it easy to mischaracterize them. Add to that the mistrust on campus of the "corporate university," and money that comes from large corporate bodies will, for some students and faculty, be suspect from the start. It's important, then, for universities to set out clearly the terms of agreements for significant donations and to make those terms public. Just as it's a fundamental principle that the results of research must be publicly accessible, not hidden from scrutiny, so it is fundamental to fundraising that the purposes and terms of gifts not be hidden.

The second comment is that private money is not a quick solution to the financial challenges universities face. The basic operations of the institution aren't all that attractive to donors, nor should they be in a system where government support is supposed to keep the institution's lights on and its salary bills met. When donors are moved to give generously, they might provide student awards that, though welcome and attractive for recruitment, can't meet the needs of the operating budget. Moreover, donors often fulfil pledges and bequests on a timetable beyond the university's control, and endowments take time to yield returns.

My third point is that university fundraising is an enterprise for the very long term. Universities work on a timetable that stretches over years, not weeks or months. It takes time to plan, initiate, or ramp up a program, and even more time to close one as students move through its years. Success can be determined only over a few cycles of admission and graduation. Funding, then, must be correspondingly available over years, not months. For this reason, universities are best assisted by flexible endowments, rather than by expendable money. And endowments are usually the gifts of long-term friends of the institution. Those friends have been around long enough to appreciate the university's strengths, its needs, and its opportunities. They know they are valued for their commitment, not just for their "capacity." They wouldn't think of compromising the integrity or autonomy of the university, because they understand its founding principles and its mission. Most commonly they are its alumni, with a loyalty to the place stretching back into their formative years.

For this reason alone, the administrative and functional relationship between alumni affairs and advancement – whether called that or development or fundraising – should be seamless. Moreover, although it is tempting to develop quantitative measures of success within specified periods, the rewards of alumni engagement, like those of friendship, are complex, not easily quantifiable, and difficult to predict.

It's easier, then, to protect the autonomy of the university when it comes to its friends, who understand and care about the institution and want to give back, than in the case of government or other external authorities whose main interest is, to put it crudely, in the products of the system. Autonomy is critical for the success of the knowledge functions of the university, and it must be defended. But that defence is a challenging task, for several reasons.

The Challenges of Defending Autonomy

The first difficulty in the defence of autonomy is that it can appear self-serving. Underneath this appearance lies an unarticulated association with adolescent cries for freedom, which might be suspect as barriers to interrogation of action and motive. Likewise with most institutions: when they speak about autonomy, recourse to such language is sometimes seen as an attempt to escape from public scrutiny. When it comes to universities, however, there are no grounds for such suspicion: universities are publicly accountable, and work diligently at responsible and appropriate transparency. I will say more about accountability and transparency in Chapter Five, but here it is enough to point to a few practices demonstrating that autonomy is no cloak shielding the university from scrutiny.

Meetings of governing committees and councils are open, except when confidential personnel issues, such as senior appointments or disciplinary actions, are under consideration. Universities, moreover, must adhere to government access-to-information policies, and report to government frequently on many different measures. Universities also operate as self-regulating professions on academic matters, accountable to peers at the national and international levels. No new programs are approved without careful academic scrutiny by knowledgeable experts in appropriate fields; and in many jurisdictions, established programs are reviewed on a regular schedule, with results reported to a central body. In Ontario and other places, the results of these program reviews are posted on public websites, as are student satisfaction surveys and many financial details.

University accountability might be only hazily understood, however, and here universities could educate the public about its processes, but the more serious challenge to the defence of autonomy is what recourse universities have when it's threatened. Earlier I proposed that autonomy is a way of protecting academic freedom within the institution. But it now strikes me that there is a significant difference between defending academic freedom and defending autonomy. In the former case, there are usually well-defined dispute resolution procedures: in most Canadian universities, if I claimed my academic freedom had been infringed, I could enter a grievance; the claim would be resolved by due process, usually involving peer review of some sort. If dissatisfaction persisted, I might have the support of national associations devoted to the vigorous pursuit of academic freedom. Even if my zeal stretched the limits of academic freedom, still, the issue would be debated, and there would be a determination of the matter. I might not like the outcome, but a panel of experts would have reached its conclusion about my academic freedom.

For the determination of issues of institutional autonomy, however, there is no such defined and accepted procedure. Suppose a university felt that an external body had intruded inappropriately into its decision-making processes and outcomes: there are no established routes for determining the matter, no obvious court of appeal. In the case of government, if the usual channels of quiet communication and diplomacy didn't work, the university would have to decide whether it wanted to make a public – and therefore almost always a political – fuss out of the alleged intrusion. Since in particular cases the facts are usually a bit murky and the justifications for involvement not utterly implausible, universities might decide it's not worth disturbing a delicate power-and-purse relationship.

Without any clear mechanism for appeal, the challenge for universities, then, is to cultivate a wider public understanding of the paramount value of certain freedoms. In a society that appreciates the fundamental importance of these freedoms, there is a kind of *shared social conscience* that assesses and guides behaviour more effectively than does legislative decree. In fact, this social conscience grounds particular legislation about freedoms; it's only because of these convictions that rights are affirmed and laws created. Think of freedom of the press, guaranteed in section 2.b of the Canadian Charter of Rights and Freedoms: this is fundamental to the functioning of a healthy democracy. Information must not be controlled by the powerful; government must not insulate itself from comment and criticism. State control of the media, or ownership of the major forms of media concentrated in a few hands, is readily understood as antithetical to democratic values. Likewise with the independence of the courts. Canadian judges are guaranteed independence in the Constitution Act, 1867, Part VII, on the judicature. Citizens understand without needing long persuasive arguments that interference with the judicial system denies justice to those without influence. That understanding grounds the value of judicial independence, and is more fundamental than any legal protection. While it's good to have that protection, as Justice Ian Binnie has pointed out, the "principal bulwark to outside interference ... is the deep-rooted acceptance of the need for judicial independence in Canadian society."[34]

Freedom of the press and the autonomy of the courts follow from, and support, basic human rights. So it's relatively easy to justify these freedoms. With universities, it's not quite that straightforward. What human rights need protection by university autonomy? There is consternation both private and public if government intrudes into the business of the courts. When was the last outcry about a perceived invasion of university autonomy?

Just below the surface of the public mind (and sometimes finding voice), two countermanding attitudes play out here to suggest that university independence is either unnecessary or ill-used (and probably both). When there is expectation that universities will train immediately employable graduates, why would they need independence from government direction and society's expectations? Shouldn't they serve market needs, especially when it's hard for young people to find ready employment? And worse, the freedoms already enjoyed aren't necessarily a good thing: popular writers and commentators complain that professors belong to an elite class, pursuing their private interests regardless of their social utility. They have jobs for life, and are underworked and overpaid – so goes the familiar tune, resonating with populist suspicions.

Criticism that strikes at the heart of university autonomy, however, is wrong for a simple yet deep reason: *the university is the very place where other essential freedoms are inculcated, cultivated and defended.*

Because the university occupies a protected place for its knowledge functions, its students are exposed to and educated in the importance of independence from power and influence in a robust democracy. The university instantiates and promulgates freedom of inquiry and freedom of expression. It educates the journalists and jurists of the future in the ways of responsible integrity, including critical judgment and independence from the corrupting influence of power, prestige, and money. A little thought experiment should demonstrate my point: imagine a society where universities have no independence from external control, and ask how the press and the courts would function in that society.

Universities need integrity and trust to function effectively, and if my argument holds, they also need autonomy for the sake of integrity. Their protected place should be accepted by a democratic society, and universities should be celebrated not only because of their social utility, but also because of their unique status as guarantors of our most essential freedoms.

Responsibility for Defending University Autonomy

I'll close this chapter with one last challenge about defending the autonomy of the university: the question of responsibility. One hopes that all members of the institution understand the centrality of freedom from external constraints, and weave this theme into their conversations both public and private. Ultimately this must be the fundamental duty of institutional governance. The board, whatever its configuration or founding legislation, must develop and maintain a shared understanding of its authority vis-à-vis other centres of power, especially government in the case of public institutions, religious bodies for other schools, and donors or other interested parties. Board members must appreciate, within the institution, the role and scope of an academic decision-making body, and safeguard its independence from both outside interference and internal meddling.

Although formal responsibility sits with the board, the day-to-day challenges of upholding the university's independence belong to the president. As we have seen, encroachment can be subtle, unclear – the result of good but ill-informed intentions. It is hardly ever blatant. Sometimes what appears to be intrusion is just benign advice. Sometimes what's presented as advice is not benign. Distractions come in many forms. A president, then, needs judgment and wisdom, the ability to understand what autonomy means not just in principle, but in the particular circumstances that make up the daily life of the university. I'll return to the importance of presidential judgment at the end of Chapter Five.

chapter four

Academic Freedom Is Necessary and Messy

Ah, freedom!

The experience is elemental: the long clear draw of breath after a bad cold, the carefree amble in the woods with no particular end in mind. The noun "freedom" is abstract, but the breath drawing and woods ambling are concrete actions done freely, without constraint or compulsion. Constraints bar us from what we want to do; compulsions force us to do what we don't want to do – such as sitting in a windowless room for an obligatory two-hour meeting.

From our earliest days we push against barriers and resist external forces. Climbing out of the crib or kicking the air as we're picked up and dunked in the bath are elemental attempts to establish our own agency – early expressions of the urge for freedom as unconstrained or uncompelled action. To be a person in one's own right is to exercise personal agency, the ability to make and implement choices for oneself. Those choices are particular, but freedom as an abstract noun requires a setting in which to operate meaningfully. The adolescent struggling to assert individuality might wish to be "absolutely free," but that is like wanting "absolute stuff." There is no "absolute stuff": there's the stuff in the bottom drawer, and the stuff you were supposed to read last night, *this* or *that* stuff. Likewise, there is no absolute freedom, but rather the freedom to do or be *this* or *that*.

The contexts for being or doing freely that interest us here are institutional and political, in the broad sense of having to do with the exercise of power and authority in a social system. Those in authority use various forms of power to constrain and compel: physical coercion in banishment, imprisonment, or death; restrictions on assembly, expression, or movement; fines or seizure of property. More insidiously authorities can control information to inculcate certain beliefs so that agency is unconsciously restricted – an erosion of freedom not by overt constraint or compulsion, but by "compelling," in an extended psychological sense, those beliefs. In authoritarian regimes, the very threat of power can curtail free action through intimidation as effectively as through its actual use.

The history of the struggle for forms of freedom is vast and complicated – far beyond the purview of this chapter, let alone the ability of its author. The basic theme in the political realm is the effort to limit the powers of the king or dictator or bishop – however the ruling authority is constituted. Put that way, the struggle is about competing freedoms, where a few have too many and the masses have too few, and about getting the right balance of abilities to act.

Fundamental Freedoms

For our purposes, the most relevant freedoms are those having to do with beliefs, practices, and expression. These have been enshrined in declarations, charters, and conventions in various combinations. For example, articles 18, 19, and 20 of the 1948 UN Universal Declaration of Human Rights deal, respectively, with freedom of thought, conscience, and religion; freedom of opinion and expression; and peaceful assembly and association.[1] In 1950 the European Convention on Human Rights included these freedoms in its articles 9, 10, and 11. Over thirty years later Canada's Constitution Act, 1982 included the Charter of Rights and Freedoms, which in section 2 sets out four "fundamental freedoms": (*a*) freedom of conscience and religion; (*b*) freedom of thought, belief, opinion and expression, including freedom of the press and other media of communication; (*c*) freedom of peaceful assembly; and (*d*) freedom of association.

It might be noted that freedom of thought, conscience, and opinion sometimes are linked with freedom of religion, but religion is a set of practices as well as of convictions, whereas thought, opinion, and conscience are internal epistemic states. That's why expression is so important: it would be nigh impossible for an external authority to forbid certain thoughts, since these are inaccessible to other observers. Practices, rituals, expressed speech, and publications, however, are available to and knowable by others. That's why their free exercise matters. As for the other fundamental freedoms, the Charter assumes a difference between assembly and association that is worth noting. The freedom to assemble has a political context in which is guaranteed the right of the people to gather to contest decisions or directions of government outside the cycle of elections. The freedom to associate is much broader, granting power to form unions and other forms of social organizations with or without political objectives.

Suppose a visitor from a culture alien to these notions asked how we justify these freedoms. Why are they important, and what reasons could we give someone who claimed they were unnecessary? Freedoms that are foundational don't rest on some other values even more basic; they are expressed in statements that are self-evident. One way to show this – and *showing* is different from arguing from other statements – is to imagine if it were otherwise. Think of someone who doesn't enjoy freedom of thought or conscience: their beliefs would not be *their own* in any meaningful sense. They would not initiate, adopt, or appraise those beliefs; they simply would discover them within their consciousness. To say, "that's my belief I'm defending" is different, then, from saying "that's my leg you're pulling." They both belong to me, but I've claimed ownership of my belief by deliberately accepting it; I don't have to do anything else for my leg to be mine. Those without freedom of thought, opinion, or conscience are the mere repositories of other people's beliefs, not their own epistemic agents making up their minds for themselves. Our answer to the visitor, then, is that these freedoms are essential to *who we are*, as thinking, caring, feeling human beings. Humans without these freedoms wouldn't be mature persons as we know, value, and cherish them; they'd be the creatures of other agents and forces.

Likewise with the freedoms to practise and express publicly the convictions we have adopted and wish to live by. The kinds of beings we are – thinking, caring, human persons – need families and communities in which beliefs are shared, exposed, expressed, challenged, corrected, supported, and celebrated. When these freedoms are denied or curtailed, as they have often been by those with social, religious, or political power, human dignity and agency are eroded. Human life is impoverished, although the powerful few always manage to benefit. That's why the freedom to *associate* is fundamental to the sociality of human persons,[2] while the freedom to *assemble* is a secondary form of freedom necessary to safeguard the other freedoms when challenged by political power. Another way to put this would be to call the freedoms of thought, expression, and association *constitutive* freedoms: they are essential constituents of what it is to be a mature human agent – a thinking, communicating, social being. One cannot be that sort of being without the agency to exercise those functions and activities freely. It isn't quite the same with the freedom of assembly, since that freedom need be exercised only if those in authority encroach on our constitutive freedoms – then, of course, the ability to protest becomes necessary to safeguard those freedoms.

Academic Freedom

In the previous chapter we saw that university autonomy is necessary to protect the academic enterprise from undue influences arising from government decisions or the interests of influential persons, corporations, or organizations. I now turn to the kind of freedom unique to the internal life of the university: *academic freedom*.

I'll consider more detailed descriptions of academic freedom in due course; for now it's enough to speak of what's involved in fairly general terms. When we take our fundamental freedoms to the campus and the academic life, it's understandable that faculty members should be able to pursue their interest in creating and generating knowledge without undue influence. They should also be able to express their scholarly ideas and conclusions both in their teaching and in their publications. (Here, and throughout this discussion, I am employing the expansive view of creating and publishing "knowledge" to include the creative and performing arts as practised in a university.) They should be able to meet with one another and form groups interested in issues relevant to their pursuit and transmission of knowledge. Looked at this way, the idea of academic freedom gathers up in one label freedoms of thought, conscience, belief, expression, and association in the context of the academic life – and it's that context which provides the label "academic."

But now the question becomes: is academic freedom necessarily a separate kind of freedom? Members of the university have the same freedoms that everyone in a democratic society enjoys; what is different about academic freedom? In some places, declarations of fundamental freedoms are only aspirational and rhetorical; in Canada and other democracies, such freedoms are upheld legally – indeed in several countries these fundamental freedoms are constitutionally guaranteed.[3] Is there something special about *academic* freedom beyond its use as a handy label for the context in which fundamental constitutive freedoms are exercised?

To arrive at an answer, we need to recognize that the context is the relationship between members of an institution and the power that has the authority to structure, grant, or terminate that relationship. That power is usually referred to as "the university," and it resides in the board, or in the president as determined by the board. The obvious form of relationship is economic: the university hires and determines the duties of faculty members as employees, and can discipline or dismiss them. But there are other forms of status that don't have to involve money, such as rank or some privileges. Call all of these features of the relationship the "benefits" conferred by the university.

The issue is this: these benefits do not confer fundamental freedoms on members – they already enjoy those as citizens. Removing such benefits, therefore, would not affect their fundamental freedoms. It might be the case that someone whose contract is terminated would find it very difficult to do research and publication without a salary, but their freedom to do so would not be abrogated. Moreover, in Canada, members who claimed the university had infringed their rights and freedoms would have no recourse to the Charter, which applies only to governments and their agencies, not to universities.[4] If the benefits of membership are to be retained when freedoms are exercised in ways that perturb the university, then there must be some other form of guarantee of those benefits.

Perhaps human rights legislation and employment law already provide sufficient recourse against discrimination and unjust dismissal, universities are like any other institutions, and a distinctively *academic* freedom is not required. Universities are indeed employers, and subject to the relevant regulations and legislation. But universities can muzzle the expression of research without transgressing laws about discrimination, and they can dismiss under employment laws with adequate notice or severance. So these laws don't necessarily address the academic enterprise that is at the heart of the university.

If there is to be protection of the freedoms to explore ideas regardless of their popularity or social acceptability and to teach and publicly in oral or written form the results of scholarship, then some particular and distinctive form of guarantee is required. That's all the more important when we add two more features to the context of free expression in the university. The first is teaching: faculty members aren't simply expressing freely their opinions in the classroom; they are exercising the authority of scholarship in explaining, defending, or criticizing received opinions, assessing their students' understanding, and conferring on them the benefits that lead to their degrees. Second, when faculty members speak or write publicly about their scholarship, they do so as members of the university and the academy, not merely as private citizens. Their work colours directly the reputation of the university, which, as we have seen, is so significant for its flourishing. Teaching and public expression might incur social or political disapproval, creating embarrassment for the university.

What's needed, then, is the commitment that the university will refrain from imposing disciplinary measures and sanctions, up to and including dismissal, even when the research, teaching, or public expression of faculty members causes perturbation that would otherwise be actionable under other legislation. That's why the conferral of this commitment is termed *academic* freedom.

I don't intend this yet as a precise definition of academic freedom – for one thing, I haven't discussed the limits to this kind of freedom – there are some important ones – or which members of the university get to enjoy how much of it. First, however, we need to determine why academic freedom is justified.

Grounding Academic Freedom

One justification for academic freedom advanced several decades ago is that it is a moral right conferred on faculty when they are hired. Faculty are required to seek and promote truth as they sincerely understand it. Where there is a duty to do something, it is morally wrong for the one expecting the duty to be performed to prevent its performance.[5] On this view the duties and rights of universities and faculty members follow the same pattern as those of any employers and employees. Nevertheless, when it comes to the duty of truth seeking, this principle is both too broad and too restrictive. As expressed, the university's duty could confer positive rights as well as the right to be free from sanctions and dismissal. If I am hired to seek truth in ancient philosophy, I may well argue that I am prevented from discharging this duty without regular travel to Greece, a greatly enhanced library collection, and a teaching load that does not interfere with my current research. That's too broad. On the other hand, if the university doesn't want me to spend all of my time seeking truth in areas I wasn't hired to teach, it might write a very restrictive contract about the kind of truth I should be seeking (maybe just about Plato's early dialogues) – and then this moral right would be too restrained to count as academic freedom.

There's a different justification of academic freedom – a broadly utilitarian one: the claim that *society is better off* if its universities permit and encourage the free exploration, teaching, and publication of ideas without fear of sanction or reprisal. That way, more truth gets out, so to speak, and society benefits when there is more, rather than less, truth. The interests of society, then, justify academic freedom. That's a noble hope, for which there is good evidence, especially in the case of scientific advances. It's relatively easy to point to the social benefits of engineering and medical research, though it's less clear that these discoveries are necessarily dependent on the academic freedom of the researchers – R&D scientists in pharmaceutical labs don't have these freedoms. The problem arises in determining just what the interests of society are, and especially in agreeing on who makes that determination. Government plausibly could claim to represent those interests and to be unable to discern what possible social benefit might arise from some arcane field of study – or worse, from scholarship and teaching critical of reigning orthodoxies. Ironically, universities themselves might lay the best claim to possess the history, expertise, and independence required to understand the long-term interests of society. That would make them feel better about the consequences of protecting academic freedom, but self-justification has never been as popular with audiences as with speakers.

Despite the challenge of securing agreement on controversial claims about what's beneficial for society, there is abundant evidence that universities contribute significantly to the public good. But might there be a second way to ground academic freedom as a value particular to universities? I propose that there is. Recalling my defence of foundational personal freedoms, think of academic freedom as *constitutive*: the kind of value that defines and constitutes the identity of the institution, in similar fashion to the freedoms of thought, expression, and association that constitute a responsible human agent. A university that doesn't safeguard its faculty's freedoms to discover, teach, and publish is not a properly constructed university. It might be something else – perhaps a think tank, a directed research institute, or a training school – but it is not a fully formed university. The reason is that the epistemic functions of the university have to do with discovering, assessing and critiquing ideas, beliefs, and practices. Not all of these are well founded or worthy; some are false, even if for a long time a great many people have thought they were true. If a group or society as a whole held certain beliefs or practices as sacrosanct and beyond legitimate questioning, and the university were pressured into sanctioning those who investigated, taught, or published disputed material, the institution would not be functioning as a university.

Further, as we saw in Chapter Two, universities must be trust-worthy if they are to be effective in their knowledge functions. Trust depends upon integrity. Universities must be seen to have robust policies on academic integrity, and crucial to that integrity are guarantees that neither external nor internal forces will interfere with the proper business of inquiry, assessment, and publication.

It's for the sake of that integrity, then, that universities (as employers) voluntarily limit their freedom to discipline or sanction faculty members for their views. Just as the state creates a protected place for universities by respecting autonomy, limiting its power to interfere in academic matters, so the university creates a space for its faculty, protected from adverse consequences by respecting academic freedom.

Determining Limits to Academic Freedom

Ah, but no freedom is completely unfettered. What are the limits on academic freedom and, just as important, who determines if those limits have been transgressed?

Some limits are obvious. When a faculty member is no longer deemed able to perform adequately the duties of the position, he or she should not be able to claim the freedom to carry them out incompetently. Likewise, if the exercise of freedom involves breaches of academic integrity, such misconduct would subvert the functions of the university and might cause this freedom to be abrogated. Sometimes "gross misconduct" is invoked as a reason to limit academic freedom. Egregious cases of criminal behaviour such as assault or fraud don't necessarily involve academic integrity, but such conduct affects the safety and security of the university's members and, therefore, its ability to carry out its functions.[6]

Now the crucial question: *who gets to determine* whether a faculty member is no longer competent or that the member's behaviour constitutes an academic offence or "gross misconduct"? If judgment is left absolutely only to those in power, academic freedom is but a fragile promise, one that can be made and broken by the same authority. If academic freedom is to be a constitutive freedom defining the university, then decisions made about conferring, diminishing, or removing the benefits of membership cannot be thought arbitrary. Faculty members are not chosen and their careers advanced except on the recommendation of independent peer review. Neither should they be disciplined, sanctioned, or dismissed without the assessment of their conduct by competent peers. Exactly how that process works will depend on the particularities of the case and the policies of the university in question. In minor cases the judgment of internal colleagues might suffice; in egregious cases, especially of alleged academic incompetence, it would be wise to seek beyond immediate colleagues for evidence and assessment. Peer judgment is not infallible, but as I argue in the next chapter, it is fundamental to the decision-making processes of universities.

The answer to the crucial question depends on the difference between *determining* and *deciding*. Legally the university, as employer, must *decide* on sanctions and impose them on its members. But the *determination* of incompetence and misconduct should involve peers who are experienced in academic assessment, not simply reflect the sole judgment of those in power.

So far I've argued that academic freedom is peculiar to the university as a constitutive but not absolute freedom, conferred upon its members to enable them to carry out the essential functions of the institution, and withdrawn only when that purpose is frustrated, as determined by competent academic judgment. I haven't yet attempted a definition of "academic freedom," or discussed whether tenure is necessary to guarantee this freedom, or even asked which members of the university actually enjoy it. Let's start with tenure, then move to freedom of speech and some reflections on how academic freedom plays out in religious institutions where freedom of conscience and religion might bump up against it.

Academic Freedom and Tenure

Briefly, holding tenure is having the guarantee that your contract will not be terminated until the normal age of retirement except under very strict conditions, generally known as *for just cause*. It's often argued by faculty associations and unions that the only effective guarantee of academic freedom is a system of tenure. It's also argued, often, by commentators in the media and occasionally by some board members that tenure is a bad and unnecessary thing. Sometimes it protects actual incompetence; for some its guarantee of a continuing paycheque encourages laziness and low levels of productivity; and, as even deans know, it sometimes has a sclerotic effect on the flexibility required to address changing enrolment patterns.

For the record, it should be stressed here that well-functioning universities grant tenure after a very rigorous process and only to faculty members who have demonstrated accomplishment and promise in their scholarship and teaching. Although cases of dismissal of tenured faculty are rare, university agreements do set out conditions under which a tenured appointment may be terminated; they are usually the kinds of conditions set out in the previous section on the limits of academic freedom. Appropriately, the standard of evidence for termination of tenure is high. Many agreements include financial exigency among "just causes" for which tenure may be revoked, though this is contentious; it is a challenge for a university not only to demonstrate this financial condition, but then to justify the termination of faculty in a particular area.

The link between tenure and academic freedom is strong. In fact, tenure is usually justified by its protection of academic freedom: that is its principal reason, according to the Canadian Association of University Teachers and the American Association of University Professors.[7] Some make the corresponding claim that without tenure there is no academic freedom.[8] Of course, it doesn't follow that, if X is the principal reason for Y, there can be no Y without X; something else might make Y possible. That's the difference between sufficient and necessary conditions. Tenure is sufficient for academic freedom: if you've got tenure, you've got academic freedom. But is it necessary?

The answer has to be no. Academic freedom is not a metaphysical state that descends upon a faculty member the moment tenure

is conferred. It's a relationship between the university – the institution, as employer – and the faculty member in the form of a commitment to refrain from imposing sanctions on the free exercise
of academic expertise and convictions. That commitment is the
university's to make; it could provide a similar guarantee of freedom of inquiry and expression, including of teaching and publication, *during a contractual period of time shorter than "until normal
retirement."*

And in fact, since academic freedom is constitutive of the very
institution, it's crucial that the university respects the academic
freedom of all its academic staff, tenured or not, full or part time.
There is evidence that an increasingly high percentage of faculty
is not tenured – one US survey places the share of tenure-track
faculty at less than 30 per cent (see Table 4.1) – and it's commonly
believed that very high numbers of Canadian undergraduates are
taught by part-time contract faculty.[9] It's difficult to get an accurate
picture of such numbers,[10] and defining who is and is not in this
category poses some challenges; for instance, some professionals –
poets, novelists, lawyers, executives – teach only a course or two

Table 4.1. University Faculty by Type, United States, 1975–2014

	1975	1989	1993	1995	2003	2005	2007	2009	2011	2013	2014
Faculty type	(per cent)										
Full-time tenured	29.03	27.61	24.99	24.82	19.26	17.73	17.19	16.82	17.73	21.60	21.45
Full-time tenure-track	16.12	11.40	10.22	9.61	8.77	8.20	7.98	7.65	6.84	8.09	8.05
Full-time non-tenure-track	10.33	14.09	13.59	13.56	14.96	16.33	14.87	15.06	12.95	16.41	16.73
Part-time	24.00	30.36	33.07	33.19	37.04	39.07	40.50	41.11	41.45	41.14	40.93

Source: American Association of University Professors, "Higher Education at a
Crossroads: The Economic Value of Tenure and the Security of the Profession,"
Academe, March-April 2016, fig. 2, available online at https://www.aaup.org/sites/
default/files/2015-16EconomicStatusReport.pdf.

by choice. Nevertheless, my point is a simple one: whatever the percentage of non-tenured faculty, the university cannot be said to fulfil its knowledge functions if it does not extend academic freedom to those with whom it contracts to teach and engage in scholarly work.

That doesn't mean, however, that all members of the institution enjoy all forms of academic freedom, or that claims to academic freedom are always justifiable. We need to look at the scope across membership of this freedom – do librarians, or students, possess it? – and across content – does it pertain to issues outside one's academic area of expertise? Before that discussion, though, I need to make sure that my claim – that tenure is not necessarily the only safeguard of academic freedom – is not misunderstood. Tenure is indeed important to the academic enterprise, in more ways than one.

First, tenure is indeed strongly linked to academic freedom. Holding a permanent position makes it possible to speak openly and honestly, especially when subtle disapproval from others might counsel reticence. They might be colleagues or officials near the bottom of the hierarchy, not the university in its full authority. It's just wrong to believe that threats to academic freedom always come from Above; sometimes it's the work of an academic administrator to protect colleagues from each other.[11] Although the university can profess its support of academic freedom for non-tenured positions (often referred to as contingent positions), the possibility of non-renewal of one's contract can have a dampening effect on freedoms of inquiry and expression within the academy.

Second, the university's fundamental functions of knowledge generation and discovery need to be carried out in time allotted for research, and over significant periods of time. Contingent faculty are hired mainly to teach, not to engage in scholarship that demands longer periods of research. Permanence provides that space necessary for sustained scientific research or the mature scholarship reflected in books and articles. An institution that hires mainly for program delivery might manage with a preponderance of part-time people, but it would limp seriously in trying to do what universities are supposed to do with knowledge. Those guaranteed permanence create and discover knowledge; indeed, they are required to do so in addition to their teaching.

Third, the academic business of the university requires collegial discussion and deliberation in councils and senates, as I'll discuss in the next chapter. Contingent faculty, especially part-time instructors, are hired to perform specific duties around teaching in particular programs, and do not normally participate fully in developing curriculum or debating policies. They have neither the time nor the responsibility to interact with students beyond their assigned contact hours or to contribute to the wider intellectual and cultural life of the institution. They can't carry the weight of decision making about hiring and promotion, nor should they take on significant academic administration. To function as an academic community, a university requires a substantial body of permanent faculty.

I've just said "permanent," rather than "tenured," deliberately, because the functions of research and academic service don't actually require tenure in the strongest legal sense. As long as full-time faculty enjoy guarantees of academic freedom in continuing positions that can't be terminated without just cause and due process, including appeal, that will suffice.[12] But those conditions look very much like tenure, in substance if not in name.

Now, back to the question of scope: who should enjoy academic freedom, and for what kinds of behaviour?

The Scope of Academic Freedom

So far I have argued that not only permanent faculty, but all those engaged in the creation, expression, and transmission of knowledge should enjoy the protections of academic freedom. The university, however, has many more members who participate to some extent in its knowledge operations. What about them?

Who Has Academic Freedom?

Should academic freedom be extended to members of university groups beyond the faculty? The answer is, perhaps, but not fully. It all depends.

Take librarians, for instance. In many institutions their work is covered by policies similar to those for faculty members. If the freedoms of academic life are constitutive of the university, then any defining knowledge function that librarians perform should be protected. These could include such decisions as acquiring unpopular material that has academic merit, mounting exhibits, or publishing reports and accounts.[13]

And students? Some statements refer to students' exercise of the freedoms of learning and expression,[14] although it's far from clear what this means or how it works out in particular cases.[15] It would subvert the purpose of the university to do away with prerequisites or degree requirements in the name of the freedom to learn whatever one wants to learn; and freedom of expression doesn't mean that anyone's opinion is as good as anyone else's. I suggest, then, that the process of education, especially at the undergraduate level, is learning the proper acquisition, assessment, and expression of knowledge – an apprenticeship in the functions of the university. Put another way, it's a honing in the academic context of the fundamental freedoms of thought, belief, expression, and association. One needs to distinguish a good idea from a bad one, clear from shoddy thinking, effective from muddled discourse, and so on – all that is involved in the responsible exercise of one's freedoms. This means that students do not have the full-blown academic freedom that faculty members are accorded in their employment relation with the university; but they should have a nascent freedom within the academic enterprise to develop their own thinking and expression under the tutelage of their instructors. Not paid by the university, students have no employment benefits to be protected by academic freedom. Nevertheless they seek the benefits of grades, degrees, and diplomas, which are withheld under certain conditions, such as academic misconduct. Might there be pressure to deny such benefits for academically responsible, but perturbing, behaviour?

Here are three possible scenarios. In the first, an undergraduate in an independent study course chooses to write on a topic approved by the instructor, but then, without the instructor's explicit approval, expounds controversial views that are reported in the student press. The instructor is pressed to reject the student's paper or ask for revision. In the second, a graduate student, teaching in a prescribed curriculum, offends some parents with a disturbing interpretation. The university is pressured to express its disapproval of such conduct and to sanction the offending student instructor. In the third scenario, two senior undergraduates become uncomfortable with their supervisor's instructions to alter some conclusions on research. They disclose this to the chair of the department, uncertain whether they might suffer adverse consequences from the faculty member.[16] In such scenarios it's the freedom of the students that is in question – and not just their freedom of expression, but their freedom with respect to academic matters. If they act with academic integrity, their freedoms should be protected by the institution.

That I've resorted to scenarios is an indication of the difficulty of determining any general principles about the academic freedom of students. Best, I think, to see those with the status of student as learning how to practise the relevant freedoms in the academy, but exercising them on their own only in particular contexts. The protection of academic freedom is accorded them in specific circumstances in which the university would properly protect the academic freedom of a faculty member.

One more class of persons in the university community should be considered: academic administrators such as deans, vice-presidents, and presidents. The short comment is that they do enjoy academic freedom *in their own academic work*, as faculty members. As administrators? That's more problematic. Deans, for instance, hold power over budget, appointments, and other benefits; they are therefore the guardians of the academic freedoms of those under their authority. One can claim academic freedom only where it is, or should be, protected by a higher authority. Presidents, then, should protect the research, teaching, and publication of deans just because they are faculty members. As we will see in the next section, because they are faculty members, they also have the freedom to criticize the university – but in the same way that they don't have *decanal* freedoms of research and publication, they don't have *decanal* freedom to criticize the university. Whether it is right to criticize is up to the president to determine. The academic administration of a university needs a shared commitment if it is to be effective. A wise administrator encourages debate and welcomes criticism within the team, but a member who can't accept the outcome of deliberations is free to dissent by leaving the team. Open dissension subverts the purposes of the university, and administrators should not claim immunity in the name of academic freedom. If the complaint is serious and not a peevish expression of a thwarted will, freedom of conscience would be a much better ground. If a faculty member is to be dismissed as an administrator, it should be done humanely, with due process, and the individual must retain tenure – unless, of course, the person's behaviour constituted grounds for academic dismissal.[17]

What's Protected by Academic Freedom?

Let's turn now to scope in the second sense: what sorts of activities are protected by academic freedom? Thus far I've listed scholarship and research and the expression of knowledge claims in teaching and in publication. It's understandable that the sphere of freedom, given this list, would be one's academic discipline – the area in which one stakes the claims of familiarity and expertise. But this is too narrow, for two different reasons.

First, over the course of an academic life, the boundaries and focus of one's intellectual interest continue to shift, as does the character of academic disciplines. I, for one, have published in areas in which I've never been formally educated or in which I have never taught. I wouldn't be happy with any attempt to designate only certain kinds of questions belonging to the discipline in which I was hired as protected by academic freedom. What matters is not what I claim as my territory, but, rather, whether the community of scholars (a deliberately vague notion) would agree that the territory in question is academic.[18]

There's a second concern about limiting the scope of academic freedom to issues rooted in a field of knowledge. Many statements include the freedom to criticize the university itself and society at large.[19] Critique of the university must surely be appropriately considered "academic," not just a general guarantee of free speech enjoyed by citizens. As I noted above in explaining the importance of permanence, the business of the university requires informed deliberation on curriculum, degree requirements, and policies about dozens of issues listed across the alphabet from Absence from Class to Withdrawal from a Course. Very few policies arise from specific areas of study in which faculty are expert; they are forms of structuring the general academic experience of students and the conditions under which the university carries out its functions. It's not only good practice for a university to encourage informed debate on policies and regulations; it's also right and proper that the provisions of academic freedom should extend beyond scholarship and teaching to include participation in the critical assessment of the university's decisions and practices. That means that the cranky and eccentric, as well as the respectful and astute, may comment on how the university (usually the president) performs and is perceived, without fear of the adverse consequences of poking and prodding those in authority.

What of the freedom to criticize society at large – extramural freedom, as it's known in US institutions; is it properly called academic? One might argue that (as some statements have it) faculty members enjoy the freedoms of expression and assembly of all citizens in democratic societies,[20] so there is no need to confer this right on them. Nevertheless universities can be pressured by external authorities and powers, including influential community members, to sanction their members who give offence. As we saw in the previous chapter, such intrusion into the university's space would compromise the university's autonomy. Pressure might also be internal, from those concerned for the university's reputation when faculty members speak out about societal issues. In fact, reputational concerns account for the requirement in some statements that, when faculty members speak out on public issues outside their area of competence, they should not take advantage of their university affiliation.[21] It's clear – how could it be otherwise? – that faculty members who are citizens enjoy the right and privileges of citizenship, including, in our societies, freedom of expression and the right to criticize government and public institutions and agencies. This freedom is not in dispute, even when it is incorporated into statements of academic freedom. What is at stake, though, is the use of discipline or sanctions on the part of the university when one of its members exercises a democratic freedom in a way that cannot easily be linked to the speaker's area of academic competence. A scientist in environmental studies may comment authoritatively on public policy about climate change, but a scholar whose expertise is generative studies in Basque linguistics could criticize that policy only as a citizen. If the linguist's university affords extramural academic freedom, it would not impose discipline even if pressured to do so by forces within or outside the institution – unless the expression of opinion demonstrated incompetence or inability to carry out normal responsibilities.[22]

Since there is no necessary connection between one's professional expertise and the subjects of civic debate, I propose that, instead of thinking of extramural expression as a feature of academic freedom per se, we regard it as a fundamental freedom, with academic implications and consequences.[23] It is *academic* in context only where utterances are known to be *from an academic*, who is a *member of an academic institution*. It's important, though, for the university to accord its members this freedom. Otherwise it would have to determine on every problematic occasion whether an expression was warranted, which would mean not only assessing the competence of the speaker but also taking a stand on political and societal issues. It would also mean that, if the university were willing to censor some expression, it could face pressure to sanction research and expression that is more closely related to academic expertise. Its faculty members would live under uncertainty about just how free they were to pursue ideas that might perturb others. As a practical measure, then, universities should include among the freedoms of faculty members the freedom to criticize society at large, both as competent experts and as citizens. In the former capacity their freedom is fully academic; in the latter role they enjoy, if not full-blown academic freedom, then its benefits, just because they are academics, regardless of their field of expertise.

The Responsibilities and Irresponsibilities
of Academic Freedom

One more issues needs addressing in this section on the scope of academic freedom: its responsible use. I follow some comments on the attendant responsibilities that faculty members assume in their positions by observations on the potential for misuse of this important value for the academic life.

No one seriously believes that academic freedom gives licence for irresponsible behaviour. The debate, rather, is over how responsibilities are discharged, and who decides when there is a difference of opinion. Universities have not only developed statements on responsibilities; they have also articulated policies that govern many aspects of the academic life in which freedoms are exercised. A typical list of topics would include research ethics and integrity, conflict of interest and commitment, grading practices, teaching assessment, academic appeals, sexual harassment, and criteria for tenure and promotion. These and other documents structure the works and products of scholarship, teaching, and assessment, and relationships with colleagues and students. In so doing, approved policies create responsibilities in the exercise of freedoms, and may be relied upon in assessing behaviour, providing redress, or imposing penalties in some cases.

Many universities provide a paragraph or two on the responsibilities that accompany academic freedom; they stress fairness in discharging duties of teaching and scholarship, and enjoin participation in the committee work that collegial processes require.[24] Some institutions use terms like respect or restraint in setting out expectations for responsible behaviour, and include injunctions not to speak in the name of the institution in extramural expression (as I noted earlier).[25] It is well and good to hope for civility in interpersonal relationships among academics; nevertheless, it's very difficult to achieve general agreement on what constitutes disrespectful discourse, or whether your being offended by my strong language constitutes lack of respect. I'll consider below the possibility that free speech need not always be respectful; but here it's enough to acknowledge that university administrators require patience and a high level of tolerance for the few whose behaviour habitually skirts the edges of civility. One exhaler of bad air can take up much of the oxygen in a department.

When academic freedom is invoked to justify behaviour that would not be tolerated in other organizations or even families, universities are hard pressed to respond appropriately. That concern prompted Canadian university presidents to include, in their 2010 statement on academic freedom, the sentence: "The university must also defend academic freedom against interpretations that are excessive or too loose, and the claims that may spring from such definitions."[26] Just as there might be interpretations of academic freedom that are too narrow – I've argued that limiting it to one's field of expertise is too restrictive – so there are some that might be too loose, too vague, or far too generous, and are used to justify kicking against unwelcome constraints or compulsions. My teaching a contentious text in a curriculum approved by my peers should be protected, but my insistence that I can teach only in the late afternoon on Tuesdays has no justification in any notion of academic freedom. My proposal to teach a particular course should be debated by my colleagues, but if the department or council determined that it didn't fit in the curriculum, my preference would have been denied and my ego bruised, but my freedom would not have been abrogated. If my merit increase were diminished by my deliberate refusal to engage in minimal service on committees in order to spend more time on research or teaching, I couldn't wave the flag of freedom to claim unjust treatment. The invocation of academic freedom works where there are threats to my academic investigation and expression, not where I fail to perform the duties expected and required of a member of the collegium. Academic freedom cannot privilege me above my colleagues.

Since there will always be disputes about interpretations of the meaning and implications of academic freedom, university administrators need wisdom and judgment as well as patience and tolerance. It would be perverse if those in power were the sole arbiters in challenges to their authority in the name of academic freedom; this freedom is intended to provide protection against that very practice. That's why peer assessment and determination are crucial. They take from the powerful the ability to impose arbitrary penalties, locating in those who are academically competent the responsibility for determining the limits or abuses of academic freedom.

From this understanding, two practical suggestions emerge. First, universities should engage in open and periodic discussion about the nature of academic freedom. Surely all members of the institution – faculty, senate, board, administration – have not only an interest but a duty to gain a more than superficial understanding of this defining value of a university. We require knowledge of health and safety regulations, but seem content to live with folk wisdom about this thing called academic freedom. That's not good enough.

Second, when there arise challenges in the name of academic freedom to administrative decisions, prudence as well as principle counsel determination of the claim by peers, rather than by fiat. Sometimes that calls for using a grievance procedure, as long as the procedure involves the academically competent. Informal resolution, however, can often be effective as long as the parties agree. Every institution has a few wise and hoary heads lifted above the fray; it can occasionally help to call upon their experienced judgment before festering issues require surgery.

Can Academic Freedom Be Defined?

It's time to conclude this discussion of academic freedom with a brief comment on its definition, before moving to its relationship to freedom of expression and a consideration of the fundamental freedoms of conscience and religion in its relationship to the notion of academic freedom I've been exploring.

I have refrained from offering a succinct definition of academic freedom. The answer to the question of whether there can be a definition is, of course, yes: it has been defined in many documents and statements, and what has been done can be done. The real question is whether it can be *done well*. A definition done well minimizes ambiguity, making it possible to pick out just the right things from a clutter of cases, examples, imaginary scenarios, and the like. A strict definition of a word like "cousin" will screen out lots of relationships, leaving only the offspring of one's aunt or uncle in the bin. It will also explain extended and metaphorical uses of the term, as in "kissing cousin" or "our American cousins." With other terms, effective definition isn't so easy, and we often end up giving lots of examples and uses in the hope that describing uses will do the work of definition.

When it comes to academic freedom, there is a double challenge, one for each of its terms. Freedom, as we saw at the beginning of this chapter, is a concept as elusive as it is important – it always needs a context in which to situate its meaning. As for the adjective, I haven't even tried to elucidate what "academic" picks out, leaving that as an adjective connected to "advanced" or "higher" learning and teaching in institutions devoted to making and critiquing knowledge claims. Still, universities meet this double challenge by offering up definitions on which they rely in defining the fundamental values of their employment and other relations with members. Their definitions often have legal force in collective agreements. Where they don't function in contracts, definitions of academic freedom might be more aspirational statements than negotiated articles formally adopted by boards and associations. Nonetheless, they are relied on, regardless of their status.

We have also seen that the language in definitions or statements requires interpretation – and that the interpreters should not be simply those with the authority to make decisions. The ideas, commitments, and practices clustering around academic freedom have grown out of the lived experience of faculty members and institutions over many long years and in many different countries. That collective experience provides rich material for understanding, especially in the details and disposition of actual cases of alleged infringement of academic freedom.

A statement of the principles of academic freedom need not be as precise as, and can be more expansive than, a strict definition. It should include the areas I've been discussing here: research and scholarship, including artistic creation; teaching; publication, in the sense of making publicly accessible the results of investigation or creation; the freedom to be critical of the university; and the freedom to comment on issues of wider societal import.

There are many ways of expressing these ideas that are central to the concept of academic freedom, and it would be wrong to privilege just one, even if it's the one you've lived with or perhaps written about. Why so? Because there's something perverse about insisting that this particular statement is authoritative, beyond revision. When a statement is about the freedom to interpret and express ideas, that very freedom has to be applicable to the statement itself. In consequence, interpretation of the language of any statement is crucial, and is never finished, as new situations arise in which the principles need to be worked out. That will always be a messy business.

More important than statements, however, are the policies and practices that give effect to the principles of academic freedom. Academic freedom remains but a promise unless there are policies spelling out what constitutes "just cause" for discipline or termination, and unless procedures involve peer assessment. It's helpful, then, to include in any statement of academic freedom reference to the university's relevant policies, and also to set out the responsibilities that structure and inform the exercise of freedom in the generation and expression of knowledge at the heart of the university's life.

Academic freedom, I've argued, is a defining freedom of a university, without which the institution would be something else. It's necessary. But, as this chapter has demonstrated, there's nothing neat or straightforward about how it actually operates. A messy necessity indeed.

Before moving on to the final condition for the successful operation of the university, effective administration and governance, let me offer some reflections on two complicated issues arising out of the relationship of civic freedoms to academic freedom. The first is freedom of expression (in speech, publication, and assembly), especially for students. The second is freedom of conscience and religion as it finds institutional expression in certain universities committed to a particular religious creed and life.

Academic Freedom and Freedom of Speech: Disrespect, Dissent, Disruption

I've just argued above that, although freedom of expression is a civic freedom, faculty members should have this freedom protected by the university even in areas outside their academic competence. The reasons are prudential: censoring a faculty member would commit the university to take sides in civic disputes, and sanctioning free speech would chill the climate on campus, since the notion of academic competence is fluid. But what about students? Since I was hesitant to accord them full academic freedom, they wouldn't enjoy the protection it affords. But they are highly engaged in many forms of expression: in writing for the student press, debating, inviting speakers on controversial topics, protesting, demonstrating, mounting provocative artistic exhibitions and plays. Their activities usually bear some form of the university's name, and they use university spaces and facilities. What should be the limits on this freedom, especially when the university's reputation – that precious commodity – is at stake?

The question is sharpened when one remembers that, with respect to expression under the aegis of academic freedom, the appropriateness of what's expressed is subject to peer assessment, and faculty are accountable for their views. The point of free speech and expression within civil society, however, is to let anyone say anything, regardless of its cogency, propriety, or truth, as long as it's not contrary to law. (Laws differ in jurisdictions, but slander and libel, and incitement to violence, are usually impermissible, and Canada has laws against hateful propaganda as well.) Since universities are places where claims to knowledge are subject to critical examination, there's something unsettling about permitting expression that might be unrestrained by that scrutiny in the protected epistemic and social space of the university.

So, why promote, in this special place, unfettered expression as long as it's legal? Let's examine two responses to whether there are limitations on this freedom, one essential answer and one inadequate.

The essential limit first. If one thinks of instances where limits on expression have often been imposed in university settings, they form clusters of activities: the disinviting of controversial speakers or the shutting down of their presentations; the banning by student groups of morally or socially suspect presentations; the withdrawing of publications. The agents in these cases exercise the authority of the university or student government, or they exercise power by disruption, blocking access or making it impossible for the speaker to continue. I have in mind specific cases, but no doubt a casual perusal of university news will reveal weekly examples.[27] In any story there are particularities that one must know in order to make an informed judgment about the proper exercise of free expression or the proper imposition of limits on that expression. But one fundamental principle must guide judgment: legitimate freedom of expression cannot be negated by the actions of others, even in the name of their freedom. That is, the very conditions of free expression must be respected, not denied or removed.

What are those conditions? It depends on the events in question, but they include the ability of the speaker or presenter to carry out the invited or announced task, the safety and security of the venue and attendees, the uncensored media story or article. Given the variety of possibilities, perhaps some elaboration will uncover more of the underlying principle.

Take public events first. If one wishes to protest the event – picketing, making pointed remarks in question periods, clapping or booing at certain times, or walking out in anger, disgust, or silent disapproval: all of these measures express disagreement with the speaker or the purpose of the event.[28] Measures such as blocking access to the event, continued noise making to silence the speaker, or triggering fire alarms shut down the event and prevent the exercise of free speech.[29] Disruption on this order should be contrary to university policy and should carry sanctions if necessary. When events are cancelled in advance, the rationale is often the inability of the university to guarantee safety and security. An experienced administration will anticipate difficulty – not always successfully; these judgment calls are not easy – and have alternate venues or modes of delivery in mind. Cancelling a contentious event rather

than restructuring or rescheduling must be a last resort for an institution that protects freedom of expression.

When student groups themselves attempt to limit free expression, it's tempting for the university to mitigate responsibility by
affirming the independence of student societies. The same distancing strategy is used when student freedom of expression causes
offence to alumni and society. Unfortunately the university's
reputation does not enjoy that independence; events occurring in
university space and under its name create guilt by association.
The main challenge in specific incidents is damage control, with
patient explanations of the fundamental importance of free expression, pointing to specific policies adopted by the university, but
also sanctions where that freedom has been violated. Prevention
is better than cure, but it isn't always possible. Some measures,
however, do help. Clubs and societies should go through a process
of formal recognition by the university, which usually collects fees
on behalf of the student council. Enshrining in agreements actual
policies about fundamental freedoms and disruptions would give
the university some leverage if freedom of expression were threatened. Further, problematic events are always worse when student
leaders experience alienation from the administration. Undoubtedly they often intensify that alienation, perhaps for their own
purposes. Nevertheless, if the university can find sympathetic faculty members to support or advise student groups, some issues
can be resolved through negotiation, rather than the imposition of
authority.[30]

The student press affords one other category for comment. I
must begin with the confession that I think some of what is put
out in student newspapers is one-sided and often inaccurate, written without adequate consultation with knowledgeable sources.
Some of it borders on the puerile and scatological. But that negative appraisal must be balanced with the happy acknowledgment
that at other times the journalism can be excellent, bringing to the
community's attention issues that require the light of day. Especially these days, it is crucial to affirm the importance of a free
and informed press. Although freedom of the press and media is a
fundamental one, it is under attack from more than one direction.

Social media, with all the analytical sophistication of an emoticon, are vehicles for venting personal prejudice and – especially at presidential thumb-and-fingertips – demeaning, dismissive disgust without a shred of evidence. The power of a handful of wealthy media owners to control messages and thereby opinion damages the crucial independence of the press. Even without that control, in a digital era with shrinking subscription revenues, it's increasingly difficult to fund investigative journalism, at a time when we need sustained, independent analysis of social and political issues. A democracy built on ignorance eats away at its very self, unwittingly welcoming control by the shrewd and rich powerful few. It's even worse when the few in power accuse independent media of lying and dishonesty, eroding confidence in evidence and reasoning.

The time is opportune, then, for universities to educate students about the role of the media, and to support and encourage intelligent campus journalism. If that requires restraint when the limits of the decent and respectful are stretched, so be it. For what would it mean for the university to shut down free expression in the campus press? It would use its authority and power to silence, rather than to engage in further discourse, an outright denial of the fundamental freedom it is supposed to be promoting.

I don't say it would always be wrong to invoke the university's authority by requiring a campus paper to be taken off the stands, or demanding retractions. There are legal limits to free speech. And gratuitous expressions of prejudice or hatred must be dealt with.[31] But that an article is disrespectful or causes offence, even deep offence, does not seem to me sufficient reason to remove a paper from circulation.[32]

Reference to offence brings me back to what I termed the inadequate answer about limits on expression: it is that limits should be imposed, and preferably self-imposed, in the name of minimizing offence to others. It's often claimed that, in a truth-seeking community such as the university, discourse should be civil, with the interlocutors demonstrating respect for each other even though they disagree. Even if one has the freedom to express certain ideas that might be hurtful, restraint would demonstrate respect through silence. "Civil discourse exists on a higher plane than does free speech, setting limits that are often not enacted by law but are rather agreed upon by individuals within society."[33]

It's hard not to be in favour of civility, especially towards those who have experienced enough of life's slings and arrows. One must have sympathy for those deeply offended by a particular form of free expression, not least because almost all of us can imagine like offence being given by some other form: one person's biting wit may mean another person's hurtful wound.

The question for a university, however, is not about social norms but about the very meaning of civil discourse – that is, discourse about issues in the civil society we inhabit. Civic discourse is not always "civil" in the sense of being comfortable. Sometimes it is passionate and engaged, far from cool and polite. Its very civility lies not in manners, or in the social conventions of a group, but in its attempts to create, challenge, and enlarge understanding of issues. Discourse that is truly "civil" is the expression of a culture that embraces communities of difference who may passionately disagree but nevertheless continue to talk and to listen. Properly civil discourse will not remain silent about the appropriate limits on free expression; it will debate laws and customs; it will call prejudice to account even if it must shock to do so. Bland speech might not offend but it might also mask injustice. Civil discourse must sometimes be provocative discourse.

No one should take delight in the offence of others. But a free society must be willing to give voice to the arts and to the press even when they are scandalous or disrespectful, because power and prejudice love respectful silence. Within a free society, the university has a special obligation to protect the space for free and civil discourse. Different societies have different limits on free expression. Where else may these limits be discussed, criticized, defended, or debated, if not in a university? Where may the passionate learn to think and speak effectively about their passions, by opening them up to discussion and debate with others, if not in a university? Universities must be places where freedom flourishes, for there is no better place to explore and determine what civil discourse actually is.

That is why the fundamental question about the limits of freedom must be the simple one of whether the very conditions of free and informed discussion are violated. Offence should call forth more discourse, not shut it down. So even where disagreement is experienced as disrespectful or worse, the vehicles of expression should not be silenced either by appeal to good manners or by recourse to disruption.

One other issue about the campus press deserves a mention. I've written as though the campus press is the student press, but universities these days staff up their communications departments to promote the role of the institution in the community and to attract new students. Their publications are really house organs, with the result that faculty in particular lack a vehicle for comment and reflection on matters of importance. Communication takes place within departments or perhaps faculties, but not across the institution. Newsletters and bulletins are generated by particular employee groups, reflecting their special interests, but without a campus-wide publication, sponsored by the administration but enshrining freedom of expression, it's hard to build a sense of community especially across a large institution. Memos from the administration are good, but they are only one-way.

At the beginning of this section I referred to the scrutiny of peer assessment in the proper exercise of academic freedoms, noting that this is missing in freedom of expression. If anyone can say anything in the protected place of the university, why should the university promote unfettered expression as long as it's legal? The answer must surely be that the university is just the sort of place where ideas and beliefs need to find expression *in order to be assessed*. Even if there's firm conviction in one group that the ideas in question are unworthy of any consideration, others will disagree, wanting to hear the case for themselves. On each campus, issues of the day or hour will arise, many beyond prediction. Members of the university, given the restlessness of the academic mind that faculty hope to instil in their students, will want to explore these issues. The worth of ideas can't be measured by some timeless complete menu of truths to be expressed or falsehoods to be exposed. Better, then, to foster freedom of expression within legitimate limits, in order to create opportunities for debate, dialogue, and even dissent. It doesn't follow that a university needs actively to invite charlatans and spin doctors in order to expose their deceptions. Nor is there any obligation to rent or offer space for other groups to promote ideas and values contrary to those of the institution.[34]

Events, displays, productions, and publications are a little like the books in a university library that are not assigned for courses: no one is compelled to read them, but they are available to open up minds to areas of exploration, sometimes where discovery is unwelcome or disturbing. Lectures, plays, speeches, performances, debates – these are living books that should not be censored. There's a difference, of course, in that the mind of the librarian is on accession according to approved policy. We wouldn't want an Arbiter of Events, in a properly constructed university, to keep us from unpleasant surprises. That's why freedom of expression is even messier than academic freedom. What's expressed lacks the academic integrity required of academic freedom. But it produces material, sometimes memorable, for that scrutiny.

Academic Freedom and the Freedoms of Conscience and Religion

As I noted at the beginning of this chapter, freedom of conscience is usually connected to freedom of religion, and the latter is a matter not only of interior belief but also of practice and association. Religious commitment is life involving; it structures habits, choices, and relationships. Put in other words, it's a way of living out authentically the knowledge that the faithful understand to arise from a relationship to transcendent reality.[35]

Many statements stress that academic freedom does not require neutrality on issues, but rather makes commitment possible. There is room, then, in a university for those with religious convictions, as well as for those without; for those who propose belief and for those who oppose belief. Where there is academic freedom, however, there can be no reigning orthodoxy dictating the consciences, ideas, and expression of faculty members. How could there be?

Built into the very concept of academic freedom is freedom of conscience, exercised in pursuit of knowledge; no subject of academic investigation may be forbidden, no results of honest scholarly endeavour suppressed.

There's a difference, of course, between the freedom of individual faculty members and the institutional freedom of a religiously oriented institution[36] – that is, institutional *autonomy*. The point of autonomy is to protect academic freedom within the university, although autonomy in itself does not guarantee academic freedom, any more than staying out of the business of the family next door ensures that they will all get along happily. And, as we saw in Chapter Three on this topic, lack of formal autonomy doesn't entail that there will be actual interference – studied or benign neglect has similar effects to declared autonomy. But any institution with little autonomy *in practice* can't properly fulfil the functions of a properly constructed university. Some religiously oriented institutions are directed by a denominational board that exercises an effective hand in controlling who teaches and what is taught. Although there are perfectly good reasons for a religious denomination to develop members who are like-minded graduates committed to the creed and way of life of that denomination, an institution without effective autonomy is more properly called something other than a university.[37]

Should an institution of higher learning with a distinct religious or theological perspective join the conversation at this stage, it would want to point out that it had the overwhelming burden of history on its side in claiming membership in the class of universities. Some of the most distinguished universities in the world have grown from religious roots. And – this might be controversial, but it's a defensible position – such a university does not have to be transplanted into secular ground in order to fulfil the proper functions of a university. The condition is a straightforward one: the institution must create and preserve a protected place for the academically free exercise of its knowledge functions.

If this condition is met, an institution may have a religiously inspired mandate – a theologically informed mission. It may include in its curriculum theology – as academically responsible reflection informed from within faith and practice – and not just the phenomenon of religion studied by the social sciences, or religious texts as literary artefacts, however valuable such studies. Further, to engage in theological scholarship and teaching, the institution should want to hire faculty members in accordance with its mission. That's not unusual: all universities hire in accordance with their mission, even where the "mission" is tacit and might be better expressed as an approach or perspective on its discipline. Literature departments might look for particular kinds of theorists; philosophy departments might hire analytic, rather than Continental, philosophers. If its mission is confessional, the institution would hire faculty who are best able, academically, to advance that mission. Academic competence would still need to be judged in the customary way, and usually would include thinking and writing from a standpoint sympathetic to the institution's stance.

But here's the heart of the matter: as in all properly constructed universities, in a religiously oriented university the hiring is done on the grounds of academic competence in the subject, including familiarity or sympathy with the approach or perspective. Further, once hired, a faculty member must come under the provisions of academic freedom, which include the institution's commitment to permit, without discipline or sanction, unfettered scholarship and expression.[38] When it comes to religiously oriented universities, however, there are three caveats to this general philosophy: one about hiring, a second about the conditions of continued membership in the institution, and a third about non-discrimination.

The first arises out of a practice in some institutions that articulates standards of belief and behaviour for its faculty members and requires them to sign an agreement that, if they violate those standards, they may be disciplined. This practice was referenced in the American Association of University Professors' 1940 Statement of Principles on Academic Freedom and Tenure: "Limitations of academic freedom because of religious or other aims of the institution should be clearly stated in writing at the time of the appointment." Such an agreement on the part of a faculty member is not just a limitation, however; it amounts to a voluntary denial of the fundamental principle of academic freedom. Although there are proper limits on the exercise of academic freedom, as we saw above, surrendering freedom with respect to certain ideas is a contradiction of the very notion.[39] Indeed, thirty years later the association's council adopted, among several new interpretations of the Statement, the observation that "most church-related institutions no longer need or desire the departure from the principle of academic freedom implied in the 1940 'Statement,' and we do not now endorse such a departure."[40] Properly constructed universities cannot require the surrender of academic freedom, even if done voluntarily, as a condition of membership.

A second caveat relating to religiously oriented universities concerns the conditions for remaining a member of the institution. Consider a hypothetical faculty member, academically able and hired in good faith because of scholarship sympathetic to the institution's stance. In this scenario, when joining the community, the faculty member had no difficulty identifying with its orientation, but now has had a crisis of conscience and no longer can affirm some article of the institution's creed or agree with a condition in its code of conduct. I've made this an example of freedom of conscience, partly because minds do change upon continued reflection and enlarged experience, but mainly because academic freedom is so closely related to constitutive freedoms. Assuming the parties act in good faith, the faculty member cannot be disciplined or dismissed if the school is to honour its commitment to academic freedom.[41] Depending on the circumstances (and circumstances will vary widely), existing duties should be carried out as initially agreed, or reassigned after consultation. But – as should be abundantly clear by now – actual beliefs and their expression cannot be constrained by the threat of sanction. Moreover, I have argued that academic freedom must include the freedom to be critical of the institution and society at large. Changed belief can lead to changed views about conduct, and if a faculty member expresses reservations or concerns about a code of conduct, surely an undistracted university must respect that freedom. Again the principle is simple: hire on mission, but once hired, all faculty come under the protections of academic freedom, including scholarly investigation and its results, teaching, publication, and freedom to criticize the university.

The third caveat concerns the complex business of human rights and discrimination in hiring. As in many jurisdictions, Canada has federal and provincial legislation setting out prohibited grounds for discrimination, including race, national or ethnic origin, colour, religion, age, sex, sexual orientation, marital status, family status, disability – the list varies slightly in different jurisdictions but has a strong core. And it is relevant to this discussion in two areas in particular. In hiring a faculty member, a university may not discriminate among candidates on the basis of religion,[42] but a religiously oriented institution might well wish to engage in exactly that sort of discrimination. Further, many such institutions have codes of conduct that could be relevant to some prohibited grounds, the most salient these days being sexual identity and same-sex marriages or unions. How issues of non-discrimination play out in properly constructed universities that are religiously oriented is highly convoluted, and highly controversial.

But there is some assistance in relevant considerations about how equality, freedom of conscience, and freedom of religion are exercised within the context of non-discrimination legislation. Recognizing that some groups have been historically disadvantaged, legislation permits preference for members of these groups in hiring for the sake of furthering equity. More, some occupations require preference for one applicant over another on grounds that would otherwise be prohibited. These "*bone fide* [good faith] occupational requirements" may include discriminating among candidates on such characteristics as age (in the case of required licences to drive or fly) or gender (such as staff in a men's locker room or in a sexual assault counselling practice). It has been argued that adherence to a particular religion is an occupational requirement for teaching that religion in a confessional school, especially in Catholic schools, and that discrimination on religious grounds is therefore justifiable. But does this exception to non-discrimination on religious grounds for the sake of *bone fide* occupational requirements apply to universities defined by autonomy and academic freedom?

Just suppose a religiously oriented university wants all its members to affirm a particular creed. It surely is a stretch to argue that, say, members of the housekeeping staff or accounting office can perform their assigned duties only if they are adherents to the religion that identifies the institution. Once that is recognized, doubt is cast upon the requirements for adherence to the creed by teachers of mathematics or physics or Spanish, or many other subjects. One might make the case for subjects directly dealing with religious belief and practice, such as theology, sacred texts, or some literatures and philosophy. But it's hard for a university committed to the principles of academic freedom to square the occupational requirement of familiarity with and sympathy for a set of convictions with discrimination against someone who cannot in good conscience affirm all the articles in a particular creed. What is the *bone fide* requirement *for a university*, which is defined by its freedoms, beyond academic competence and sympathetic familiarity? It might be good and pleasant for members of the institution to dwell together, each and every one person participating in a like-minded community. But is a *university* that the kind of community?

Similar reasoning may be applied to discrimination on the basis of codes of conduct. As I've argued, freedom of religion involves more than belief; it also means practice, ritual, and community. That's where codes enter the picture: a religiously oriented institution might argue that its members – especially those in a position to model the institution's values – should live a certain kind of life. So the occupational qualifications of mathematics professors would, on this view, include demonstrable adherence to the institution's code of conduct. One can imagine how this thinking would go: an institution would be regarded as hypocritical if it accepted behaviour in its senior members that it proscribed among its students. Either there is no alcohol on campus for anyone, or it's permissible for anyone of legal age.

The alcohol example, though, is not one of discrimination on proscribed grounds. When it comes to sexual orientation, the matter is indeed convoluted. In many countries (mainly in the Americas and western Europe), discrimination on grounds of sexual orientation is prohibited, and in a growing number same-sex marriage or civil union is legally permitted. The religiously conservative, however, hold as a matter of conscience that sexual conduct with partners of the same sex is proscribed by divine decree, whatever the state may proclaim. This is a fraught example of the clash between the power of the state and the hard-won freedom of conscience and religion, a clash that continues unabated, especially in twenty-first-century America. I can't comment on the legal and constitutional issues involved, and won't predict any outcomes in civil society. But here we can ask whether this discrimination has any place in the particular circumstances of a properly constructed university. Given the burden of this chapter – that universities must embed academic freedom as a constitutive value – can we find a link between that value and non-discrimination?

It's just a fact, regardless of how one feels about it, that beliefs about sexual identity and relationships are for some people matters of religious conscience. If the state permits as a fundamental freedom the freedom of belief, it cannot bind their conscience, although it may regulate their behaviour with respect to their convictions. For instance, a minister may refrain from performing a same-sex marriage, but not from renting an apartment to the couple. Should this individual freedom of religious conscience be extended to institutions that are religiously oriented? An institution can certainly declare that it holds to the 'traditional view of marriage as between one man and one woman," and can invite into membership those who are in agreement with that view. But should it exclude *otherwise well-qualified* potential faculty members for the *sole* reason that their conviction or even behaviour is not in accord with this interpretation of religious doctrine about sexuality?

There will be legal and political answers, but I now want to argue that it should not do so, for reasons arising out of the very nature of a university. This is not a prescriptive argument, based on a view of what is permissible or impermissible in law or public opinion. It's rather an appeal to what an exemplary university looks like when it is religiously oriented, and has its ground in the very nature of a university and the nature of pursuit of theological wisdom.[43] I argued in the second caveat above that a religiously oriented university should not discipline or dismiss a faculty member for the sole reason that beliefs about creed or conduct had changed during the course of employment. Apply that understanding of an academic community to the question of non-discrimination in hiring. Again, an institution might prefer a community of like-minded members. But that's not a principled answer in a society where the dignity of the person, surely a religiously relevant concept if there ever was one, is buttressed by human rights.

A much better view arises out of an understanding of what a university is. An undistracted university makes its hiring decisions with academic integrity, and supports academic freedom by welcoming into its community those who will exercise that freedom effectively and responsibly. The principled answer, then, is this: since disciplining a faculty member for beliefs or on prohibited grounds would violate academic freedom, choosing not to hire on beliefs or prohibited grounds would be contrary to the spirit of academic freedom – again, as long as academic competence, familiarity, and sympathy with mission are strong.[44]

This is not an argument for diluting the distinctive character of a religiously oriented university. It can affirm its convictions, proclaim its identity, and encourage membership from those who wish to participate in its understanding of God, the world, and human experience. But it should seek to build an academic community, where all are welcomed into the pursuit of truth and knowledge. It can be welcoming only if it proclaims its commitment to non-discrimination and academic freedom in that pursuit.[45]

chapter five

Decision Making Is Complicated: Boards, Colleagues, Presidents, Peers

I come now to one more condition necessary for the effective operations of the university with respect to its knowledge functions. It goes without argument that a university must be well administered and well governed; but since in different jurisdictions there are distinctive forms of university governance, and since few universities have identical administrative structures, it is almost impossible to speak in generalities about this issue. Nevertheless there are some fundamental principles relating to decision making and the exercise of authority in universities that should be recognizable in particular systems. I argue that, although one naturally thinks of boards and presidents as decision makers, the notions of peer assessment and collegial deliberation need some form of operation in any university administrative and governing structure. The anatomy here described might be difficult to recognize in some institutions, and the comment that it doesn't actually work this smoothly would often be fair; but the point of the exercise is to set out some fundamental structures for effective operation that respects the academic functions of the university.

Universities are not easily managed. In the second chapter we recognized the importance of trust and integrity in the academic enterprise, where highly valued expertise isn't generally shared, but instead distributed across particular areas of knowledge. How should we think about administration and governance in this kind of institution, where the work of some of its members is often so refined that even other colleagues in the same department don't fully understand it? Add in the issues of institutional autonomy and academic freedom we've been thinking about, and the challenges of effective administration and governance grow even more complicated.

In what follows, then, I provide a brief account of how authority is to be exercised across levels of university administration, and then move to considerations of governance, with some comment on the current concern with transparency and accountability. I do need to reiterate, however, that in many places the realities of university decision making would not be described in this way. Nevertheless I'd argue that, despite differences in governance systems, they should reflect the basic principles I discuss here.

Academic Administration

University administration is constructed differently in different institutions, but commonly one finds three levels: the department, then the faculty or division embracing a cluster of departments, and finally the centre overseeing all divisions. At the first level there is a disciplinary focus from which academic programs are delivered and research is carried out, although interdisciplinary programs have seen significant development in recent decades. In charge (though that isn't quite the right word) of the department is an academic administrator (a chair or director or head) who has primary responsibility for academic quality. That responsibility is exercised in hiring faculty members and in assessing their performance for important decisions such as tenure, promotion, and annual reviews. The chair, however, rarely makes decisions without the advice or recommendations of a committee. These academic decisions are collegial in the root sense of the term. That is, they arise not from the dominant will of one person, but from the collective authority of colleagues in the discipline as it is understood and practised by those who are expert in the area. In hiring and other personnel decisions, then, the chair must rely on the expert judgment of specialists in the candidate's particular competence and on the advice of colleagues.

The department delivers its programs through an approved curriculum, but the chair doesn't dictate the content of that curriculum. Rather, curricular changes are debated in committees, where reasons for change prevail or fail to persuade. Typically curricular matters are recommended for approval, again by colleagues, to a higher level in the university.

When we come to the next level of university organization, we move beyond particular areas of knowledge into broader groupings that form a division, usually a faculty such as arts or engineering. The head of a faculty is a dean, who oversees the workings of departments and to whom chairs or directors report.[1] Although they have their own disciplinary backgrounds, deans don't make chair-like decisions. Instead their offices supervise the processes by which chairs are appointed. Deans receive and vet recommendations from departments for hiring and promotion. Importantly (especially from the standpoint of chairs), deans allocate resources to the units reporting to them. On the curricular side, they work with committees dealing with recommendations for the shape of the curriculum and requirements for the degrees under their purview.

Although deans have considerable academic and financial authority, they, like chairs, must cultivate and respect collegial decision making. Their academic authority may include powers related to academic personnel decisions, but they can't act simply on their own. They need the experience of making second-order academic assessment. That is, although not qualified to pronounce upon the merits of a particular piece of research or scholarship (a first-order judgment), a dean must recognize the quality of someone else's first-order assessment. That involves assessing evidence and arguments. The recommendation from the chair must contain letters of reference from experts, not friends; they must persuade by giving reasons that demonstrate knowledge of the subject and the candidate's work.

At this divisional level are also found operations supportive of the academic enterprise. Since degree requirements vary by division across the university, registrarial functions such as student recruitment, admission, advising, and awards tend to be carried out under the general authority of the faculty dean. Some other student services may be delivered at this level.

The third and highest level of academic administration is the centre: the president and vice-presidents of the institution. Institutional academic integrity requires consistency of standards and performance across the divisions, responsibility for which the office of the president is charged. Other institutional operations – such as human resources, financial management, government relations, alumni relations and advancement, grounds, maintenance, and housing, and services such as health and crisis management – all likewise require consistent policy and application. Hence there will be a number of vice-presidential portfolios, with assistant vice-presidents and other administrative layers depending on the complexity of the institution. In labelling this level the "highest" in a university's administration, I am of course imagining a spatial positioning on an organizational chart. However, when speaking of the core academic mission of the institution, "highest" cannot mean that presidential authority is first-order with respect to specific disciplines. Any president who presumes to exercise epistemic authority *qua president* about a substantive issue of disciplinary knowledge treads on dangerous territory. Rather the president is charged with responsibility for the flourishing of the entire institution, while responsibility day-to-day for academic integrity and success is normally delegated to the office of the vice-president academic. Universities have complex systems of delegation, so that some matters are left to departmental decisions and others are resolved at the decanal level. But the most important academic issues are decided centrally only on the recommendation of the "lower" levels. This means that power is distributed in a paradoxically inverted hierarchical fashion across the institution, with the greatest first-order authority vested in the "lower" level of the disciplines and the ultimate approval of decisions at the "highest," central level. In this paradox of power, the point of authority is from one perspective at the top of the usual pyramid; from another the pyramid is inverted, with the crucial point at the bottom – at the "lowest" level. This latter, first-order, perspective is disciplinary, and reflects the understanding of academic decision making within the university; the former, with the president at the top, is how boards of governors see the university world.

I began with administration, rather than with governance, because it's important to understand the processes whereby decisions are made within the university. We need to move to governance, but before setting out the difference between internal governance and board governance, let's think further about the importance of peer assessment in the university world.

The Authority of Peers

Much is made of the language of "peer": we speak of peer assessment or review and decision by peers as distinct from a chain of command where orders are given downwards from the top. The Oxford English Dictionary defines the word in its sense A.1.b: "A person who equals another in natural gifts, ability, or achievements; the equal in any respect of a person or thing." This rather sweeping definition doesn't quite capture the notion I'm after. It would be better to say that the peers involved in academic assessment are those who have *a similar lived experience within a recognized professional form of life*, especially within a particular area of expertise. (They are probably not all "equal in their natural gifts, ability, or achievements," strictly speaking; some might be smarter or more prolific than others.)

Peers as Those Who Share in the Academic Form of Life

It's worth a moment to think about what it is to have a similar lived experience. The phrase "lived experience" can refer to what one feels and knows in one's personal interior life, as distinct from the descriptions and values that others assign to an individual or group. It has currency in certain ways of doing philosophy, but here I am content to use it simply as referring to a *form of life* that a group of people share when they belong to a particular profession. There are, of course, as many *forms of life* as there are identifiable groups of people whose identity consists in their understanding a common vocabulary, knowing how to perform a certain cluster of activities, sharing a certain set of values and beliefs, being able to recognize bad from authentic performance or bogus from genuine claims. One would expect, for instance, bakers to use language about flours and yeasts and to practise techniques that many of us wouldn't know. Certain religious forms of life seem difficult to comprehend for outsiders, but provide significant meaning to those who share the associated religious experiences.

The academic form of life is the shared experience of academic practices and values. It is also a *professional* form of life, a term I use to distinguish it from forms of life that anyone who wants to give them a try may enter, like becoming a home baker. One enters the professional form of life only after a long process of education, an apprenticeship that takes longer than becoming a lawyer, and much longer than the education that, it seems, will suffice to become president of the United States. The PhD or similar doctorate is the usual entry qualification, although in creative fields that has not been necessary in the past. In the sciences, theoretical and applied, most aspiring academics serve time on postdoctoral fellowships; in the social sciences and humanities, a series of contract positions, often part time, has been the customary pattern. Without publications and teaching experience, the applications of candidates for regular positions don't make it past an initial cursory glance. Letters of recommendation that glow through the envelope help get one's name on the long short list. The academic form of life might look attractive from some vantage points, but the entry hurdles are high.

What's it like inside? Rather than a neat collection of set practices, the academic life is formed by a family of related activities and attitudes, and looks roughly like this: it is basically a mindset accompanied by a series of know-hows. The mindset is intellectual curiosity, an enjoyment of what's known coupled with dissatisfaction with the existing state of knowledge claims and a resolve to discover more. In this mindset, there is *always more* – more to discover, create, impart, query. If it seems that the academic form of life is characterized by *epistemic restlessness*, that's because that's what it's like. But it *knows what to do* with this restlessness. The know-hows of the academic life are about finding things out and figuring out their relevance and worth. Call that research or scholarship. But one must add that this form of life knows how to *assess* what's discovered or claimed in a particular field of competence. Participants in an academic form of life build up experience in their field so that they know what's already been done and what needs doing. They have beliefs about the reputations of the major players in the field. Having written letters of recommendation, reviews of books, appraisals of scholarship, they can discern faint praise, snide asides, and genteel character assassination. In other words, effective participants in the academic form of life have developed mature judgment that enables them to become competent assessors of worth in their fields and in the wider university enterprise of education and research.

It would be remiss of me to pass over the high expectations and significant demands upon those who share in this lived experience. The initial gasp of relief at being hired quickly turns into long, deep breaths over half a dozen years of endurance training for tenure and promotion. Let's say that the average age for completing the PhD is thirty-six.[2] Add a couple of years for the fortunate few before the first full-time tenure-track position, then six years until the tenure decision. It's a tough-minded guild that finally accepts its permanent members in their mid-forties, with only a couple of decades to go before what used to be known as normal retirement age.

While thinking about the forms of academic life, it would also be egregiously remiss not to draw attention to the growing numbers of part-time and contract faculty members, who live under similar demands and expectations, but whose levels of uncertainty and compensation are inversely proportional – the first being higher, in case there is any doubt. In the previous chapter I argued that these contingent faculty members should have the assurance of academic freedom. Likewise, members of this class deserve to be included in the notion of academic peer; it's not hard to think of situations in which their experience would be valuable in assessing, say, the curriculum or student experience.

Peer Assessment

Take now the notion of academic peer to the processes of assessment within the university. Here I'll consider the assessment of academic performance, leaving until later the role of peers in collegial decision making about other academic matters.

When we refer to "peer review" of scholarship, we have in mind that the material in question is assessed by experts – scholars who know the literature and can weigh the quality of the contribution to the field. They write reports, giving reasons for their judgment of the merit of the work under consideration. This exercise is crucial in maintaining the integrity of the university.

This review by one's close peers is *first-order* assessment. But second-order assessment is also important. This level, a step up from review by those most knowledgeable about the subject matter, is inhabited by academics with varying degrees of appreciation of the content being reviewed. Scholars in related areas within the same discipline might understand particular ideas and claims more fully than those in cognate disciplinary areas, but even the latter can judge many aspects of a scholar's work. The reason is that, as peers broadly conceived, they *share the lived experience of the academic life*. If they cannot appraise the substantive worth of a piece of scholarship, they still know the marks of expertise in a given field and how to interpret the assessments of experts. They know the questions to ask about the character of research, and can appreciate different indicators of quality in different disciplines. What's true about peer review of scholarship pertains as well to assessing the effectiveness of teaching, especially because pedagogical effectiveness might not be tightly tied to disciplinary expertise. The concept of peer extends as well to those with shared knowledge of other academic requirements, as I point out below in discussing collegial governance.

The class of academic peers, then, has at its core those expert in the scholar's field; around that core are peers in a more extended sense, who live the life of teaching and research. As the circle of peers widens, the exercise of second-order assessment moves from the decanal level in many universities to the central academic office responsible for final approval of recommendations for hiring, tenure, and promotion, and other academic matters. At this level the decision makers must be seasoned in judgment, and should enjoy the respect of academic colleagues for their understanding of the academic life. Where the person charged with final approval is the president, it's critical for academic reputation, both internally and in the broader community of universities, that the president be acknowledged as an academic peer. That's because second-order judgment focuses on the integrity of procedures that need to be understood not from models extrinsic to university life, but from within the lived academic experience.

If academic peer review is so fundamental to the integrity of the university, one hopes it is done well. Is it?

Not perfectly, as one can imagine true of almost any practice in any institution. It's not difficult to think of the challenges in implementing fair and reliable procedures of assessment. Peers can be biased against forms of inquiry, publication, or schools of thought. They can hold grudges against individuals; they can also be too friendly and uncritical.[3] They can be incompetent themselves. They can misread evidence. They can fail to be thorough or timely. In new or emerging disciplines, the availability of arm's-length peers might be seriously limited because the community is small.

Consider, however, the alternative: assessment by those who hold power, on criteria that reflect non-academic values and priorities, or at least values that have not been scrutinized by those who share in the academic form of life. Anything but peer review and assessment would erode the integrity and reputation of the university more surely than flaws in the peer review system. That is why healthy universities develop policies and procedures to mitigate potential problems in peer assessment. The choice of individuals to carry out assessments must be approved by one level up – the dean in many institutions. A committee could include an extra-departmental member as assessor, making deliberations accountable beyond a small group that might be too friendly or too indifferent to a candidate. At the level of final approval, dossiers might be turned back where the evidence was not compelling. Should the regular process be considered to fail, most institutions have appeal or grievance procedures to address alleged bias.

The Character of University Administration

Academic administration is a peculiar calling, not suited to every person no matter how otherwise talented and erudite. If there is one especially apt analogous calling for a university academic administrator, it's that of a judge. A judge has to know the law, figure out the credibility of witnesses, assess the validity of arguments on both sides, render a verdict, and assign appropriate consequences. Judging requires knowledge, experience, and a kind of wisdom that takes into account the letter and spirit of the law as well as the particularities of the case. It can't be done well – that is, justly – mechanically or by rote. And good judging can't be assessed by measurement or reported by scores – by the number of cases decided per month, percentage of pronouncements of guilt, or revenues generated by fines. There is no "bottom line" in judging. Only those knowledgeable about the law and its interpretation and application can authoritatively determine the quality of judging. Such knowledgeable persons are "peers" who share familiarity with a set of experiences that belong to the life of the law. Yet others – such as trial lawyers, law clerks, and professors of jurisprudence – are also deeply acquainted with judicial practice, and able to make informed assessments of judging. The plural is appropriate because the process of assessing a complex performance is best as a small group activity where countervailing biases and limited experiences can be balanced.

Take the analogy of the judge, and the assessment of judging, back to the role of the academic administrator. In the university, the council and board create and revise policies. Chairs, deans, and presidents interpret and apply those policies, and in so doing must exercise judgment (the word is apt). A good administrator does this out of the knowledge, experience, and wisdom that comes from understanding not just the content of policies, but also their rationale and the ways in which they have actually worked. As with judges, the assessment of the performance of academic administrators cannot be easily calculated by quantitative measurements. There is always a seduction in the certainty conveyed by numbers, especially when comparisons must be made and when performance is linked to salary. But assigning numbers to aspects of performance requires qualitative judgment.

What should one look for in an academic administrator, given the values of peer assessment – especially second order – and collegial judgment? Ideally the successful candidate is a senior scholar, well published and widely respected by colleagues and students alike. The ideal, however, isn't always possible. At the level of chair, the demands of bureaucracy, including legal and personnel issues, complicate the role, diminishing its desirability and prestige. When administrative tasks are thought onerous, there's a tendency to share them around every few years. Since the more prolific scholars value research time above serving a bureaucracy, it's not always senior scholars who end up in the chair's office; sometimes that's just as well, given that research prowess doesn't automatically come with administrative skill. But in the end a department is well served by a chair who understands how to make fair and reasoned judgments about performance in those areas of knowledge generation and transmission entrusted to the unit. Since the chair must act as coach to colleagues in need of advice and encouragement, and also as judge of their performance, he or she must be trusted to be both impartial and supportive.

The work of a dean takes the incumbent away from close departmental colleagues and, given the significance of budget decisions, might look more managerial than collegial. Certainly a dean who bears fiscal responsibility needs to understand the financial operations of the university, and must manage business and personnel affairs prudently. But deans are not managers on a corporate or business model. They have to meet enrolment targets, and increasingly they set fundraising goals. But they don't manage according to goals and plans decided by a chief executive. Academic planning doesn't descend from higher authority so much as arise out of collegial deliberation, which deans stimulate and mediate between chairs and the centre. Rather than following corporate directives, above all deans must exercise the academic judgment I've stressed as essential to the academic enterprise.

There are corporate-like measures that might be employed in assessing decanal performance, such as ratio of student applications to acceptances, retention and graduation rates, and cost per student. Whether such indicators translate easily into assessments of academic worth and value is highly doubtful.[4] A strong university needs deans who can *interpret* what is measured mainly because it is measurable, and form judgments, like the judges in the first paragraph of this section, about the quality of the student experience, teaching, and research and scholarship.

I will leave to a comment at the end of this chapter a discussion of the character of the position of president, since that role is so closely connected to the board of the university.

Governance Structures

Thus far we've considered decision making by peers, both focused and broadly construed, in matters having to do with faculty, those who do the teaching and research in the institution. The principle of decision by peers applies as well to questions of what's taught and to whom – the educational mission of the university. Here I turn from administration to governance, where we find a fundamental division of responsibilities into two main areas. They might go by different names, but they reflect a distinction between the academic – the core knowledge functions of the university – and the material and financial conditions that enable those functions. For our purposes one can refer to the bodies with academic responsibility as councils or senates, and the enabling body with general oversight as a board.[5]

Generally speaking, then, university governing structures are bicameral – but their bicameral nature is not a system of two-step deliberation on the same matters; rather, it's the separation of jurisdiction for academic and material matters just noted. Ultimate responsibility for the entire institution does rest with the board, as we saw in Chapter Three on autonomy. But just as the state devolves its authority over universities to independent boards, so a university board devolves academic authority to a senate – if devolution is the right term when the state's enabling legislation may require the board to cede authority for academic matters to a senate body. Why this bifurcation of power? There are four main constituencies from which persons are drawn for the work of governance: faculty, students, administrative staff, and "lay" members of the public, who often are alumni of the institution. All these groups have a legitimate interest in governance, but they are not equally represented on councils and boards. Board members are typically well-educated alumni who have views about education and research; they also represent public interest in the enterprise of higher education. Faculty members are directly affected by decisions about the material and financial conditions of their knowledge functions, and understand on the ground, out of their lived experience, how the institution works. Students and administrative staff as well have relevant experience of the enterprise. Why not have representatives of these constituencies deliberate and decide together on academic and other policies, priorities and allocation of resources?

There is indeed great benefit in a shared understanding of the work of the university across these estates: the academics need to appreciate fiscal challenges, and the board members should appreciate the challenges and rewards of research and teaching. But the nub of the issue is the balance of power. Whose voice is determinative of academic decisions? And whose voice determines, in the end, all those other decisions that make the university's knowledge functions possible?

In most universities lay members have little say in academic decisions, and the internal members, largely faculty but also students and sometimes staff, don't have a controlling voice in board matters. To understand why this is the case, we should take the principle of decision-by-peers to the question of the internal academic governance of the university in councils and senate.

Council and Senate as Collegial Governance

Recalling my initial discussion of the knowledge functions of the university, it's readily seen that universities must decide a myriad academic issues. At the roots are the questions of who gets to teach and carry out research, what it is that is investigated and taught, who is admitted to programs, and what are the requirements for recognizing and certifying their learning. Of course, from these roots grow a host of related matters – to name but a few: hiring, tenure and dismissal; academic standards, integrity and misconduct; scholarship and awards policy; program development; degree requirements and nomenclature; library and information technology policies; and so on. What's significant about this list is that most of these topics do not form the subject matter of university intellectual disciplines or departments. Those disciplines do create and mount their own programs, of course; but these departmental programs are subject to approval higher up by other academics who might understand but little of their content. What substantive expertise confers authority upon senate members to make academic decisions?

The answer must be their shared experience in the common enterprise of knowledge creation, critique, and transmission. As peers sharing in the academic form of life, faculty members constitute a *collegium* – a body of colleagues. Here the notion of peer is stretched further away from its first-order disciplinary focus, and even from a second-order appraisal of the adequacy of first-order judgments. Much of the work of senates has to do with issues more general than discipline based: admission and degree requirements, scholarships and awards, petitions and appeals. Faculty members are peers in the sense that they share, from their own teaching and research, knowledge of the contours of acceptable degree requirements and content; they can assess academic policies in light of what they themselves live and observe from day to day. More important, they know what questions to ask and what answers are credible. This ability to interrogate and critique matters under deliberation by an academic council or senate is fundamental to institutional health, as I argued in discussing academic freedom in Chapter Four.

We typically call this kind of decision making "collegial," meaning that those qualified to make academic judgments form a non-hierarchical group of peers with equal voice, and that, having spoken and listened to one another, they reach a conclusion on the matter. Academic administrators such as chair, directors, deans, and the like can propose ideas and resolutions and keep order, but under collegial governance they cannot dictate outcomes. I shan't pretend that the practice is straightforward and sweetly civil – "collegial" in the happy sense. Some voices are strident; some bear more weight because of reputation. Although personality and politicking make the realization of collegial governance a challenge, it's the best we've got, and the best safeguard of the authority of the collected wisdom of the academy. But it must be added that the very notion of the collegium can be threatened, not by outside forces, but from within when a rift grows between academic administration and so-called rank-and-file faculty members. Whether there was a time when this idea of the authority of the collegium actually found instantiation in actual universities may be debated; certainly the past few decades have seen the transformation of faculty associations into faculty unions, where senior academics holding administrative positions even for a few years are regarded or act as management.[6] Criticism of a management mentality depends for its pertinence, however, upon the belief that academic decision making should indeed be collegial and not managerial.

Although peers in the wider sense discussed above carry the weight of academic deliberation and decision, for the past half-century, university senate bodies have included voting members who are not faculty: students and administrative staff often in student services areas. Since they do not fully live the academic life in all its knowledge functions, what qualifies them for this participation? It can be argued that students, especially at the graduate level, are like junior apprentices to faculty members, learning aspects of academic forms of life. Staff members can be keen observers of faculty attitudes and behaviour. When policies are unclear or have unintended consequences, it is usually those affected, not the proposers, who can point this out. There would be something perverse in a system that encouraged students to evaluate teaching but did not permit them some voice in evaluating programs and policies. It would be difficult, however, to find grounds for granting non-faculty an equal or determinative voice in deliberations and decisions.[7]

As for alumni and independent board members, precisely because they do not live the academic life they should not have a determinative role in academic decisions. Should they have a voice, if only a small one? They should certainly be aware of the conversation, and have every opportunity to appreciate the importance of academic deliberation and decisions. Perhaps, for the sake of those major twin social virtues of accountability and transparency, they should have an interrogative voice, but a significant vote in decisions would be problematic. Board members hold the power of the purse, and as the ultimate guarantors of academic freedom in the institution, they should not intrude upon the autonomy of the senate.

The Responsibilities of the Board

This is not to downplay the importance of the board for the overall well-being of the university: its fiduciary duty, its ultimate responsibility. Board members are the trustees of the institution, and must see to its good administration by selecting the president and in most cases approving appointments to senior positions. They evaluate the performance of the president, set senior salaries, and hold the power of dismissal. The board approves the budget and major expenditures on the president's recommendation, and sets important policies in the many non-academic areas in which the university operates. Board members are chosen for their life experience in finance, the law, business, human resources, property management, risk assessment, and other areas well outside the range of competencies of most faculty, students, and other members of the university. This wide external expertise is a valuable source of advice for the university as well as crucial to public accountability.

Why, then, should faculty, students, or administrative staff have any voice at the board level? After all, if board members should respect the autonomy of senate-like deliberations and decisions, should not the internal members of the university stay out of board matters?

I think not; the parallel isn't appropriate. A better comparison is with students and staff involvement in academic matters. Just as those two groups have a stake in the outcome of academic decisions driven by faculty members in a senate, so faculty members and others have a stake in the outcome of board deliberations. Independent board members need to understand the implications for the academic enterprise of their decisions, and it is one of the roles of internal members to assist in that understanding. Internal members should also have vote as well as voice, but they should not hold a majority on the board. They must act in the interests of the whole institution, not as advocates for particular issues and groups. Further, when directly affected by particular decisions such as salary and benefit schemes, they must declare conflict of interest and absent themselves from debate and resolution.

How should board members think of their responsibilities? Fundamentally, as the custodians of the university's future – its immediate future and its middle and long-term future. I want to emphasize the long term: in almost every case, the university for which they hold fiduciary responsibility will outlast them and the great-grandchildren of their great-grandchildren. Governing parties come and go, corporations and businesses diversify or shut their doors or merge, populations fluctuate, and communities change their cultural and economic character, but universities – especially those we call "established" – will persist. They will change as well, but their essential *raison d'être*, their foundational purpose for their knowledge functions – this will not change. For if it does, they will no longer be universities. Therefore, unless a university can no longer reasonably be thought to fulfil its functions, the primary responsibility of the board is to take no decision that will risk that future, and to seek to support those actions that promote the university's foundational purpose.

It is difficult to think of the longer term, since certainty about the future is not vouchsafed even to investors. Nevertheless boards must always make their best efforts to consider the trajectories of their decisions. Sometimes that means accepting deficits as part of a longer-term strategy; sometimes it means arguing for maintenance and construction plans that will enhance knowledge functions and last more than a couple of decades. Given the large percentage of budget dedicated to salaries, boards should attend to that steadily escalating cost, but also understand that changes in programs and personnel require a long period – several years in the case of program closure or development – to implement. Although it would be impossible to develop realistic plans for an institution twenty years down the road – and therefore a Far Future Task Force could work up only a piece of creative fiction – boards should encourage presidents to step away periodically from the noise of urgent business to reflect on the issues that will help determine the future of their institutions.

As I have kept insisting, the constitutive mandate of a university board is to preserve and sustain the autonomy of the institution. By "constitutive" I mean that mandate setting out the very nature of the institution in its relations with other authorities and institutions, the space in which it carries out its determining functions. In the discussion of autonomy in Chapter Three, I considered how the state, at least in some jurisdictions, cedes its authority to boards; but even if a university does not enjoy legislative autonomy, it must in practice carve out a protected place in order to fulfil properly its knowledge functions. I needn't add that, even with legislative autonomy, an institution must still be vigilant in its actual practice, since there are always countervailing social forces willing to challenge the university and its members.

At the same time, the business of sustaining autonomy cannot be mindless. This is no call for a perpetual institutional conflict with society, adolescent in its insistence on freedom for its own sake. The point of autonomy, as I argued earlier, is for the long-term good of society, culture, and civilization itself. So board members find themselves in need of judicious assessment, restraint, trust, and courage. They require restraint and trust in respecting the academic freedoms expressed in peer decision making on academic matters. They need judgment in assessing the measures brought forward by the administration to fulfil the university's knowledge functions. And on occasion they require courage – to resist unwarranted intrusion into the life and soul of the university, or to call for clearer justification from the administration should proposals be incomplete or too ambitious.

Board members with corporate experience often expect the university to come up with guiding principles such as vision and mission statements, and with strategic plans and goals. In fact, since all universities are pretty much in the same business, it would be difficult to distinguish one from another by any substantive difference in their mottos and aspirational statements. Their distinctive marks turn out to be their histories and locations – their place in time and space, as I argue in the concluding chapter. For now I only want to make a plea for boards to understand the histories of their institutions and to cultivate growth from their pasts, rather than uproot and transplant. In the university, change must be nurtured, not imposed.

That said, the administration of universities also requires a certain nimbleness of response within the context of deliberate development and change. Suddenly announced government programs, unexpected enrolment shifts from one discipline into another, unforeseen partnership possibilities – such opportunities cannot be written into plans in advance. But neither should the university yield to every temptation. Just as buying cheap is sometimes more costly in the end, so the glitter of immediate gain can later lead to grief.

Universities are well served by the dedication and expertise of their boards, especially those who are independent members through election or appointment. They volunteer their time and experience, and deserve the attention of the institution in orienting them to the academic values I have discussed in this chapter. Members from the corporate world benefit from gaining an appreciation of how academic judgment operates – a condition necessary for trust in the university's internal processes. I should add that, on some not-for-profit boards, members are selected for their "capacity" to contribute to the organization, where that term refers to money. That criterion for university board membership is a very bad one, creating an appearance (warranted or not) of undue influence in the affairs of the institution.

I've promised to say something about the relationship between board and president, but before that, some thoughts on what governance seems to be about these days.

Transparency and Accountability

If one were to choose but two watchwords that have peppered the language of governance in the past two decades, they'd have to be "transparency" and "accountability." These ideas have something in common with access to information, important in a democratic society so that citizens can make informed judgments about the performance of elected governments and officials. But the importance of a concept doesn't mean that it's well understood or employed for its intended purpose. So it's worth spending a bit of time thinking about these two ideas.

Despite their being hooked together and spoken in the same breath, transparency and accountability are not the same thing. Accountability is the thing that's sought after; transparency is a means to that outcome. And, as every child knows, when you want something there can be different ways to get it.

Further, accountability needs to be located in particular contexts in order to make sense. There must be an authority to whom the account is rendered, and a set of responsibilities and duties that the account is about. By "authority" I mean a body (or person) to which duties are owed or with a legitimate set of interests in their performance. My accountabilities are limited to the things for which I'm responsible, and they are accountabilities only to those who have some kind of stake in how I've discharged those responsibilities. "Some kind of stake" means more than mere curiosity: my neighbours might be interested in what I'm growing in the flower bed, but I have no obligation to inform them or to provide an answer to a question – unless I'm about to change an agreement with them to plant, say, only white or blue hydrangeas.

University accountabilities turn out to be pretty complex once you start to think about them. There are many *internal* accountabilities, up the chain of responsibilities, when reasons have to be given for actions. That will involve all those first- and second-order peer judgments I've discussed. Administrative reporting apart, one of the most fundamental principles in the faculty/student relationship has to do with the non-arbitrary exercise of power in grading and assessing work: faculty members are accountable not just to their students, but also to the institution, for fair and reasonable assignments and assessment. Universities have policies on academic appeals that are, generally speaking, effective guarantees of fairness. Accountability through levels of university governance is remarkably robust. I'll come to that shortly, after a word about transparency.

Transparency, although related to accountability, is a different institutional value. It has to do, not with the requirement for justification of decisions and behaviour, but with the ease of access to relevant information. Sometimes this information is important in assessing how a responsibility has been discharged; in other cases there is little direct connection with actual university obligations. For example, university performance indicators, although presented in the context of accountability and transparency, are often better seen as efforts to promote the profile of the institution, especially comparatively. There's nothing wrong with that; indeed, as we saw in Chapter Two, reputation is crucial to the flourishing of universities. But publishing the percentage of students in residence or the average class size can be related only remotely to any issue for which a university must be held accountable; such numbers alone are mute about the quality of the student experience.

Not all professions of transparency, then, assist accountability. Nor are all efforts in the name of transparency actually transparent. The relevant information can be buried in a great mass of data; charts and graphs with their neat manufactured precision can distract from more fundamental issues. Effective transparency is not only understandable to non-specialists; it is also about information that actually matters.[8] For instance, one might question whether government-mandated "sunshine" lists of salaries that name individuals in fact serve the underlying purposes of accountability.[9]

If not all transparency necessarily serves accountability, does all accountability require transparency? No – but yes, in a way. Let me explain. There is more than one reason for sacrificing the principle of transparency. Although most university governing bodies conduct their meetings in open session, the door might be closed on transparency if individual privacy would be invaded – say, when debating a senior appointment or an expulsion for academic misconduct. And no university business involving solicitor/client privilege would be disclosed. In delicate financial or business negotiations, it might not be in the university's interest to disclose pertinent information that would adversely affect its position. The principle of confidentiality is invoked, in some institutions, around senior searches. Although in some places presidential candidates make public appearances, in other universities an open process might not attract the top choices, who are usually those successful in their current positions and unwilling to commit to the public possibility of departure. In such cases, confidentiality and the best interests of the institution might trump transparency. Nevertheless universities must still be accountable for their actions, and be seen to be so. That means, I suggest, *procedural* transparency, where *substantive* confidentiality is warranted. In other words, there should be publicly available information about the reasons for confidentiality, about the persons or body involved in the decision, and about any non-confidential aspects of the procedure.

How Accountable Are Universities?

Where are the points of accountability in universities these days? In the context of this writing, those points permeate the entire institution. Here are a half-dozen.

(1) Although retired colleagues trade stories around the common room about the informality of hiring in their day,[10] current hiring procedures are formally structured by agreements, including open advertising and final approval from the academic hierarchy.

(2) One of the most active areas in university administration over the past couple of decades has been the development of policies for all manner of things. That's not always welcome, of course, because a highly bureaucratic system sits uneasily with the academic mind. In the academic form of life, one always wants to dig underneath particular rules or decrees to understand their purpose – and then to question whether that purpose is justified, and if so, whether there is a better means to fulfil it – "better" meaning anything from "more just" to "more efficient" to "not your idea but mine." The restlessness of mind characteristic of the academic

form of life sits uneasily with checklists and ramified regulations. Nevertheless written policies that have been debated and approved are, usually, a reasonable way to achieve clarity about procedures and to hold agents responsible for their administration.

(3) There is much greater financial accountability in the twenty-first-century university in many jurisdictions. In open meetings, boards approve tuition fees, investment policies, and budgets. Financial statements are audited and published, and internal audit procedures have been able to expose rare improprieties in some institutions. There are policies on expenditures for such things as procurement, legitimate travel and entertainment expenses, and one-up approvals for reimbursement. In Canada and elsewhere, presidential expenses are disclosed and posted publicly.

(4) As in many jurisdictions, universities in Ontario (for example) have agreed to submit all new programs for approval to a province-wide universities council, in a process that requires external review before going through their own internal governance. They have also agreed to review existing programs every seven years and to open their review procedures to independent peer audit. The documentation for these processes is available on university websites, so that anyone at all can learn how programs have been developed and reviewed.

(5) I have distinguished transparency from accountability, but since the former serves to provide information on which performance can be held to account, it should be noted that vast quantities of information are available to members of a university and to the general public. In fact, there is so much information that the *effectiveness* of transparency must be a concern, as I noted a few paragraphs back. That notwithstanding, it's also possible in most jurisdictions to invoke access-to-information policies or legislation to raise questions of accountability.

(6) Universities have highly developed appeal procedures, on everything from grades on assignments and academic standing to denials of tenure or promotion or performance assessments to grievance over personnel decisions. Further, when regular processes run their course, there is in most institutions recourse to the services of a university ombudsperson – and now, as we

saw in Chapter Three, in Ontario and other jurisdictions, a provincial ombudsman.

These examples of a pervasive system of accountability in universities could be multiplied throughout all administrative units and across the experience of students, faculty, and staff. In fact it's hard to imagine what kind of decision, for which a university actor is responsible, would or could fall outside the scope of accountability. One couldn't have said that fifty years ago. Whether the system always works effectively is another matter; but that's not news.

A Concluding Comment: The President and the Board Chair

Earlier I considered the character of university administration, discussing the qualities and roles of chair and dean within the structure of the institution. What about the president?

The president sits at the top of the complex organization. There's no need to spell out the complexity very much: it has to do with real estate, labour relations, financial management, endowments, residences and food services, publicity and communications, deferred maintenance, municipal, provincial and government relations, alumni affairs and fundraising, international recruitment, and – oh yes – with the creation, transmission, and certification of knowledge.

The university is, of course, an academy, a place of learning. I've put that last on the list only because it's often assumed that the president's time and focus of attention is on all those other things, not on the university's *raison d'être*. That assumption is not unwarranted, given the nature of the position, but all these temporal, financial, and material concerns are *in the service of* the academic enterprise; and the president must always make judgments about temporal matters that will advance that enterprise. A good president understands that. Great presidents embody academic values in their characters and accomplishments. In their public presence, demeanour, and pronouncements, they are able to articulate and defend those values and to argue effectively about the need for resources and expenditures to promote the academic enterprise.[11]

That is why, in seeking out candidates for the presidency, the board should place high on the list of qualifications *a lived experience of the academic form of life*. Effective presidents need not be the most accomplished of academics, although the challenge of gaining the respect, if not the trust, of faculty members will be easier if they have gained some academic distinction in their careers. Further, the greater their academic reputation and accomplishment, the more credible their advocacy. But if they lack this distinction, they must at the very least demonstrate competent academic judgment and genuine interest in the academic life.

Presidencies are often paradoxically lonely occupations. There isn't a moment when one is not "on." Face and profile are public commodities; in airports, restaurants, and streets, even in large cities, alumni recognize and assess what the president is wearing, saying, doing. Yet in this very public persona lives the very human individual who bears the responsibility for the entire institution, made up not just of its present members, but also of the many past and future students who form a living community. The president, wisely surrounded by a talented team, will take advice and counsel; but in the end it is the lone individual who is responsible to the community and to the board, the one judge who must weigh evidence and argument, and render a verdict.

One would hope, then, for a supportive relationship between president and board chair. The board hires the president and assesses performance; it has the authority to dismiss. The chair and the president need mutual respect and trust, nourished by frank and confidential communication. It's not uncommon, unfortunately, for the relationship to be more tentative. The chair's form of professional life might be very different from the president's, making it difficult for the one who hires to understand, advise, and appraise the life of the person hired. Where the two forms of life diverge significantly, the president's job becomes even more isolated.

The first decade and a half of the twenty-first century saw an unusual number of resignations of Canadian university presidents.

Although presidential inexperience or misjudgment will have played their part, tensions and stress in the relationship between president and board were also cited as reasons.[12] It is incumbent upon boards not only to seek out candidates who are properly and academically presidential, but also to cultivate the relationship through ongoing transitional support that includes academic colleagues. Spending informal time together to build confidence and trust in experience, values, and judgment isn't a bad idea, either.

PART II

Three Questions

chapter six

Is It Now All about Students?

Imagine yourself a graduate returning to campus for your fiftieth reunion. You would exclaim about how some of your old classmates hadn't changed, while trying to remember that lecture on Locke's theory of personal identity over time, because you can't quite figure out how this person talking to you is the same as the one who was your roommate for two years. For some things, like people, change is a ripening; for other things, it's a transformation into something you could not have imagined.

Should you be given a campus tour, some buildings would be familiar, though the library would have many pieces of technology unimagined when you were thumbing through the card catalogues. You'd still find faculty offices. More than likely, there would be a much more prominent building called a "student centre," a focal point for the campus in a way that a chapel might have been long ago. That would not be the only expression of the university's commitment to students, however. Had you not visited your old haunts since graduation, you undoubtedly would find surprising the number of offices with names of unfamiliar positions, all related to the provision of services to students. Those services extend from recruitment through all aspects of their education to graduation and career advice. And most of them have to do with assisting them to succeed in ways unavailable to you when you arrived that late summer morning long ago.

Had you time to investigate these services thoroughly, you'd be impressed by the commitment to enabling success for current students. You'd be a little puzzled sometimes too. But how long and how deeply should you scratch your head? This attention to students and their experience is undoubtedly a good thing, but how does it relate to the fundamental knowledge functions of the university? Is it an unmitigated good? How is the transformation of the campus actually working?

Hard questions; but to begin to investigate them, we should remind ourselves of the multiform transformations in the institutional role of students in the mid- to late twentieth-century university. This is not the place for anything but a brief reference to the political engagement of students in the 1960s, especially in the United States over Vietnam. In many strikes and marches in Europe and America, students experienced the effectiveness of protest. On campuses, university administrators awoke to a new reality, and over time involved students in the decision-making processes of the institution. In Canada and elsewhere this involvement took several forms. They included, among other things, consulting students in the review of curriculum and degree requirements instead of simply telling them what they had to study, incorporating students into governance systems, and soliciting student opinion in assessing faculty members.

These days, student contributions are so ingrained in university processes that it's hard to imagine those earlier times. Not only do students contribute to governance in departmental committees, councils, senates, and boards dealing with academic programs and policies; they also participate in hiring procedures for faculty and for presidents and vice-presidents. As I argued in Chapter Five on governance, although students are not academic peers, they nevertheless have an important perspective on the enterprise of the university.

The involvement of students in all levels of decision making is but one manifestation of the university's heightened attention to students – some might say, its awaking from somnolence about just who these people are and why they are on campus. I want in this chapter to paint in broad strokes how students have come to be at the forefront of the university's consciousness in two different areas: teaching and student services. That done, we need to pause for some assessment of this refocusing, which will lead into the following chapter, on what a university education is all about.

Teaching Matters

First, teaching. A common journalistic topos is the preoccupation of highly paid faculty members with their own erudite but irrelevant research, ignoring their undergraduate students, who are unwelcome intrusions into their true calling. Those neglected warm bodies have to make do with whatever help their teaching assistants can offer in crowded tutorials.

Really? There might have been a past when The Professor swept into the classroom, chalk dust on sleeve, emoted for forty-five minutes, answered a couple of timid questions by repeating the relevant part of the lecture, and left in a swirl of more chalk dust. Even if that past is not entirely the work of creative memory, it certainly has no relationship to the present. To achieve some idea of the teaching life of faculty members in universities these days, one should rely on neither fiction nor the cranky press. Look, instead, at the evidence of the ways in which universities have refocused attention upon teaching. I'll mention four areas.

(1) The importance of the knowledge transmission function of the university has been entrenched in policies for hiring, tenure, and promotion. Candidates for faculty positions typically add evidence of teaching competence to their dossiers, including having taken courses in the pedagogy of their discipline. In the interview process they are usually required to give an undergraduate lecture. Once hired, their annual performance assessments include those on classroom performance and interactions with students. Criteria for tenure and promotion require competence in teaching. It's often possible for faculty members to progress through the academic ranks based on excellence in teaching.[1]

(2) How is teaching effectiveness assessed? One obvious way is to consult students, and over the past few decades teaching evaluations have become standard, even mandatory. Although they are imperfect measures of scholarly and pedagogical effectiveness,

student evaluations can help identify outstanding teachers as well as expose consistent shortcomings in the performance of some others. Further, the practice of publishing the results is widespread, offering students an opportunity to warn or encourage others about particular courses and instructors – and giving one's colleagues some comparative information. But evaluations alone are insufficient. Student opinion is balanced by additional evidence such as statements of teaching philosophy, syllabi and sample assignments in teaching portfolios, and classroom visits by colleagues. For confirmation that a university's interest in teaching performance is not trivial, simply ask someone who has recently had to assemble material for tenure or promotion consideration.

(3) Another relevant policy development has been the creation of faculty ranks for those whose duties are pedagogical rather than research-related. Although titles have varied with institutions, it's becoming more common for these ranks to be professorial: one can hold the rank of assistant, associate, or full professor, *teaching stream*.[2] One can be sceptical about the reason for introducing these ranks. Those who hold them have greater teaching loads than their research-and-teaching colleagues – many of whose loads have been significantly reduced over the past few decades – and their salary scales are often lower. With diminishing resources and mounting enrolments, universities needed to increase their teaching capacity, and creating this faculty rank, along with more contract and part-time appointments, was one way to do it.[3] There are also concerns about the nature and quality of universities that are too dependent on faculty without research interests and duties. Nevertheless, in the broader scheme of things, the validation of teaching-stream faculty should be seen as an important indication of the centrality of students and their education.

(4) One more type of evidence can be adduced: it's the development of centres for teaching and learning, set up to assist new faculty with course development and delivery and to provide remedial services for those who have fallen into bad habits, no doubt because they imitate the teaching they themselves received. Initially those centres advised individual instructors, but many of them have morphed into offices of educational effectiveness

assessment and development. They can assist with integrated learning, blended learning, writing across the curriculum, curriculum mapping, developing and assessing learning outcomes, and continuous improvement.[4] They are staffed with a new category of professionals whose discipline is educational development. Their degrees are typically from faculties of education. Although some might have graduate degrees in other subjects, they have found their way into this new professional life. Where they fit on the map of those whose work is academic rather than administrative will depend on the institution. If teaching courses for degree credit is the work of faculty, and those who assist students with counselling and advice are administrative staff, the educational developers sit somewhere in an ill-defined space. They don't teach students; they don't profess expertise as members of any established department; but their focus is clearly academic in the broader sense, concerned with how content belonging to someone else's particular expertise is taught and learned.[5] In this way they are like their colleagues in writing centres, who provide instruction and assistance to students, sometimes in short courses and sometimes in individual sessions over particular assignments.

We can't pretend that these developments have resolved all the challenges in teaching undergraduates. As I noted, for faculty engaged in scholarly and research activity, publishing has become even more important for their careers. Reduced teaching loads mean more time in the lab or library; research grants may buy out teaching obligations. More courses are delivered by part-time and contract teachers, as we saw earlier in this book. The fact that challenges remain, however, should not negate the main contention of this section. In the initiatives just described, universities are embracing their mission to teach, assessing their effectiveness with students, and structuring their policies and institutional resources to improve the success of their faculty as teachers.

Were you back on campus for your fiftieth reunion anniversary, all this would be new. None of these initiatives were in place when you were a student. Your own children probably didn't see much of this when they were at university. Your grandchildren are much better cared for.

And the attention to teaching is just the half of it. Where you might have had a registrar's office and a nurse to help with the usual problems of being an undergraduate, today's students have a panoply of services to get them in, through, and out of, the university.

Serving Students

The particular organization and array of services for students depends, of course, on the university and the character of its student body. For some institutions, recruitment and retention are a challenge, and resources are directed to measures that assist at-risk students to succeed. The populations of some schools are residential, or significantly international, or culturally diverse. In what follows I am not attempting to set out all the services a university should provide, but instead to develop an account of the kinds of services to be found at a representative (if only notional) group of universities – although the account does reflect my experience in a large urban university.[6]

It's difficult to come up with a classification system covering all the services on offer. One set has to do with advising and counselling, another with physical and mental well-being, another with financial and career issues, yet another with social and recreational opportunities – but the list can't be neatly organized because the scope of activities and responsibilities is so large. We can start, though, with those services most closely related to the educational functions of the university in teaching and learning.

Among those essential student services, we'd want to place academic advising about degree and program requirements. That would appear to be straightforward, but the business of steering students through regulations, petitions, and appeals is complicated by the predilection of the university for regulations and the ingenuity of young people for getting things mixed up. So a seemingly simple problem can have multiple dimensions.

The ability to complete a course, for instance, can require a loan or grant; financial counselling might be necessary. Maybe the problem is poor performance, so referral to the writing centre is appropriate. With a less structured experience in university, time management requires attention. Or perhaps it's note taking or writing tests. The learning strategist, in another office, can help with that. Perhaps there is a need for accommodation because of physical, developmental, or psychological constraints;[7] then the accessibility office can assist.

Some services, then, deal with academic issues such as degree regulations and course selection, and others with the conditions that impede progress in learning and make it difficult to succeed, especially in undergraduate education. Those conditions might arise from lack of preparation in earlier schooling, or other disadvantages, requiring services that are remedial or accommodating. The percentage of students for whom such services are helpful depends, as I noted, on an institution's population.

More pervasive issues, however, have recently attracted a good deal of public attention: sexual violence and mental health. Each has required universities to increase services to their students. In Canada, the United States, the United Kingdom, and elsewhere,[8] incidents of sexual harassment and assault, usually involving students as perpetrators, have surfaced in recent years, provoking justifiably strong condemnation and even government directives on policy and procedures. It has been difficult to ascertain how widespread are instances of sexual violence for students because not all (perhaps the majority) are not reported or (worse) not recorded, although it is not at all difficult to state categorically that one case is one too many. According to a US survey of 150,000 students, the majority of incidents go unreported for different reasons: embarrassment, emotional difficulty, concern about legal proceedings, because it "wasn't serious." The survey found that almost a quarter of women undergraduate students had experienced non-consensual sexual contact since they entered university.[9] Other sources might not have the same figure, but it's commonly claimed that one in three women will experience some form of sexual assault in her lifetime.[10] There is no doubt at all that this is a pervasive, difficult social problem in need of addressing at many levels. And since sexual violence is more common among younger people of university age, universities and colleges cannot ignore the problem any more than they can ignore issues of mental health and well-being; indeed, there are direct consequences of sexual misconduct upon the mental and emotional states of their victims. Universities have in recent years been reviewing and improving their policies on sexual harassment and assault, and the support they are able to offer to those who come forward with disclosures.[11] More resources are dedicated to offices with this mandate across the university sector; in Ontario the government requires universities and colleges to establish policies and services to deal with complaints and provide support. These initiatives demonstrate a heightened attention to students and their well-being. How this sits with the university's fundamental purpose is a question we'll need to think about, especially where deep social problems are concerned. Let's return for now, though, to that second pervasive challenge, mental health.

If our society has kept much guilty silence about sexual violence, issues of student mental and emotional well-being by contrast are widely discussed and reported. Any university advisor or dean of students can provide evidence of the alarming number of students in need of assistance. The spectrum of issues is wide, from pronounced anxiety and crippling self-doubt, to suicide. This generation of undergraduates is more medicated, more self-harming, and more suicidal than one would like to think, and their numbers increase steadily every year.[12] A few are clinically mentally ill and need hospitalization – a service that the university cannot itself provide, any more than it can perform appendectomies. Undoubtedly alcohol and drugs are implicated in endeavours to deal with emotional distress, but many students do seek counselling and assistance from the university. Resources for these services are stretched, with higher priority given to serious cases that involve high risk. In some institutions the less risky find it hard to get timely appointments for psychological services.

It appears that universities with residence students might find greater need for personal support services, partly because students are usually some distance from home and its familiar forms of assistance, and partly because they can be challenged by time management, roommate interactions, or too familiar temptations. International students are especially vulnerable to loneliness and anxiety if the culture and language are unfamiliar; for some, the very notion of mental illness might be problematic.[13]

All this seems to signal an epidemic of emotional fragility and insecurity of the self among undergraduates.[14] It's difficult to pinpoint the causes. These students are, by and large, better "cared for" than were previous generations. Their parents are much more involved in their lives, even at university – the hovering helicopters become on occasion irresistible bulldozers, or so one hears. Perhaps unrealizable levels of expectation have been thrust upon them; perhaps social media have generated idealized images of others, increasing a sense of inadequacy in a competitive generation. Traditional institutions of support might be weak: the family, the local community, the synagogue, mosque, or church might not hold the same power for stability and growth as they once did. Avuncular counsel, whether from relatives or trusted figures, might be supplanted by professional but impersonal advice, psychologizing or medicalizing what have always been the usual human perplexities and uncertainties.[15] I throw up possible explanations, but only to report common-room conversation among university staff and faculty who care about educating their students in this milieu – a milieu veneered with their paper-thin applications boasting of their accomplishments but covering over their silent, whimpering insecurities.

Of course this malaise doesn't lurk in the heart and bowels of every student who looks confident and well put together. And there are other populations coming to universities than the one I am most familiar with. With what's inelegantly known as the massification of higher education, a far greater percentage of youth in their late teens and early twenties is seeking university degrees, and they don't all come from folds or pockets in the social fabric like the one just described. But they will have their own anxieties and uncertainties, and universities will have to develop services to address those needs.

So far the services for students I have discussed involve giving advice and support, broadly speaking, for academic success and for coping with the multiform barriers to that success – barriers arising from mental health concerns, trauma, or assault. The array of services is much greater than that, however. I've said nothing about food services, housing and residences; nothing about all the activities that occur in dozens of clubs and societies, nothing about physical fitness and wellness, nothing about sport and the huge role it plays, especially in US collegiate life. Some of these – such as housing for small residential liberal arts colleges – are essential conditions for carrying out the university's educational functions, and some provide important experiences that enrich learning generally – as we will see in the next chapter. Others, such as career offices, provide a welcome service to graduating students, but are more tangential to the functions of the university. The same with collegiate sports: they create spirit, loyalty, and cash, but it's hard to see how the knowledge functions of the university would be seriously diminished without them.

These assorted services all share one feature: they require resources, and lots of them. That includes dedicated and appropriately trained staff. I remarked on the emergence of a new kind of professional, the educational developer, when discussing teaching in the previous section. For some years, parallel professionals have been emerging in the wide area of student services,[16] especially in offices of deans of students. Personnel costs are not trivial for universities. Nor are space and maintenance costs for all the activities related to students outside the classroom. Funds must come from one source or other.[17] The willingness of universities to meet this obligation is yet one more indication of the seriousness with which students are taken in the twenty-first century.

What's Good for Students Is Good for the University

Universities do believe that students matter, and that they matter a great deal. If the evidence alluded to above about efforts to enhance and reward teaching and the expansion (some would say mushrooming) of services across a spectrum of needs does not convince the reader, there is more. I've adduced examples about practices and policies elevating teaching in career advancement decisions, and about services offered to students, in this or that university. Beyond particular institutions, there is further evidence of commitment to student well-being and success across whole systems of higher education.

Look at the pervasive, almost ubiquitous, employment of surveys such as the National Survey of Student Engagement. Survey results can benchmark performance over time and against national averages, and be used to promote a university's attractiveness to prospective applicants. To be sure, in the competitive bid for enrolment, universities have an undisguised interest in demonstrating high levels of satisfaction of their students and holding out promises of special attention and unparalleled opportunities. It pays universities – to speak of financial as well as other benefits – to treat students well. So what's good for students is indeed good for the university's public presence. Reputation, as we saw early in the book, is everything in a competitive world.

A second system-wide indication of commitment to students? Their role in quality assurance processes across many countries. In Canada new programs must be approved by a quality assurance body, which may also monitor the continuing program reviews carried out by each university. A fundamental principle is that these processes must include consultation with students. External reviewers, visiting the university to determine the adequacy of its resources and policies to deliver the program in question, typically will meet with a representative group of students to gather their assessment of the quality of their educational experience. In the United Kingdom, the role of students has extended to membership on panels of peers engaged in reviews. The focus of quality assurance in that country is very clearly centred on students: the Quality Assurance Agency for Higher Education website announces "[w]e are dedicated to checking that the three million students working towards a UK qualification get the higher education experience they are entitled to expect." All the photographs on the site relating to expectations for higher education feature students.[18] It is the same across the European Higher Education Area, where the role of quality assurance is to ensure "the qualifications achieved by students and their experience of higher education remain at the forefront of institutional missions."[19]

A significant element of quality assurance processes is the place of learning outcomes, an approach to education across elementary, secondary, and postsecondary systems that has become enormously popular around the world.[20] Instead of asking what one wants to teach in a course or program, the question becomes what students are able to know and to do as a result of having taken the course or program.[21] The difference in approach is the difference between objectives, which live in the mind of the teacher, and outcomes, which are exhibited in the understanding and actions of the student. Whether outcomes have been achieved requires, of course, assessment, and assessment is most easily carried out where there is behaviour to be measured. That might be one reason the use of learning outcomes is more prevalent in subjects and disciplines that require skills where performance is measurable than in areas where understanding depends on developing a more seasoned judgment over time. The challenge of assessment aside, however, the dominant language of learning outcomes in the development of university curricula demonstrates yet again the pronounced shift of attention to students and their experience.

To restate the point: it's good for universities to treat students well. But it's also good for students that teaching and support services are directed to their learning and well-being. It has meant accessibility, for one thing, and achievement, for another.

University education has become much more accessible as a result of this attitudinal change. Where once physical and financial constraints created such difficulties that some young people would not have been able to contemplate becoming university students, these barriers have been reduced. They have not been eliminated: financial issues still loom large, particularly in socially disadvantaged groups where postsecondary education is perceived to be beyond ambition's reach. There is much work still to be done. Nonetheless accommodation practices and financial aid have opened up for many the possibility of the goods of a university education.

As for achievement, universities strive to support students in danger of failing. All those strategies for learning discussed above, and the counselling around emotional and personal difficulties, are designed to assist those who seek help to achieve decent grades. Those who don't seek assistance may be contacted during their first year if their grades indicate academic difficulty. Again, there is more to be done, and not every student can succeed at what they had hoped to be their major area of study: not all can be lawyers or doctors. Some will fail courses because they don't have the requisite aptitude, or don't work at it properly or very much at all. But the will to succeed might be guided to more appropriate studies, for willingness on the part of the student is usually met, these days, with a sense of care on the part of the institution.

No doubt we all have our stories of hard-hearted, rules-bound bureaucrats who present the implacable face of the institution, unmoved by the plight of undergraduates. The realm of the university is not the kingdom of heaven, and the last are seldom the first. Nevertheless, were you to spend a few days with those who teach and provide services to students, you would in most institutions find them committed to their calling. They do, by and large, care about students. In Chapter Five I wrote about the academic form of life. It's characterized, I said, by epistemic restlessness, a curiosity dissatisfied with the existing state of affairs and seeking to know better. That description, however true of the impetus for research, lacks an important element: the satisfaction of teaching. All teachers know the happy feeling of completed effort when students demonstrate they have grasped the concept or argument being taught. It's a special satisfaction to witness the furrowed brow relaxing as the eyes crinkle with understanding. It's even better, though, in the university, because teaching is a bit like working with apprentices, some of whom are so gifted that they might question your way of doing things. You end up learning from them, and as they engage with you in the pursuit of knowledge, they are inculcated into the freedoms and virtues of the life of the mind.[22] To witness the maturing and independence of mind in someone you've taught: there are few experiences (to speak personally) that provide such satisfaction and provoke such gratitude for one's profession.

Those in other branches of the university's administrative ranks will give similar testimony about the rewards of their work. Having some part in the education of the next generation is a very good way to live, particularly if one is fortunate enough to see how a piece of happily good advice, the removal of a barrier, or support in an hour of crisis works out in the long run.

What's good for students is good for those who work with them, as well as for the university itself. But – I raised this question at the beginning of the chapter – is this an unmitigated good? Must we acknowledge attendant difficulties that trail along with the university's reorientation upon students?

What's Good Is Not Unqualifiedly So

There is more than one way a good might look better than it turns out to be. Although it is indeed properly thought a good in itself, it could fail to meet its target, so to speak. And it could have adverse consequences that cling to it, so that its very goodness is mitigated by what happens along with it. Both problems, I'll argue, qualify the beneficial attention to students that marks the contemporary university.

Unavailed Benefits

For a good to be effective, it must be taken up. The question arises, then, about how students take advantage of the many services available to facilitate their studies and enrich their experience. There's no general answer; it depends on the university. But experience in a large urban university suggests that students in residence are disproportionately engaged in the extracurricular activities that make much of the meaning of university life. Living and eating together makes it easier to join clubs, attend guest lectures, and get involved in campus politics.[23] Commuting students just don't have either the time or the connections. Nor does the high percentage of students who find it necessary to work at part-time jobs in order to afford their education. Sometimes there are cultural expectations at play: young women still living with their families might find it difficult to attend evening events, especially social gatherings. Low participation in campus events is mirrored in participation rates for campus elections: the voter turnout varies from around 10 per cent to an average of 20 per cent.[24]

There is no easy way to know what proportion of students in need of academic advising and support actually avail themselves of services such as the ones I've described. The number of visits to writing and academic skills centres can be tracked, of course. But sometimes they are used by good students seeking the key to top grades – not an utterly bad thing, unless motivated by an unhealthy competitive spirit that masks the pervasive anxiety reported above, but not always a good thing either, when resources should be directed to those in real difficulty.

Not that everyone in sustained or occasional difficulty takes advantage of this assistance. Some evidence may be found in the amount of cheating that reputedly takes place on today's campuses. In Canada the popular press puts the figure at half of all university students.[25] In US surveys of over seventy thousand students between 2002 and 2015, 68 per cent reported cheating on a test or written assignment.[26] In the United Kingdom, the *Guardian* reported in April 2018 that cheating at the top universities had soared by 40 per cent over the past three years.[27]

There are multiform reasons and even more excuses for this behaviour, but the most common – at least for plagiarism – is the kind of panic that sets in when time or ability or both fall short. Although knowingly done, it's often a matter of yielding to temptation, rather than cunning malice, exhibited in forging credentials, collusion, impersonation and bribery; desperation can play its part too. So while some academic misconduct is a deliberate and premeditated assault on the integrity of the institution for the sake of personal gain, much of it wouldn't occur were students to use the academic and personal supports available to them. Universities might publicize the details and penalties concerning egregious cases, including suspension and expulsion,[28] but there often isn't sufficient institutional deterrence for run-of-the-mill offences such as failure to cite sources. Prosecuting an offender requires the faculty member to assemble evidence and to go through a series of steps that might result in a modest penalty.

Universities therefore tend to stress prevention. If assignments are varied and essay topics phrased so as to require more than stock answers, and with classes small enough for instructors to know their students, academic misconduct is much less frequent. That last condition, however, isn't possible in most institutions, where large classes mean impersonal learning. Where students experience only remote connections with faculty, the trust that's betrayed by cheating is only notional – it has no personal content. And trust, as I argued in Chapter Two, is unsurprisingly related to integrity.[29] But there I also argued that trust requires belief in the integrity of an institution; here the point is that trusting and being trusted encourages academic integrity.

There's something unsettling about the state of affairs in which unprecedented attention to student welfare is accompanied by student behaviour that constitutes an unprecedented erosion of the integrity at the heart of the academic enterprise. It suggests that a social malaise has infected the student psyche, eating away at honesty, and it isn't being cured by the measures the university has so far offered. Maybe it's related to the malaise of insecurity of the self that requires propping up. If your vaunted confidence in your abilities is hollowed out when you hit university, and cheating is the obvious way to keep up appearances, what then? Your moral fibre might be as weak as your inner certainties of the self. Perhaps you'd rather risk being caught than lose face by admitting that you need help.

There are different reasons, then, students don't take up the benefits available to them: lack of opportunity because of the constraints of time and distance from campus, and lack of motivation because of the desire to preserve an aura of competence. No doubt lack of knowledge about how to access services, peer pressure, and plain old failure of nerve also play their parts. The success of the university's attentiveness to students is a mitigated good, then, insofar as it fails to be realized.

It's also qualified, as I mentioned, by unintended consequences. One of these is the attitudes this attention might encourage. That is the next topic, to be followed by some comments on the challenges occasioned for the university itself.

Inappropriate Expectations

Providing an array of services to students creates expectations about the university's obligations to meet perceived needs and interests. Charging significant fees also might generate a sense of entitlement. It's easy to imagine how these concepts slide over into the world of commerce, for the language of goods and services brings with it the notions of customers, consumers, and clients. Goods are what producers come up with, to be purchased for use, enjoyment, or consumption by customers. Services are what providers, often professionals of some kind, offer clients. Are students, then, customers for the goods produced in the university – clients of the services on offer?

It's not uncommon to find this vocabulary used of students and their experience. The context is often concern about attracting and retaining students in a competitive environment: "Call it customer service, or call it something else. Either way, colleges and universities – the market leaders, at least – are starting to adopt it. Institutions that understand their students and provide them with rapid and personalized service stand to increase enrollments, improve retention and reimagine market potential"[30] – that's from a US publication on college management. For another example, a dean at Syracuse University claims that university leaders must have a customer service mentality, for we have to provide students with "the level of service they're expecting."[31] In the United Kingdom, since the Dearing Report in 1997, the government has referred to students as customers, and that language peppers policy discussions.[32] Whether most students actually think of themselves as customers is less clear, but there are some manifestations of the consumer/client mentality, especially where their tuition costs are high. After all, if one pays money, isn't the expectation of value for dollar a reasonable one? Isn't the customer entitled to get a quality product, especially where the advertising has created high expectations? And doesn't the investment in the enterprise and the product mean a say in how it all works?

Those questions raise complicated issues, two of which I'll comment on: the appropriateness of language and labels, and the obligations of the university upon which expectations should depend.

Students Are Really Students

I referred in Chapter Two to models of the university that employ the terms of markets and competition, and pointed out the particular nature of the goods available in a university education. Education can't properly be regarded as a commodity, although perhaps in the root sense higher education is *commodious* – that is, beneficial and useful. But the adjective commodious is no longer common parlance. A "commodity," the Oxford English Dictionary tells us, is "a kind of thing produced for use or sale, an article of commerce, an object of trade." When you trade something, you don't have it anymore. You have instead the thing you traded it for. And you can trade that for something else again, so you don't necessarily keep it. But knowledge doesn't work that way. You share knowledge with someone, and they learn what you know. But you don't give your knowledge away in the sharing.

The point here is that the *language* of commodity is just wrong when applied to education. It doesn't work, any more than would talk about "trading" one genuine memory for someone else's memory. You can understand each word in that sentence, but it makes no sense as a claim. Further, there might also be a moral objection to this language. When critics complain of the commodification of knowledge, they could be making a point about the inappropriateness of placing a monetary value on a human value such as knowledge, insight, or wisdom, just as it is inappropriate (even plain wrong) to monetize friendship and love.

Even more, there are practical problems in this mistaken and confused thinking. As we saw in Chapter Two, the benefits of a university degree aren't consumables that are desired or required within a short span of time. You can't easily decide you don't like your current degree "provider" and try another next week. The goods take time to be realized, often past graduation. So although there are broad ranges of salary typical for graduates with particular degrees – engineering pays more than art history – it's not right or possible to put a dollar figure on the value for one's life of having been at university. The best anyone can do is to guess whether the expense of the experience will have been "worth it," where worth is a matter of individual judgment about the good life.

How we use language is important. It not only describes roles and relationships; it also creates expectations. The language of the market works for the market, but it doesn't work for families. It doesn't work for many other experiences. Think of museums and art galleries. These institutions don't have customers or clients; they have visitors or guests. Concerts, symphonies, and the opera have audiences and patrons. Sporting events have fans, not customers. However, just because organizations and institutions don't use the language of commerce doesn't mean they are indifferent to the experience of those who enjoy and support them – quite the contrary. They want to serve them well, just for the sake of the experience they offer.

Those who come to university to learn become members of the institution for the sake of the knowledge they will gain. At the end of Chapter One, I did note that people attend for additional, non-knowledge-related, reasons – for socializing, friendship forming, and the discovery of life partners. They might even say they were attending for the sake of a diploma, the credential rather than the knowledge it represents. Nonetheless their primary and defining relationship with the institution is that of the knowledge seeker. They are not customers or clients; but neither are they fans or visitors. They are there to learn, and in that sense are learners. But learning is an activity that goes on regardless of one's status,[33] and those who attend university for the sake of knowledge and degrees have a different status from other members of the institution. They are, plain and simply, *students*. And that is what they should be called.

Universities do want to serve their students well. When they purchase goods such as food or textbooks, the principles of effective marketing and customer service are appropriate; and when they use services such as psychological counselling, they are clients as well as students. In some aspects of the relationship, then, universities are under commercial and legal obligations, and must observe professional standards. The quality of residence life, food, bookstores, and the like has an important effect upon student experience, and it behoves universities to seek "customer satisfaction" in these areas. But the customer mentality is inappropriately carried over into the classroom.

Obligations and Entitlements

Let's characterize the "customer mentality" as the belief that, in paying for a good or service, the payment creates an obligation on the part of the provider and a corresponding entitlement on the part of the purchaser. Although the provider's obligation may or may not be legally enforceable, "entitlement" is the belief that the purchaser is owed – has a right to – the satisfaction of expectations. There should be no rotten potatoes in the bag; the sweater should be the stated standard size; the room should be painted the chosen colour.

There's good reason for the customer mentality. But only in certain economic transactions. For not all expectations, even legitimate ones, create obligations and entitlements. You expect the team to win, the lyric soprano to sing well, the gallery to curate a show effectively. If your expectations are disappointed, that's life. You don't get your money back. You paid for the experience of an event, and experiences are hard things to predict because they depend on so many factors, including your own attitudes and preparedness.

Being a student isn't like being a fan, a visitor, or a patron. It's a matter of seeking the experience that constitutes becoming educated, whatever that is – we'll see about that in the next chapter. The university holds out as its aim to create that experience for its students. It thereby creates expectations, but very little by way of entitlement. The university does have some obligations: to offer courses required to complete an announced program; to set assignments that can be completed in reasonable time and with reasonable access to the necessary resources; and so on. Students might arrive, however, with expectations that create no obligation upon the institution. If they have been afforded all kinds of support in order to achieve high grades, they might find transition to a life requiring self-motivation difficult. If they've always been at the top end of the class, they might suffer self-doubt in joining a competitive cohort that's composed only of high achievers. If their road to educational success has been smooth, with no failures, low grades might unsettle self-esteem. And if, added to all this, they have absorbed the mindset of the consumer, they will want their expectations met to their satisfaction – especially when the university makes a great deal of the importance of Student Satisfaction.

There is a chain of potential consequences here that can erode the significant goodness of the all-about-students turn. In promoting its teaching function and providing student services, the university elevates student experience. In that elevation it valorizes student satisfaction. Student satisfaction involves meeting expectations. Expectations can arise from a sense of assumed entitlement, an attitude closely related to the mentality of the consumer. But education is not a commodity, and students need to be students. The rest of us – especially governments and promoters who want to create beliefs about their intentions towards those seeking education – need to watch our language.

The Social Burden of the University

One more aspect of the university's shift to students is unintended, but not at all inconsequential. And it contains a sobering ironic twist. I call it the social burden that the university is now required to shoulder.

It's not as though the challenges weren't already weighing on the institution. With the "massification" of higher education, universities must educate a vastly greater percentage of the population. That percentage is increasing rapidly: one report claims that global growth in enrolments from 2000 to 2010 averaged 7.6 million each year.[34] Resources cannot keep pace with increased participation rates, so universities have to find more efficient ways to educate students. Especially in areas where growth was pronounced fifty or sixty years ago, the facilities that were built for expansion need renovation and refitting. In Canada alone the estimated cost of university deferred maintenance is $8.4 billion.[35]

But put those financial and material burdens to one side for now. Put aside as well the educational burden of remedial work that often has to be assumed when students arrive with barely adequate preparation in numeracy and literacy. Instead I'm thinking of the *social* burden the university is required to carry as it attempts to serve students in those areas I discussed above.

In loco cuiuscumque?

In place of whomever? At the start of this chapter, I went back in imagination to a time when you'd have three offices on campus to take care of your needs: the registrar for academic advice, the chaplain for spiritual problems, and the nurse for minor health issues. Mind, spirit, and body. It's not so simple these days. In fact it's hard to think of an area of human life that isn't addressed by the university in one form or another. From day one at orientation through to graduation, somebody is giving advice, offering assistance, arranging a session, reviewing or assessing or improving or remedying this or that. Nutritional choices. Exercise. Safe sex. Roommate relationships. Financial planning. Time management. Study habits. Sleep. Alcohol. Consent. Drugs. Writing multiple choice tests. Accommodating disabilities. Constructing essays. Avoiding plagiarism. Anxiety. Choosing a career. Suicidality. Taking time for fun. Dealing with the fraud complex. Sexual harassment and violence. Walksafe programs. Getting involved in the community. Healthy meals on a budget. How to write a resumé. Table manners, interview strategies. If I've neglected a topic or issue, that's the fault of memory, not because the university has ignored it.

Here's the ironic twist. Back half a century or so, students rose up against the idea that the university's relationship to them was *in loco parentis*, in place of the parent. That legal doctrine, developed in eighteenth-century British common law, granted school authorities the right to exercise parental discipline over pupils when the parent was not present. Until the mid-twentieth century, universities assumed this stance, treating their students as immature and in need of moral and character development; just as parents could discipline at whim, so could universities.[36] The doctrine slid out of favour, sometimes with the push of protest and with the approval of the courts. Universities no longer had parental duties with respect to their students.

Until very recently. Not that the courts have actually reinstated *in loco parentis* obligations; rather, it's the world that has turned things round – and not just back to an earlier time, either. The list I have generated places the university not just in the role of parents, but of whole extended families, places it indeed in the various social services roles of entire communities. It's not your dad telling you what to eat, your mother advising you about relationships, your uncle or aunt suggesting career options, your village or town providing facilities. The university is now in the place of … well, *whomever*? Whoever fits the need. Rather than proclaiming their independence and claiming the autonomy of a fresh maturity, students need (want, expect, demand – the verb depends on the subject and object of the sentence) the props and nets that make freedom safe. Reluctant fledglings, they.

Let me be clear. This description doesn't fit all students, and I mustn't be taken to suggest at all that the university should not be fulfilling these roles. It's important to acknowledge that this is the way the world is. If it's ironic that today's students seek a relationship with the university that their grandparents rejected as paternalistic, that's just another irony of history. If it's unsettling that, despite the university's broad-spectrum remedies, the social malaise it addresses also erodes the integrity of its degrees – the university cannot simply tell its students to grow up or go home. The students are who they are, and if the university is to fulfil its functions in educating them, it has a practical imperative to assist them. Regardless of its legal duties, the university's very mission gives it a moral imperative to ameliorate conditions that impede education, insofar as it is in its competence to do so.

When institutions must bear a social burden that stretches their mandate, they struggle to keep afloat. They also need to identify problems that surface in the struggle so that their identity and mission won't be corroded by the salt tides of social forces. I propose that there are three areas of potential concern. The third has to do with government, but the first belongs to the way administrative organization within the university has unfolded, and the second to mandate and focus.

Responsibility Diffused

There's no easy solution to the internal structural problem, which I'll call the *administrative diffusion of responsibility* for the educational experience, broadly conceived, of students, particularly undergraduates. One way to appreciate this is to make a mental list of all the academic and administrative members of the university with some level of responsibility for their experience that a typical undergraduate would encounter just in the first year. There'd be five to ten faculty members, a similar number of teaching assistants; three or four registrarial persons; likewise with staff in the dean of students office, residence dons, and more than likely over the course of the year staff in at least some of counselling services, accommodation services, academic services, writing centres, and health services. Some might require the assistance of a crisis or sexual assault response team. That's a large set of people sharing responsibility for a student, and chances are high that only the administrative staff will know, or remember her or his name. Given entirely proper privacy concerns, even if instructors made a point of learning their students' names, they wouldn't know who needs accommodation for exam writing, who is suffering from deep anxiety, who committed plagiarism in another course. Given the size of the class, neither would they know who is on the volleyball team or who attended the student production of *The Tempest* last night. In other words, they won't know anything at all about their students apart from their performance in their particular class. Of course this isn't a situation brought about by the pronounced growth in student services – faculty members rarely discuss their own students with others who teach them because the curriculum, at least in almost all universities, is atomized into courses and credits taught by different people. Academic instruction is divvied up among those five or ten faculty, and no academic has primary responsibility for assessing overall progress – that's an administrative task subject to privacy provisions, so that one can't know how students are faring in other courses.

With increased attention to the rest of the student's experience, however, the diffusion is more pronounced. I argue in the next chapter that universities should take an expansive view of undergraduate education as encompassing the university experience and reflection upon its manifold meanings: to situate education, whatever that is, within the full lived experience of the student – that is, to take students seriously. What's learned about forgiveness in *The Tempest* might turn out to be much more important than what I said in class about deontological ethics. "Studies show," as they say, that for many people what happens outside the classroom has more lasting effect than what's studied for the sake of the degree.[37] But when it comes to the business of "student life" – meaning all those clubs, residence events, and programs under the purview of deans of students, as though the "life" of students has nothing academic in it – the interactions between those responsible for this "life" and faculty members are rare. Each group goes about its work in untroubled ignorance of the daily work of the other, although they each create experiences for the same students.

As a result, the mind, so to speak, of the university is fragmented and distracted when it thinks about its students. Everybody, it will be said, is responsible for the student experience. But faculty members, chairs, and deans think about how students follow the curriculum, are graded, and meet degree requirements, and not a lot more, apart from the activities for the department's student society. Deans of students think about student behaviour and about enlightening events that give relief from the grind of study. Academic counsellors think about timely interventions and plausible petitions. I need not go on – every office worries about student experience, at least that slice of the experience that concerns them. But where everyone is responsible for bits, nobody is responsible for the whole thing – except maybe the president, who does have a few other things to do.

So the diffusion of responsibility, exacerbated by the increased number of "service providers," is an issue – and a knotty one that's difficult to disentangle and allow the university to focus on its central functions. For the university must accept the social burdens laid upon it only for the sake of facilitating and enhancing its knowledge functions. Additional burdens and responsibilities only distract and siphon energy and resources away from its fundamental reason for being. Deciding what's an essential service isn't straightforward, nor is it easy to redraw the lines of reporting structures or to develop processes where policies and practices emerge from deliberation across the current silos of responsibilities.

Although I can't offer concrete solutions about shared responsibility here, I will return in the next chapter to the question of what's involved in an exemplary undergraduate education. Before that, though, there are two more issues related to the shouldering of what I've called the social burden of the university.

Diluted Mandate?

As the university shifts its attention, quite properly, to students, seeking to improve teaching and to offer more services for student success, the rebalancing of priorities and resources can begin to affect the mandate and focus of the institution. Let's remind ourselves, yet again, that the university is fundamentally about knowledge.

And not just about knowledge in any old way. Although the function unique to the university is the certifying of knowledge attained by the awarding of degrees, the meaning of those degrees is intimately tied up with the creation, discovery, and critique of knowledge claims – the defining characteristics of a university. Teaching, after all, is carried out in many different institutions and at many different levels. What's distinctive about university teaching is that it is carried out by those who themselves have attained standing as creators, discoverers, and assessors of knowledge. Further, they maintain this standing through continued professional activity – they "remain current in the discipline," as it's put. It's not enough to be able to repeat in different ways the assigned textbook;

university teachers must be able to assess the claims made, the procedures advocated, the underlying assumptions – and thereby contribute to the growth of knowledge in their students. Students don't merely listen; they watch and assess, learning by example how they should relate to knowledge claims themselves. (More on this in Chapter Seven.)

The exercise on which good teaching is predicated is scholarship or research, and it's that exercise into which students are being inducted at some level or other. Hence the worry, mentioned earlier in this chapter, that the development of teaching streams without research duties might dilute the mandate of the university. And I don't mean just teaching-stream faculty, but part-time and contingent faculty too. If students are taught by a large percentage of faculty who have no research obligations, universities, over time, will become less like themselves. The implication, for any university that wants to remain properly constructed and undistracted, is that it should build into its academic personnel policies a minimum requirement for some scholarly activity, however defined by the collegium, for all faculty who teach.

It's also possible for the focus of an institution to be blurred by the effort required to deliver the services it offers, with all good intentions, to its students. Those services must not find their justification only in supporting the academic mission; the institution must reinforce that *raison d'être* in its public rhetoric and staff development – a small step towards dealing with the diffusion of responsibility discussed above. Further, the focus must not wander from the proper concern for behaviour and attitudes related to academic success to areas that belong to other spheres and authorities. The old *in loco parentis* was discarded in part because it gave universities licence to order life and to discipline more or less arbitrarily in the name of "character development." The determination of what constitutes "character" is not up to the university any more than it is up to the state. The past, in which hazing rituals were said to inculcate manly stamina, or etiquette sessions to teach feminine graces, is well past. That's understood. Now the university must be vigilant about how and why it orders the lives of today's students – for it does continue to do that.

Order, Discipline, and Autonomy

Students' lives are ordered in various ways: by convention and the traditions of a particular institution, by regulations and rules, by rewards and sanctions, and by discipline. It is in the university's power to withhold credits, to refuse or revoke degrees, to impose fines, to issue orders of non-contact or non-trespass, and to suspend or expel from the institution. Almost all these sanctions have a direct connection to the academic mission of the university, and are imposed for academic failures or misconduct. Some discipline, however, does not relate to the offender's academic performance directly, but rather to other behaviour – the kind that compromises or invades the health, safety, and security of others, disrupts the legitimate activities of the university, or damages property. Such behaviour impinges on the ability of others, and of the university, to carry out their academic functions. It's right and proper, then, for the university to protect the integrity of the institution and its members through appropriate codes and attendant sanctions.

Outside those bounds, however, the university should not stray into the regulation of conduct.[38]

Civil and criminal laws, and the authorities that enforce them, exist with respect to the behaviour of persons who are citizens as well as students, and these spheres need to be acknowledged and respected. Arson and assault, for example, should be dealt with by the state, even if the university imposes its own sanctions for the sake of the integrity of its operations.[39] It's dangerous for the university to assume the judicial functions of the state where the behaviour in question is covered by the laws of the state. The university has neither the expertise nor the authority to do that. Likewise, the state should not regulate the academic behaviour of students *qua* students; it doesn't have the expertise and shouldn't have the authority, under the conditions of university autonomy that I affirmed in Chapter Three.

That raises the last issue added to the increased social burden the university carries – namely, government interest in the vexed case of sexual violence. As I've just argued, universities do have responsibility for the safety and security of all their members, without which the fundamental functions of the institution cannot be carried out. It has particular duties for students in its residences. Clearly the university cannot tolerate violence. How does this obligation relate to government?

As I noted earlier in the chapter, in 2015 the Ontario government decided it would take a series of steps to deal with incidents and complaints about sexual violence across the population by amending various pieces of pertinent legislation. It included universities in that legislation. The Sexual Violence and Harassment Action Plan Act, 2016 now requires every provincially assisted university and college to develop a policy on sexual violence and harassment. The policy must state how the institution will respond to complaints; it applies to students registered in the institution; and it must be reviewed every three years. Students must be consulted in the development and review of the policy. Further, the institution must report the following information to the minister of training, colleges and universities, presumably whenever the minister so requires, and to its board of governors annually: the number of times support services related to sexual violence are requested by students; the initiatives taken to promote awareness of the policy; and the number, and character, of incidents and complaints about sexual violence. The minister also has the discretion to order a survey of students at any time in any particular institution to ascertain the effectiveness of the policy or the number of incidents. And the government may make regulations specifying how the provisions of the act will be implemented – around processes, consultation, training, publication, and support services.[40]

There can be no disagreement that having an effective university policy on sexual assault is important for the proper functioning of the university, especially where that policy provides support for those affected by harassment and violence. How the university's responsibilities and procedures for students intersect with government's responsibilities for citizens is not at all an easy matter to decide. It's made even more difficult when sexual harassment, assault, and violence are concerned, especially in these days of heightened awareness.

It's perhaps worth pointing out that Manitoba has also enacted legislation on sexual violence awareness and prevention, but its act stops short of asserting ministerial power to assess and directly regulate university policies and practices.[41] As we saw in Chapter Three, sorting out the proper and appropriate spheres of university autonomy and responsibility is a tricky business. When society and government place upon the university expectations and obligations unclearly related to its knowledge functions, achieving clarity about its responsibilities is one more burden the institution must carry.

Conclusion

The undistracted university devotes its attention to knowledge. It also attends to students, but students as knowledge seekers. They're human beings as well, with the curiosities, fragilities, and potentials of the human condition. To be successful in the search for knowledge, they need to be taught well. Their very human needs also need attention. In the past half-century, universities have sharpened their focus on teaching and expanded greatly the services required for success. That's been good for universities and for students. This turn to students has not been without its challenges, however. It's a struggle for the university to cope with the social burden that manifests itself in insecurity, entitlement, cheating, sexual violence. Responsibility for students is diffused, and the need to advance teaching and services can weaken the university's fundamental mandate for knowledge creation and critique.

Yet despite all this, the university persists in its functions, and students gain knowledge. They continue to graduate in staggeringly large numbers. But if it's about students as knowledge-seeking persons these days, what sort of knowledge should they gain in a properly constructed, undistracted, university? Especially in undergraduate education? To that question I now turn.

chapter seven

What Knowledge Should Undergraduates Gain?

In the previous chapter I set out the many ways in which universities have recognized the importance of teaching as central to their knowledge functions. The unrelenting growth in enrolment has challenged the effectiveness of these measures, and I noted in particular the increase, correspondingly unabated, in the percentage of non-permanent, usually part-time, faculty without formal responsibilities to engage in research. At the same time, the past few years have seen an interest in reshaping the undergraduate curriculum to serve changing student interests and societal needs. Just who determines what are those needs isn't clear. There is no one authoritative voice: government announces special programs, business asks for certain skills and competencies, the professions and trades predict labour surplus or shortage. The vocabulary of skills and training permeates official documents, to be countered by educators – often joined by business leaders, if not their human resources personnel – who speak instead of the need for critical thinking and the ability to communicate effectively. Since economic development depends on innovation, and innovation is linked closely to technology, and technology requires science, which requires mathematics, there's strong interest in the STEM disciplines (science, technology, engineering, math). That interest is reinforced by laudable efforts to increase the number of young women in these areas.[1] As enrolments slip away from the humanities and social sciences, there's concern that the very notion of a liberal education is under siege just as the world needs the critical thinking and communication skills fostered by liberal studies.

How are we to navigate these swirling currents of advocacy and anxiety? The most superficial survey of books and articles on what makes for a good undergraduate education in the twenty-first century would be exhausting, and would leave us incapable of assessing their value unless we had some fundamental convictions about *the kind of knowledge* that undergraduates should gain from their university experience. I'll attempt to think through a set of such convictions in this chapter, not to prepare a curriculum, but to propose for deliberation an answer to the questions: what are the characteristics of someone who has had a decent undergraduate education? What sort of knowledge should have been gained in those formative years? In a world saturated with information bits, surely an educated person must have come to know about how to gain knowledge – but what does that involve?

The task in this chapter involves comment on the terms peppering the first paragraph: skills, training, competencies, critical thinking, effective communication, innovation, technology, liberal education. There's nothing wrong with such words, as long as we think carefully about their meaning in relation to the fundamental knowledge functions of the university. If their natural habitat has been elsewhere, they might have acquired a flavour that doesn't blend well with what the university should have on offer. At least, on offer for undergraduate education, which is my focus here. I'll argue that, although the common understanding of the current vocabulary for the aims of that education point in the right direction, on inspection they don't really deliver what the university should be seeking to accomplish – or what students themselves, their parents, their potential employers, and indeed society at large should expect from an educated person. That done, I'll set out a paradigmatic example of what's sought in liberal education, extracting some fundamental principles about human knowing that can be taken to the guiding question of what knowledge undergraduates should gain in their university experience.

Skills?

Let's start with the language of skills, closely related to competencies, techniques, and training.

Skills are important to have. They usually take effort to develop, because they are what are called *dispositions* to behave in certain ways, and dispositions are habits that are engrained in their possessors. Skills are also teachable by those who are good at explaining and demonstrating how they work, correcting behaviour and improving techniques. And they have the advantage of having a product, aim, or outcome that can be assessed, so that we know when someone is exercising a skill properly. Put these characteristics together, and you get as "skilful" some activity that's not just a matter of luck, but of practised technique that has come about through experience guided by teaching and training. One can add that competencies are what we attribute to those whose skills are successful. Not all of us can be skilled at many different things, which is why we're impressed with the kidney specialist who plays the flute so well, or the Syriac specialist who sets metal type and produces beautiful hand-printed books.

Take the language of skills, now, to university education. If we expect universities to turn out skilled graduates, we might be thinking of specialists in particular disciplines, and we'd want them to demonstrate the effective mastery of the techniques and competencies particular to their disciplines. This is especially true of graduates of *professional* programs at the undergraduate and graduate levels, where the name of the degree conveys the claim of competence in the area. Although there are some professional bachelor's degrees, say, in business or education, nowadays learning the practice of a profession or occupation is often done at the master's level, for which a solid undergraduate degree is requisite. The proliferation of professional master's degrees is one of the most striking things about program development in twenty-first-century universities. In Ontario alone, the twenty-one universities have submitted ninety-eight new master's programs for approval over the past five years, more than the eighty-two new undergraduate programs, although there are five undergraduates for every master's student.[2] The names of new professional graduate degrees reveal just how specialized advanced study has become, especially where it involves professional practice – as a quick glance at the list in the endnote will show.[3] There's been a similar development in professions where the initial degree had been at the bachelor's level: we've skipped right over to professional doctorates. From the LLB to the JD in law; from the BPharm to the PharmD in pharmacy. It's increasingly common for these professional doctorates to be built upon a more general undergraduate program.

For these kinds of degrees, their conferral signifies the attainment of the relevant competencies required by professional practice. The professions know what graduates should be able to do when they finish their programs. Those are the skills they need, which they should have learned and be able to demonstrate.[4]

From there it's an easy step to expect something similar from students graduating from programs in the arts and sciences. They should have learned the skills society wants, and be able to demonstrate their competence.

But not so fast: the words expressing this expectation seem to make sense, but I'll argue that the notion of skills gets pressed into service that's not fit for this context. That requires thinking about the contexts in which the word sits easily and understandably in everyday speech.

If you check out "skill" in the Oxford English Dictionary, a glance through its early meanings shows that the word's history is complicated. The original sense doesn't work in everyday speech now; it had to do with the mind, the ability to discern difference, to discriminate what is proper and reasonable from what is not. That meaning, linked often with reason, is now obsolete. We have moved away from the mind, to "know-how" – the ability to perform some task well.[5] To call someone skilled is obviously appropriate where dexterity is involved.[6] When we appreciate the handiwork of an excellent craftsperson, the delicate operation carried out by a surgeon, or the stick handling of a hockey star, it is natural to praise their skill. This is because, as I noted about skills in general, their know-how results in a specific product or outcome. A skilful person knows how to do something, but also does it well – where there's a shared appreciation among a community of knowledgeable persons about what "doing it well" involves.

Although the result of skilful practice is often tangible or definite (a cabinet, a vitrectomy, or a goal scored), in other cases we still speak of skill as *techniques to bring about an outcome with standards of success*. That condition is important for my argument. Hence a debater can be skilful when debates are habitually won or a lover when – well, enough said; point made. It's telling, however, that we *do not use the language of skills in some other cases*, which is also important for the argument. To call pianists or novelists "skilful" might suggest that they have excellent technique but lack the quality of, say, interpretation or character development that marks great art. Technique, after all, is *impersonal*. No matter how complicated, a technique can be taught and repeated by anyone with the requisite ability. Mere technique by itself, however praiseworthy, won't give us the unique experience or performance that expresses the personal relationship of the artist with the work. It's the same with many of the intricate webs of relationships that constitute human life. A parent who was merely "skilful" at parenting would apply a set of techniques to relationships as though there were nothing unique about being a parent to *this* child as distinct from any other child. We all know people who follow the manual without making independent judgments, and with sad results. They don't seem to know the difference between what is the case most of the time and why, and what is different here and now, with this particular person in this particular circumstance. In a word, they lack *judgment*. Judgment sits *above* skills, deciding what's the right thing to do with respect to the exercise of this or that skill, and whether the outcome of the techniques employed is valuable or desirable. Like a judge, it weighs the evidence and arguments for using skills in light of the complex of human desires and values interwoven in the circumstances concerned.

I must add immediately that, when we praise the performance of a surgeon and a hockey player, it's because they have more than technique: they too exhibit judgment about when and how to employ techniques, and when to alter them. I'd argue, then, that the word "skilful" is doing some additional work related to its original meaning in this case – the surgeon and the skater are discerning and discriminating about how to employ their skills.

But, it will be retorted, in talk about skills education there's another use of "skills" these days, having little to do with techniques and manuals. They're called "soft skills" or "people skills," and employers prize them. There is no canonical list of these "skills," but if one were drawn up it would include being a good communicator, team player, time manager, problem solver; in addition, the list would characterize those with these aptitudes as respectful, good listeners, persuasive, and confident. If these are "skills," they warrant the name only in an extended sense; in fact, I'd argue that these qualities don't fit easily in techniques-skills-competencies discourse. That's because a proper skill has associated techniques and outcomes that, as I've maintained, make it possible to figure out whether the skill has achieved its intended function and purpose. "Soft" or "people" skills might include some associated techniques: remember people's names by association with one of their characteristics, look them in the eye, make your handshake firm but not crushing, plan your week to include some leisure. But relating well to others is more a matter of judgment than of rules. Being a persuasive communicator involves a lot more than following steps in a manual: one needs to attend, in the moment, to whether the other person is listening with understanding, which is a different matter from *remembering the rule* that one needs to attend to the other in the moment. Likewise with a "skill" called problem solving. That's far too vague; we all know people who throw up their hands in the face of difficulties and those who roll up their sleeves instead. But that's because the latter are *that kind of person*, not the result of some technique they've learned. In fact, one technique to solve a problem might well mess up attempts to solve a different problem. Techniques might give the impression of being a good speaker, but they won't necessarily guarantee that one is listened to.[7]

My point is that "soft" or "people" skills shouldn't properly be thought of as skills at all, as long as skills language carries its connection to techniques designed to effect a certain outcome. Such so-called skills here are interpersonal and relational attitudes and behaviour, and arise out of the kinds of people we are, our values, loves, and commitments. If they are "skills," they are skills (although "qualities" would be better) of character, in the Oxford English Dictionary's obsolete sense: skills of discrimination and judgment.

What does this have to do with undergraduate education in the arts and sciences? Despite the many roles the university has assumed in the past few decades, surely it doesn't want to be in the business of forming and judging the character of undergraduates. Let's grant that the point of a proper undergraduate education (a "liberal" education) isn't about teaching particular skills related to occupations or professions. That wouldn't be helpful, since graduates of particular disciplines commonly end up in positions with little overt connection to their undergraduate studies.[8] What knowledge, then, should they be gaining? I'll return to these questions, but first I should confront another phrase in the current vocabulary of educational expectation: critical thinking. Is this yet another "skill" that the university should be inculcating in its undergraduates? It's related to problem solving, but it is not exactly a "people skill" since presumably it can be exercised in solitude. But what exactly is critical thinking? And how does it relate to those other "skills" of effective communication and team work, which do involve other people?

Critical Thinking?

Whatever critical thinking is, it's good to be in favour of it; otherwise one seems agreeable to shoddy or impulsive thinking or to parrot-like repetition of somebody else's thoughts. "Critical," of course, means "properly assessing," "weighing up judiciously," and that sort of thing, not negative reasoning that sets out to pick apart and destroy the rationalizations of others. Here's one oft-quoted statement about critical thinking: "The ability to think critically – ask pertinent questions, recognize and define problems, identify arguments on all sides of an issue, search for and use relevant data and arrive in the end at carefully reasoned judgments – is the indispensable means of making effective use of information and knowledge."[9] But saying more than this takes one into a fascinating morass of literature on "CT," in which experts come up with different views, not only on what critical thinking is, but how to measure it.[10] There's a whole industry out there: a quick library search yields 2,582 books and 990,696 articles with the two keywords included.[11] I can't add much to the conversation, but I have three observations that might be useful.

First, it helps to understand what critical thinking is and whether it's up to snuff, when it is about a particular profession with its set of skills and competencies. When we talk about thinking, we need to be thinking about something or other, and the quality of our thinking will be measured against what works in that area. Thinking like an engineer, or a pastry chef, or a pastor each has its own distinctive forms of reflective thought. Coming up with flaky pastry isn't at all like dealing with flaky people, so while "defining problems" and arriving at "reasoned judgments" about how to proceed might sound like the same activities, in the end we'll know whether the chef or the pastor have thought critically – not just automatically or half-heartedly – if things work out as they should.

Second, thinking is a complicated business. It's not just reasoning, the ability to draw conclusions from premises and to assess the validity of arguments. You can assess that sort of reasoning by administering logic tests. But logic won't tell you whether a particular premise is in fact the case. You can pile up masses of information without leaving your desk these days, but whether it's reliable and should be believed – that's a different question. Good thinking needs proper beliefs to work on, so an essential aspect of good thinking is knowing what to accept, what to query, what to investigate further. What's more, thinking often requires intellectual curiosity, which involves the work of imagination in asking what could or might be the case. There's also the work of moral judgment, asking what *should or should not* be the case. Neither of these activities is reasoning plain and simple.

Third, sometimes "skills" such as effective communication and team work are treated separately from critical thinking. That should not happen. Effective communication requires clarity of expression, and clarity of expression requires clarity of thought – that is, good critical thinking. Although some forms of dexterity might be difficult to explain in language alone (tying a bowtie, for instance), dextrous thinking depends on explanation. In fact it's often the attempt to explain that assists in clarifying our thought. Clear expression forms an essential aspect of critical thinking, then, even if there is more than this in communication that is persuasive and rhetorically satisfying. Likewise with "teamwork." I'll have more to say about interactions with others, but here the point is that our thinking is affirmed and usually improved when it is shared with interlocutors who bring their own critical faculties to bear upon it. I was half-right to have said that critical thinking didn't involve "people skills" and could be carried out as a solitary activity, but half-wrong too. If critical thinking is self-reflective, the self is better reflected by exposing it to others.

The upshot of these observations? We should abandon any idea that good critical thinking consists mainly in analysing, inferring, deducing, and arguing well – that it's the skill of "reasoning logically." Logical reasoning is indeed a good thing, whereas credulity, even if charming, is not. But thinking that deserves to be called critical involves all the mental faculties, including curiosity, imagination, moral sense, and judgment. It's certainly not just a set of techniques. In fact "critical thinking" is just *very good thinking in particular contexts.*

But if this is anywhere right, what follows for undergraduate education? I ended the last section by recommending that the language of skills and competencies ought to be left to professional education, since the "soft" skills advocated for graduates of arts and science programs are about relationships and judgment, rather than techniques. Now I've concluded something similar about critical thinking – that it's not properly called a skill either. Sometimes, of course, the thinking is about a particular profession or occupation, which makes it easier to say when it's well done. When the thinking is instrumental to some identifiable end, it's "critical" to that enterprise. But what sort of good thinking should we look for in a properly educated undergraduate?

Liberal Education?

Here's a common, and obvious, reply to these insistent questions. What a properly educated undergraduate needs is *a liberal education*. That might trigger a couple of immediate reactions that should be put to one side. One is trivial: the very notion of "liberal," which in some places in the world remaining unidentified is a Bad Word, although "freedom" and "liberty" are Good Words. The other reaction is that calls for liberal education are cries and whimpers from humanists, whose enrolments are sliding south and threatening to erode even the meagre resources the administration grudgingly allows their disciplines. Salvation for the humanities, they hope, lies in the requirement that students take their courses in order to get a "liberal education."

I'm not very interested in the politics of the disciplines here, for there are much more fundamental issues at play in figuring out what has been meant by liberal education and how it does or doesn't answer the question of what kinds of knowledge should be gained in a decent undergraduate experience. As with other significant topics in higher education, the literature is vast, with a library catalogue search for the phrase yielding over 1,500 books and almost 650,000 journal articles. A helpful survey of themes in the liberal arts tradition reminds us that its proponents may have different aims: the cultivation of the mind for its own sake, the education of future leaders in social values and virtues, the questioning of traditional values and social norms, or freedom from the constraints of ignorance and self-absorption.[12] Rather than trying to address these conceptions directly, one would do well to find a paradigmatic example of the experience that has inspired this way of thinking about education – a model that captures its essential features. Fortunately there is such a model, with two strong advantages. The first is that it has influenced the fundamental ideas about liberal education in Western culture for twenty-five centuries; the second is that it depends upon no particular discipline, curriculum, or course to deliver the relevant education. In fact the example I have in mind has no institutional or organizational structure. It is the quest and mission of Plato's Socrates.[13]

Liberal Education as Socratic Education

In Chapter Five I pointed out that there's an *academic form of life* characterized by dissatisfaction with the current state of knowledge claims and driven by intellectual curiosity. Its mindset manifests epistemic restlessness. Those who identify with this epistemic stance are the true progeny of Socrates, renowned for his profession of ignorance and his relentless quest for knowledge. Socrates sets out to discover his own epistemic and moral condition, but then generalizes his findings to all human knowing and striving. His quest involves interrogating himself and others; despite not finding satisfactory answers from his interlocutors, he persists in the search as his highest and most serious duty. Socrates never does come up with a fully articulated account of what a good human life should be. Nevertheless Plato presents him as achieving that life, not in human companionship, but through an uncanny love of what lies beyond the realm of the contingent and human.

There is much to debate in Plato's account of the Socratic mission, but there's no denying its influence, even if its method is sometimes misunderstood.[14] That influence is well deserved, for there is much to be said about its understanding of the conditions for gaining and imparting knowledge. I'll make bold to propose seven propositions, broadly Socratic in their origin, that can be woven into a view of undergraduate education. These claims lie at the heart of a view of liberal education as socratic, with a lowercase "s" to signify that Plato's Socrates is its inspiration, rather than its author. The first four claims are about attitudes towards the human search for and grasp of knowledge and truth; the last three deal with how the search is to be carried out.

1. The most fundamental convictions about what constitutes a properly constructed and flourishing human life are difficult to articulate fully and accurately; they are always contestable.
2. There's an inborn desire for certainty in human beings that inflates epistemic confidence and leads to hubris and conceit – the

presumption that one actually has knowledge that is not available to human beings in general or to the claimant in particular.

3. Given the first proposition, knowledge claims are perennially revisable. There are indeed truths to be known, but the human grasp on truth is tenuous and liable to misconstruction. Nevertheless the seeker must persist courageously in the search.

4. The enterprise of gaining knowledge is a serious quest, involving the very meaning of what is a good and flourishing life for human beings.

5. Education requires self-interrogation and the thrust and parry of conversation and deliberation with others, so that claims to knowledge can be challenged, defended, modified, or abandoned.

6. Since the knowledge gained comes primarily through interrogation of and by others, education is *relational*, depending on personal interaction between teacher and student.

7. The process of such education is not dependent upon institutional structures or particular curricular content.

It would be self-defeating, of course, to claim that these seven propositions are not themselves revisable, that they must hold in all times and places for all kinds of people. Nevertheless I offer them as material for reflection and as foundational convictions on which to construct an understanding of the kind of knowledge that undergraduates in the twenty-first century should gain.

The Freedoms and Responsibilities of a University Education

Put aside for a moment these convictions of a socratic education, and return to the fundamental freedoms I discussed in the early part of Chapter Four. There I argued that freedoms of thought, conscience, expression, and association are constitutive freedoms, essential to *who we are* as human beings. Without these freedoms of thought or conscience, we wouldn't be mature persons, each with our own ideas and convictions; we'd be simply the epistemic echoes of other minds. Likewise with the freedoms to practise and give public expression to our convictions. The kinds of beings we are need communities in which beliefs are shared, corrected, supported, and celebrated. If we are to belong to communities, then the freedom to *associate* is fundamental as well.

These freedoms have usually been affirmed as civic – that is, as limiting the power of the state over its citizens; that's why the freedom to assemble has been included in most statements of human rights and freedoms. But in grounding them in what it is to be the kinds of beings we are, I've widened their scope and significance. In a parallel move I've argued that academic freedom is the exercise of these fundamental freedoms within the university, making them constitutive of what a university is. A university that doesn't safeguard its faculty's freedoms to discover, teach, and publish is not a proper university.

There's another issue from that chapter that's relevant to our current concerns with undergraduate education. In asking whether students should enjoy academic freedom, I suggested that the process of education, especially at the undergraduate level, is a honing in the academic context of these fundamental freedoms of thought, belief, expression, and association. Distinguishing good from bad ideas, clear from shoddy thinking, figuring out what's persuasive discourse and what's effective social action – all that is involved in the responsible exercise of one's freedoms.

If it's granted that the overarching aim of a university education is the honing and responsible exercise of freedoms fundamental to human flourishing, then one can begin to work out how the basic features of socratic education come into play. I'll argue next that they are relevant to the understanding and cultivation of virtuous epistemic convictions that should shape education, then examine how these convictions express themselves in attitudes towards knowledge and knowing. Thereafter I'll venture some observations about the particular challenges of a university education in the twenty-first century – about character, professional programs, and the structure of the undergraduate experience – not for the sake of specific curricular recommendations, but rather as material for deliberation on the undergraduate experience.

Seven Epistemic Convictions: Knowledge about Successful Knowing

The epistemic freedoms are those having to do with our beliefs and claims to knowledge; I include here (without further argument) moral knowledge and the dictates of conscience. Although the state must not impose beliefs on its citizens, an educated mind doesn't just accept any old claim to knowledge; it seeks to winnow out false or unfounded beliefs and to inform conscience in moral reasoning. What does socratic education have to do with this? I argue that the fundamental knowledge to be gained in an undergraduate education is *knowledge about successful knowing*.

I don't mean that everyone should have a course in epistemology, although that wouldn't be an abhorrent idea. Still, it's not necessary to be able to think up theories, criticize other theories, or write papers about the epistemic capacities of the human species. One can *know about knowing* in the sense of being self-aware and developing appropriate attitudes and habits that will assist in gaining knowledge, as I'll now explain with respect to the seven propositions fundamental to socratic education.

Convictions One and Two

Start with the first couple of planks in socratic education: the difficulties of articulating beliefs accurately, and the tendency to inflate epistemic successes beyond warrant. Proper knowing begins in the recognition of ignorance and limitations, in facing with intellectual honesty and courage one's own not knowing. There's a memorable instance of this in John Williams's 1965 novel, *Stoner*, which enjoyed late-blooming popularity a few years ago. The protagonist, William Stoner, went to university to study agricultural science in order to bring new knowledge to the family farm. He found his science courses, including soil science, of general interest. But he had to take a required survey of English literature, and that "troubled and disquieted him in a way that nothing had ever done before." The reason? When asked by his professor to explain a sonnet by Shakespeare, Stoner could not find the words. He had bumped up against the limits of his ability to articulate some deep feeling, to find a meaning he knew was there, hidden and elusive. His other courses had "things to be written in notebooks and remembered by a process of drudgery." This was different. This was the beginning of his education.

There might be a different novel, of course, about a literature major bumping up against walls of ignorance about science and discovering a yearning to enter that unknown, intriguing, or disquieting world. What's important is the *recognition of one's own epistemic condition*, and the cultivation of attitudes and behaviour appropriate to that condition.

If human beings are so limited in their epistemic capacities, and if all knowledge claims are contestable, one existential reaction to epistemic numbness might be despair. A socratic education doesn't stop there, however. Sometimes and on some matters, it's important to come to terms with the limits of knowledge and to learn to live with ambiguity. On other matters, it's crucial to seek to overcome limits. Instead of despair, our *curiosity*, the desire to find out more, must be awakened, the numbness become an itch. Not everyone has the same itch, fortunately, else the world of knowledge would be even more lopsided than it is now.[15] And not everyone has a life-changing experience of what Plato calls *aporia*,[16] stunned into silence by an insistent socratic encounter – curiosity might arise in a more mildly Aristotelian fashion. But even then, its impetus is not knowing, and wanting to know.

Conviction Three

Curiosity is fed by the epistemic conviction that there is truth to be known – or, if you prefer, that there are truths to be discovered, articulated, connected up into stories and theories that help us understand ourselves, each other, and the world. That our grasp is tenuous and our articulations revisable doesn't mean that there is nothing to be sought, any more than the halting nature of our description of last night's concert means it never happened or that our experience was imaginary. Indeed sometimes discovery is unexpected, an experience of *being granted insight*. That might be one reason the language of knowing often resorts to visual meta-phors, especially when what's made clear to the seeker has par-ticular import for the quest.[17]

Conviction Four

The impetus to discover is also sparked by the conviction that *knowledge matters*. Getting things right isn't a parlour or video game to be played as an idle pastime on a lazy afternoon. Even when we don't know the outcome, finding out the truth is an important task for human beings. To be prevented from or frustrated in that activity is a fundamental denial of a freedom that constitutes who we are. To inflict this denial on ourselves, through neglect, care-lessness, or disdain, is even worse. A socratically educated mind *cares about truth*. It especially cares about knowledge that has to do with what makes for human flourishing, those goods we prize as individuals, families, institutions, and societies.[18] These convic-tions reflect the third and fourth planks in socratic education, but what about the fifth?

Conviction Five

The fifth plank is that knowledge requires interrogation by the self and by others. It emerges that this is crucial to the entire enterprise of *coming to know how to know successfully*, and I'll spend several paragraphs on its implications. If it's the case that each of us is susceptible to the inflation of our epistemic capacities, we need help in deflating that pretense. Or maybe that's too strong a state-ment for those who are just mildly befuddled about what's the case. The successful search for knowledge has to be *a joint effort*. Just as none of us can see or hear ourselves, literally, as others see and hear us – mirrors always reverse images; sound recordings of our voices surprise us with how our words are heard, rather than how we hear them – so we can't easily evaluate our own think-ing and speaking from multiple points of view. Coming to know successfully requires coming to appreciate how what we claim is perceived and assessed by others. Listening demands not only rejoinder, but sometimes revision of our beliefs. The socratic conviction that education (descrying and coming nearer to truths) is communal, conversational, interrogative, and deliberative – that conviction is hugely important. I'll point next to four significant aspects of university education that follow from the character of that education as interrogative; I'll also mention a fifth, but discuss it more fully in the next chapter.

One: a properly constructed socratic undergraduate education is not accomplished (as Stoner came to realize) by the writing down of things to be remembered. Naturally there are indeed things to be remembered, but with vast quantities of knowledge now available in a small phone, having a good memory has become less important.[19] When knowledge claims are not just repeated as someone else's, but *interrogated* instead, they have to be restated with different vocabulary, clarified, or expanded. They become *one's own*. That's the point I made in claiming that freedoms of thought and expression are constitutive freedoms, essential to our being autonomous and responsible human agents. When I said in Chapter One that "transmission" is too weak a term for what must transpire in successful pedagogic interactions, the inadequacy of the "carrying-across" metaphor for socratic education was back of mind.[20] There is, to be sure, a certain amount of information transfer required in a decent undergraduate education, but that is fodder for interrogation and conversation, not the whole point. Hence the title of this chapter: it's about what knowledge is to be *gained*, not what knowledge is to be imparted. Gaining requires effort – the effort of answering and participating in interrogative conversation – on the part of the one who comes to possess knowledge.

Two: the interrogative process can include many participants across time. The library holds vast numbers of them, although they speak *to* you and not *with* you. As Plato pointed out in the *Phaedrus*, they don't answer any questions you pose directly to them, but only say the same thing over again. It's best, then, to regard the information deposited in paper and digital forms as material over which conversations may be had. Of course, many articles and books interrogate previous books and articles, and the reader is able to observe – listen in on, so to speak – the discussion. But there's nothing as good as *being interrogated* by others who are knowledgeable about the issue in question ("in question" is a telling expression here).

Who is best situated to conduct the interrogation? Those who are authorized to act as teachers, by virtue of their own education and experience. They obviously have a special role to play in the process, which can be explained this way. Education is not *just* conversation or discussion, or even deliberation. Conversation may be less formal than discussion, without any particular topic or end in mind – one has different expectations in joining a discussion than in joining a conversation – but in either form participants may be expressing only their personal opinions. They may say what they think, without being required to give reasons – indeed, good manners might sometimes prevent that challenge. The person in the role of teacher, however, does have the authority to ask why, and to assess the appropriateness of the answer. If unfortunately the notion of *inquisition* trails along with "interrogation," that might arise from memories of intimidating teachers with "interrogation techniques"; but bad practice and misuse of power do not invalidate the interrogative character of education or the authority of the teacher. Interrogative education, however, isn't a simple question-and-answer procedure, like call-and-response preaching. Nor is it an exercise of unquestioned authority. To raise the right issues in the right way, the teacher must *listen* to the student. And so that the teacher may continue to learn in the process of teaching, the student must be able to interrogate the teacher's claims.[21]

In properly constructed socratic education, then, students learn by example and by practice how to interrogate their own assumptions, reasoning, and knowledge claims. This means that, although the teacher has a special role, other partners in conversation can play an important part in providing material for reflection and deliberation. That includes not just talk among friends, but also the insistent, even raucous, demands of passionate debate. As I noted in Chapter Four, on free speech, sometimes campus discourse can be offensive, but the university must be a place where communities of difference continue to talk and to listen – and where, I now add, they question themselves and each other.

Three: not only actual, but possible, selves and stories are involved in interrogation. The process of examination places the object of interest in a large patchwork of ideas, events, and persons, asking how it is with this object over against others in different times and places. The business of interrogating and being interrogated thus requires the lively operation of imagination, a function or faculty that is able to present not just what is the case in more vivid colours, but – as we saw when examining "critical thinking" – what *might* be the case. Without the ability to imagine, human lives would be far less than human. Although the exercise of the imagination is not a specific plank in the convictions of socratic education as set out above, Plato was himself an immensely creative writer. Intrigued by paradox, he acted it out: he used writing to criticize the written word, employed powerful rhetoric to demote rhetoric in favour of philosophy, and in the constructions of a brilliant imagination he criticized the arts. It's no accident, then, that successful socratic education must develop this facility; it cultivates what Northrop Frye called the "educated imagination." Although closely related to creativity, imagination isn't restricted to making "creative works." It's employed in any inquiry into what might have been or could be the case, in developing hypotheses or thought experiments, in the exercise of moral empathy, and so on. The deliverances of a disciplined imagination assist not just self-reflection, but all inquiry into what might be the case under what conditions.

Four: it's worth noting that the foundations of the "critical thinking" and "communication skills" so desired in university graduates are laid in interrogative education. Since this education is reflective, it involves internal debate and the honing of judgment. Since it's also relational, demanding attention to the other person, it cultivates a condition essential to effective communication: the ability to figure out how the other person's epistemic state relates to what you want them to learn. Those whose education is deeply conversational have had their thinking, and their speaking, exposed for assessment and refinement. If they don't know how to use PowerPoint, they do understand what communication is.

Five, the promised mention: although there can be "conversation" mediated by technology – conference calls, video conferencing, chat rooms – until the past few decades the interactions in socratic education have been carried out in face-to-face encounters. Is that a necessary condition? Optional? Optimal? In the final chapter I'll consider whether a properly constructed undergraduate experience of coming to know how to know should be carried out in an actual (as distinct from a virtual) human community.

Conviction Six

This issue is, of course, intimately related to the sixth conviction of socratic education: that it's relational, depending on personal interactions between the teacher and the student. Regardless of the medium, one-on-one relationships are essential to socratic education. Brilliant lectures in cavernous classrooms can inspire, especially where they demonstrate the ways in which the lecturer raises and resolves questions. Even poor lectures have potential to provoke debate and reflection. But where the teacher does not know if *a particular student* has understood what is being taught, whatever has transpired isn't socratic education. It's mass education, impersonal, taught to nameless faces, and assessed anonymously, with grades entered beside student identification numbers to be fed into databases that generate degree navigator reports and eventually transcripts. That's a little harsh, I confess; tracking undergraduate education does require sophisticated information systems. But as I pointed out in the previous chapter, chances are high that very few faculty members will know or remember the names of most of their students, at least in the large first-year courses of an urban university.

Socratic education has as its hallmark the particular relationship between teacher and student that is feebly expressed in the language of model or mentor. Models can be fictional or historical characters; mentors these days can be occasional givers of practical advice. Not all pedagogical relationships need be (should be?) as intense as the Platonic, in which the teacher is the personification of the object of the student's epistemic desires. That's a mythic presentation of human longing for the true, the good, and the beautiful. But there's something that faintly echoes it in the experience of a teacher who not only positions you to see what you've been looking for, but also knows and cares about you. The knowledge in question matters to you both, and your coming to know matters to the teacher.[22]

Conviction Seven

The seventh point in the knowledge seeking that Socrates engaged in was that it had no institutional structures to support or regulate it. It took place in the market or public square, or on occasion at a dinner party. As we've seen, if socratic education is conversational and interrogative, it can take place in any setting with conversation partners. Of course, in this book I'm asking about an undergraduate education leading to the certification of knowledge in the award of a degree, so we'll need forms of organizational structure. Whether the knowledge gained in a properly constructed socratic education must come in a formal curriculum, however, is not yet clear. That question must wait till the last section of this chapter.

In this section I've explored convictions about the conditions of any successful knowledge seeking and gaining. I turn next to the qualities of mind and character these conditions require in the seeker.

Epistemic Attitudes for Successful Knowing

Any list of desirable attitudes towards knowledge seeking is bound to be controversial, both for what it contains and for what it doesn't. I offer a half-dozen, not to prescribe so much as to provoke reflection and deliberation about the kind of mind that a socratic education requires and cultivates. The choice of these particular attitudes is dictated in part by their being necessary conditions for coming to know, but also because they seem to be especially relevant to our present age. The deliberate practice of these attitudes might go some way towards addressing the concerns, expressed in

the previous chapter about undergraduates in the first decades of
the twenty-first century.

Epistemic Humility

Recognition of the fragility and quirkiness of human epistemic
equipment should engender a sense of modesty about one's power
to know too many things with clarity and certainty. There are two
spheres in which epistemic humility should operate. The first is
at the general level, about what human beings are able to know
with certainty. I'm not talking about how humble you should be
in comparison with the people in the next room or office, because
your epistemic equipment isn't as good as theirs. I'm talking, as a
Socrates would have it, about the paltriness of any and all human
wisdom. Paltriness is a term meaning *of very little worth*, but surely
human knowledge can't be weak, insignificant, and useless; we
can't do without it. True, but the human condition is such that we
find it very difficult to resist the temptation to gather into *what's
known* all manner of things that just aren't known or even knowable.[23] The second arena for epistemic humility is about one's own
current state of knowledge. Some people are smarter than others,
as luck or grace would have it, which means that some people have
more to be modest about than others, relatively speaking. And for
everyone who is really smart about some matters, there is someone
smarter than that person about other matters, so everyone has reason to be epistemically modest about something.

Although it might be difficult to argue abstractly against the
general and specific limitations of human knowledge, actually
taking up an attitude of epistemic humility isn't all that easy. One
must navigate the rocks and shoals of overconfidence, despair,
scepticism, and cynicism. But when successfully adopted as a
stance towards knowledge claims, this attitude can help to mitigate
feelings of inadequacy, legitimizing the confession of ignorance
instead of cloaking it with pretense, bluster, or excuse. That might
also address to some extent that malaise of insecurity of the self I
referred to in Chapter Six, in the discussion of cheating as a desperate way to keep up a pretense of capability. I find myself thinking,

too, that an education that encourages students to be comfortable with epistemic humility in general, and to be honest about their own lack of understanding of particular matters, would be more true to the human condition than going on about "leadership" as a goal of education for anybody or everybody.

The Courage to Persist

Education that is socratic insists that there are truths to be discovered, that knowledge claims can be more or less adequate. This conviction is entirely compatible with epistemic modesty, so as we saw earlier the proper response to the realization that one doesn't know is not despair, but resolve to find out what one can. The itch of curiosity must be propelled by epistemic courage. Again this isn't difficult to acknowledge, but developing resolve requires failure, and getting things wrong isn't what students set out to do. If you have known only success and approbation throughout your young life, it's even harder to fail. Hard, too, to acknowledge failure in a competitive undergraduate community. It wouldn't be surprising to learn that universities have responded to student anxiety by permitting more late withdrawals without penalty from courses, on the commonsensical advice from psychological services to remove the source of anxiety. But getting up the courage to ask for a late withdrawal isn't even a distant cousin of the epistemic courage required to persist in knowledge seeking when the way is rocky, uncertain, and lonely. That courage to persist can't always be summoned up by whistling, but it needs cultivation because it's essential for coming to know how to know.

Respect for Truth

To state that socratic education depends upon, and strengthens, *respect for truth* seems either a truism itself or a statement too grand for our own intellectual climate of enthusiastic epistemic confidence about the relativity of all truth. But as I noted at the beginning of Chapter One, our time has now seen the nonsense of post-truth, factoids, and alternative facts. If one goes beyond truth there is only anti-truth, deceptions, and lies; there is no knowledge in that land. As the place defined by its knowledge functions, the university must affirm the necessity of respect for truth and the proper conditions under which truths are sought and taught. If that's a truism, so be it. What follows from it, though, could stand some spelling out.

Respect, in this sense, is "deferential regard or esteem" that places its object *above*, in worth or value, the person or thing in relation to that object. ("Respect tradition, not innovation" or "Your disobedience shows no respect for your elders.") When institutions talk about respectful behaviour, they often have in mind the values of the organization such as punctuality and civility. Universities, however, are notoriously capable of the occasional unpredictable gesture of disrespect, as I noted in the section on free speech in Chapter Three. I am not retracting anything said there by insisting on respect *for truth*. The point is this: members of the university should respect the institution, its practices, even the holders of its offices, *because of* the respect for truth – and *insofar as* the institution, those practices and those persons, instantiate, manifest, and promote the truth seeking that defines the university. I must hold the truth in higher esteem than personal preference or opinion; that's an epistemic duty embraced and enjoined by the university. And it's the ground of the relation between student and teacher. Students are *students*, as I argued in the previous chapter, because they are knowledge seekers. Because teachers assist them in gaining that knowledge, and are conductors to truths worthy of esteem, they merit respect – not because of their grade-granting power, or age, or social standing. Even if they no longer wear an academic gown in the classroom, teachers also deserve *marks of respect* for the same reason, such as appropriate forms of address that recognize their knowledge-related functions. With the unmourned loss of many class-based formalities, there has also come a loss of appreciation for ritual and form that express relationships to something of dignity beyond individual lives and interests. Universities should not be embarrassed to express in ceremony and ritual the dignity of respect for truth and knowledge. That some university traditions should be discarded because they reflect outmoded and even discriminatory attitudes does not require a descent into feel-good celebrations instead of appropriate ritual.[24]

But I've strayed into comment on institutional expressions of respect for truth. I should return to asking how that respect is manifested more specifically in the epistemic efforts of students. And here's one answer: in respect *for language*. After all, we clarify what it is we know, and express it, in words. Although I don't need to claim that all human knowing is expressible in language – indeed, personal knowing, tacit knowing, numerical knowledge, knowing how: these ways of knowing have linguistic limits – still, a vast amount of what we claim to know has to be put into words. Those words have meanings, some of them precise or technical ("demisemiquaver") and some of them hard to pin down exactly ("love," "knowledge"). Some are neutrally descriptive ("mitosis") and some carry emotive charge ("cancer"). Understanding and employing words rightly – right for meaning and for context – is highly important in the knowledge-seeking and knowledge-gaining business. That's so for passive and active linguistic abilities. Reading and listening require attention to how words work; socratic education needs careful readers and keen listeners to interrogate text and discourse. Likewise with writing and speaking: respect for language requires using not just the appropriate vocabulary but also the appropriate tone, and knowing how much or how little to say.

Those properly educated in respect for truth and language are able to judge modes of discourse, and they understand that much of what is put out on social media expresses individual feeling and emotion, not considered argument. They know the difference between rhetorical devices designed to appeal to prejudged opinion and deliberative discourse engaged with assessing reasons for beliefs. Their stance of respect for truthful language is the ground on which they live out those desired "skills" of thinking critically and communicating effectively.

Openness to Past Wisdom

It follows from what I've said so far that an interrogative education enables an attitude of openness to others as interlocutors and partners in the search for knowledge. Epistemic humility involves a decentring of the self and its preoccupations, a recognition that there are other sources of insight and a willingness to learn from them. Respect for truthful language means listening attentively to other voices, and speaking effectively in contexts different from one's own.

The concept of "the Other" has found its way from academic theory into more common discourse, signifying difference in identity and power relationships. It doesn't need saying that the properly educated will be sensitive to issues of difference and equality, but here I'm interested in the quite general attitude of mind towards those others who are now in the past. That is, I want to suggest that *consciousness of past wisdom* is requisite for twenty-first-century undergraduate education. There's a stance towards the past termed "presentism," a bias in favour of the present or present-day attitudes in interpreting history.[25] Judging nineteenth-century figures by today's moral standards has become common, although it's not clear that, from the conviction that a nineteenth-century attitude is morally wrong, it follows that the persons in question can be properly blamed.[26] The attitude expressed in presentism, however, has much wider scope than judgments on past persons. It's the view that *only the present is of value*. Few people would assent to that bald assertion, but twenty-first-century culture and technology inculcate attitudes and behaviours betraying that belief. The *immediacy of experience* compresses time into the present moment: technology gets us results quickly, shrinks space and distance, and produces vast amounts of information in milliseconds. What's on the screen is ephemeral: it can be destroyed and recreated at will. Human ingenuity has resolved many of the problems that plagued our sorry ancestors, and undoubtedly will find ways to fix things up for the future. With the geographical scattering of family members, the decline in long-term permanent marriages or unions, and the mating habits of urban young culture, even our social and personal relationships are meaningful mainly in the now.

Where the immediate and the ephemeral occupy all the spaces of the mind, there is loss of tragic proportions. Digital technology generates previously unimaginable amounts of information in a staggeringly short time, so users are adept at finding things out very quickly. There is some evidence that this very ability also is distracting, making sustained inquiry harder. But interrogative education does demand courage and persistence in the search for knowledge. It must not be distracted by the immediate. There is more wisdom to be found in the past than in the present. And more in others, whether like or different, than in the self.

Comfort with Ambiguity and Judgment

I commented earlier on the human thirst for certainty and the recognition of the inadequacies of our epistemic abilities always to give warranted satisfaction on every matter. Hence the need for epistemic modesty. As a consequence, socratic education helps the student feel at home with the fact that some questions just don't get answered in clear terms. The recognition of the very human difficulties in getting things sorted out correctly can help one make peace with ambiguities that beg to become certainties. An important mark of an educated mind is an understanding of the subtle shades between pure white and darkest black – an understanding that can generate a tolerant and charitable willingness to engage with the other.

This is the place to comment on the twenty-first-century preoccupation with measurement. Numbers are very good at expressing precision and enabling comparison. You can know with a high degree of certainty whether this or that thing is bigger or smaller, longer or shorter. So suppose someone wants to know if your work is better than mine: units of worth can be assigned to whatever we're producing, and counted up. That removes ambiguity, and gives the researcher confidence about the inquiry into better and worse work.

When one's culture is concerned with efficiency and improvement, and links success with money, the certainties of measurement are crucial. Otherwise (the story goes) you're left with opinions and subjective feelings, not hard facts. And (the story continues) that's no way to run a world.

There's no disputing the clarity of measurement or its attractiveness. But unfortunately there's a problem with the story: it's impossible to turn assessments of worth and value into numbers for measurement in any supposedly objective way. That translation requires something called *judgment*. Judgment is hugely important; we saw in the section on skills that judgment sits above skills, determining which skill to employ in which circumstances in order to achieve what's desirable and worthwhile.[27] How we determine the valuable and worthy depends upon our moral commitments; how we judge whether this particular course of action or outcome will sit with those commitments requires experience, and often deliberation with knowledgeable others. That's why judgment is often called *seasoned*. Seasoned judgment is not mere opinion or subjective feeling. It's grounded in reasoned convictions and honed in deliberation. Judgment is required to deal with ambiguity and should be the product of interrogative education.

So the hard truth is that measurement can't escape judgment but is dependent upon it. Pretending otherwise is no way to run a world.

There we have it: the qualities of mind that characterize those who successfully seek and acquire knowledge. They exhibit humility about their epistemic condition, but have the courage to persevere because of their respect for truth. They attend to the way language works. They listen well, and are open to past wisdom. When they deal with claims to knowledge, they can live with ambiguity because they have learned to exercise judgment. These qualities have been shaped and refined in the interrogative processes of their socratic education.

Character and Socratic Education

But here's a problem. Having arrived at this place, haven't we returned to a location and mission that universities abandoned in the last century: *education for character*? Recall from the previous chapter that the old *in loco parentis* attitude was discarded because universities no longer thought it appropriate to be involved in "character development." There I pointed out that the determination of what constitutes "character" is not up to the university any more than it is up to the state.

I must reaffirm that view here. Of course the university can't be in the business of turning out only nice, decent people, especially when what constitutes "good character" is contestable. Character is expressed in particular contexts saturated by culture, religion, economic and social status, and so on. Perhaps some institutions will endeavour to promote character traits expressing their special identities, but it's not easy to assess character, or to determine whether it meets expectations. Universities don't normally hand out grades on "character."[28]

Nevertheless all institutions do require forms of behaviour that are intimately related to some virtues woven into "good character": honesty and diligence, for instance, where the integrity of the academic enterprise is at stake. The university imposes discipline upon actions such as plagiarizing work, and sanctions students for late or missed assignments; but character is often taken into account in deciding upon the severity of a penalty.[29] Although in most matters the twenty-first-century university does not formally make "character formation" its pedagogic ambition, it is constantly providing guidance and advice that families and communities would have given in other circumstances – as I noted in the previous chapter. Haven't I just reinforced this quasi-parental role in advocating qualities of mind that shape character?

Perhaps, but that is not the point in the cultivation of epistemic virtues in socratic education. By contrast, the intention of character education is to shape attitudes and behaviour across a spectrum of values and relationships, turning its students into decent people with civic and personal virtues.[30] Its aim is character building, and its success is measured by what sort of person emerges from under its tutelage.

That's not the point of an undergraduate education, although its graduates might well have become different people as a result of their education. Interrogative education, as I've sketched it, is concerned with *those virtues and habits of mind that are requisite for seeking and gaining knowledge.* Courtesy and good manners aren't on that list.

Nor is caring for family members. Patriotism? No. For all that these are good things to cultivate in the right way, the university does not set out to make their display and practice the object of education.

Quite the opposite: the result of a proper undergraduate experience is *the ability to think carefully about what character is*. Why should courtesy be practised? Does family count for more than a stranger in need? Is civil disobedience a denial of patriotism? That's what the university has to do with character: instead of forming character, it interrogates its very meaning.[31]

To engage in the search for knowledge about anything, including a conversation about character, requires the participants to take up attitudes such as epistemic humility, curiosity, courage, respect for truth, and judgment. That these attitudes are good in themselves, marks of mature minds, also happens to be true.

Grant this, then. But one more query arises. Isn't this the kind of education in attitude and habit that everyone should have, not just people who are able to achieve an undergraduate degree?

Well, yes. From our earliest days, concerned and caring parents and teachers coax, inspire, cajole, and do all they can to mould our characters in ways that reflect the epistemic stances discussed here. The problem is that human beings are recalcitrant and distractible creatures, built of "crooked timber" as Kant memorably has it.[32] Attitudes need to be ingrained through habitual repetition and self-reflection across the course of one's life. An undergraduate education that's interrogative must build on those habits, but bring them into closer examination, revision, and refinement. That's important, chiefly because the educated mind makes possible the exercise of capacities for a full human life. But such a mind is also best prepared to grasp and employ the particular kinds of knowledge that belong to other spheres of human activity. For our purposes here, those are the professions. Accordingly, it's time for a quick comment on how socratic education prepares for professional education.

Professional Education and Socratic Education

At the beginning of this chapter I discussed the notions of skill and critical thinking, arguing that they are best situated in discourse that has to do with competencies to produce particular outcomes and the techniques required in exercising those competencies. To be skilful, one has to be skilled *at* something or other, where success or failure can be assessed without ambiguity by those competent to judge. Likewise with critical thinking: it's usually considered to be the kind of thinking that figures out solutions to problems where there's agreement about what constitutes appropriate resolution.

In the second section of the chapter, I observed that, when the thinking is about a particular profession or occupation, we have a context in which to judge when it's well done. Likewise with competencies: to call someone competent requires particular standards and expectations against which assessment is made. The "professions" provide these contexts, for they have standards of performance arising from the kinds of problems to be solved or outcomes to be produced. Since we're dealing with university education here, I'm not concerned with a strict definition of "profession" – the term "professional" can cover the kinds of programs that produce graduates for particular occupations. As I commented earlier, the number of new professional degrees has mushroomed across every occupational area: health and allied professions, law, education, the arts, business, engineering, applied science. These university programs are almost exclusively at the graduate level, although some still (at least in published regulations though not often in practice) accept students without a completed undergraduate degree. There are reasons for requiring previous postsecondary education for admission: success measured by grades is a screening mechanism, and some programs build on related disciplinary knowledge. One of these reasons is persuasive; another not so much.

The demonstrated acquisition, in an undergraduate program, of knowledge required for graduate study of a profession does make sense. But high grades? By itself a high grade point average is a blunt sorting instrument. What is fundamentally important for professional education is having had a socratic interrogative undergraduate education. Whatever the professional degree sought, it will be better pursued, and the profession better practised, by those who have developed the attitudes and habits cultivated in socratic education.

Better pursued, because those educated in this way are good learners of any knowledge on offer. They are not afraid to face up to what they don't know or can't quite do as yet. They are not rote practitioners of textbook techniques, although they respect the skill that might have gone into those techniques. They have learned to interrogate their own motives. They understand the differences between information, measurement, judgment, and wisdom.

They will better practise their professions as well. The proliferation of professional master's programs isn't simply market manoeuvring by universities; it's testimony to the need for highly educated professionals in an increasingly complicated world. With an accelerated pace of change driven by technology, a large premium is placed on creativity and innovation. That requires, unsurprisingly, an educated imagination. It's not accidental that we've already referred to the imagination eight times in discussing socratic education. Perhaps even more important, however, is that the professions must be put into the service of human flourishing. While no one would baldly deny this, it must be acknowledged that practitioners too are made of "crooked timber" – self-interest can be professional as well as personal. A few hours spent on professional ethics guarantees very little about social responsibility. Those educated interrogatively in their undergraduate years have developed habits of asking not just how things are done effectively, but what ought and ought not to be done for the sake of a well-constructed life and a healthy, just society.[33]

It's not news that there's no tight relationship between an impressive grade point average and the perspective on knowledge that a socratic education fosters. An excellent memory might not indicate a love for truthful speaking, nor a facile tongue a respect for past wisdom. A display of brilliance might be ignited by intellectual hubris, and self-reflection turn narcissistic. That's why admission processes demand more than transcripts, seeking evidence of who this applicant really is. The underlying question, although unasked in just this way, is: has this person been properly educated in how knowledge is sought, gained, and employed? Has she, has he, reaped the benefits of a socratic interrogative education?

How Is Socratic Education to Be Realized in the Undergraduate Experience?

Assessing the suitability of a candidate for admission often involves letters of reference from instructors who know the student, perhaps personal interviews, and certainly judgment about the quality of the undergraduate degree. Quality is partly measured by grades, but the reputations of the program and the university are also important.

It's high time, then, to face the question muttering underneath all this talk about the virtues of interrogative education. Well and good, it will be said; it would be wonderful if all students could be put through a system that assured the development of the attitudes and habits you've advocated so insistently. But haven't you been constructing the Paradigmatic Program of Epistemic Excellence at the University of Utopia? How could any of this work in an actual curriculum at a real university?

I have no satisfactory answer to the reasonable question about curriculum. Much of what's written about liberal education is compatible with the views I've expressed in this chapter, and there's good sense in proposals to include breadth in undergraduate degree programs. Compulsory writing or English courses are designed to address some of the concerns mentioned. It's laudable to stress numeracy and literacy, and to try to expose arts students to scientific thinking and science students to poetry. Everyone should study the brain these days. Education in diversity and culture difference is important, as is an understanding of the experience of the marginalized in society – knowing the shames as well as the glories of the history of one's country, too. Undergraduates should reflect on their civic responsibilities and freedoms, the role of government at all levels, the benefits and challenges of globalization.

It's clear that, if undergraduates were to learn through the curriculum even half of what an educated twenty-first-century person should know, they wouldn't need to worry about a career since they'd never leave school. I'm not going to attempt, then, to list even the general areas in which courses should be mounted. That's not up to any author. *It's up to each university to determine the shape of its curriculum for a decent undergraduate education.*

That's obvious, but worth stating. Interrogative education must take into account student and teacher. Universities don't float about in some abstract space; they are located in the particularities of location and history (more about that in the next chapter). Their student bodies have their own characteristics. As do members of their teaching staff, who have varying fields of competence. There are resource constraints and perhaps a few special opportunities.

Within each context, however, a few fundamental principles must find expression in any undergraduate education. Without them, students won't enjoy the benefits of socratic education. Or so I propose. Again the point of this exercise is to provoke deliberation about a defining function of a properly constructed and undistracted university, the cultivation and transmission of knowledge.

Education Is Interrogative Conversation

There are many ways to carry out the essential activity of socratic education – that is, an education conducted by interrogative conversation. It shouldn't need saying yet again, but education is not unidirectional – the teacher speaking to the student, who passively listens and absorbs knowledge. It's relational. That must hold for both the forms of instruction and the ways learning is assessed.

The elemental format for this education is interactive conversation, in which structured interchange takes place between teacher and student. That's quintessentially the traditional Oxbridge tutorial: the student writes a paper on an assigned topic, which is then discussed with the tutor. This format makes it possible for the teacher to attend to the expressed thinking of the student, to react to it, and to receive a defence or explanation. The teacher can assess, with immediacy, the student's attitude towards epistemic certainty and respect for truth and language, as well as encourage curiosity and the persistent search for understanding.

Although the tutorial offered by a teacher to a single student is the paradigm of interrogative conversation, the learning process can be enhanced if other participants observe exchanges and comment on them, and are directly involved themselves in interacting with the teacher. A group engaged in this way constitutes a seminar. A proper seminar must be small enough to permit participation by all, and be directed by a teacher who draws comment from the hesitant. Unfortunately tutorials and seminars in many universities are far too large, and too easily dominated by the few, some of whom might be more anxious to impress than to be interrogated.

Although the tutorial or seminar creates the conditions for the interrogative exchange between student and teacher, it's not the only way to provoke interrogative education. In practice, undergraduate education takes place in large classrooms where students are lectured. However, the lecture format can *model* interrogative education, even if actual conversations can't be carried out in the lecture hall. An effective lecture *demonstrates* how the teacher's mind works on the material. It can provoke curiosity, expose difficulties in understanding, and offer solutions to problems. As witnesses rather than conversationalists, students can still learn what it is to engage in academic inquiry. They still need to practise inquiry themselves, however, under appropriate tutelage to make sure they are getting it right.

Recently some universities have taken advantage of technology to bring something of the seminar into large classes, in what's termed an inverted or flipped classroom. Students study the lecture material online, presented perhaps in video format, before the class period, which is then used for discussion. The technology of "clickers" (personal response systems) has also enabled instructors to interrogate a large class about their understanding of a concept or argument. The question is posed, and students click on a possible answer. If significant numbers of students don't answer correctly, the misunderstanding can be corrected right then.[34] The challenge in these innovations is to discover the epistemic attitudes of *this particular student* rather than that one. Ascertaining what percentage of the class understands an item discloses very little about students' individual epistemic commitments.

Assessment is an element in interrogative conversation as long as its results are expressed to students. For the purpose of certifying knowledge, the end result of assessment is a mark or grade. Depending on university policy, a grade may be assigned to assignments with or without explanation and justification – the "feedback" essential to learning. The common way to assess students is through assignments such as papers, essays, tests, reports, and presentations – work done by *this student*, to whom *this grade* is assigned. Although written essay or examination material might not be presented in person, it's the deposit of the workings of the mind of the student, and can be assessed for the attitudes of mind it displays. The teacher can adjudicate a written conversation, as it were, between the student and the authors of the material addressed. Likewise with oral presentations. Without the teacher's commentary on the material, however, no conversation takes place.

Written examinations, too, are one-sided, speaking from student to teacher if only a grade is given, but they can reveal how a mind does its work. It's worse with multiple choice tests. Although the questions might require sophisticated thinking, the only assessment possible is the highly simplistic checking of right or wrong answers, which can be done electronically. Nothing of the student's epistemic commitments can be determined, so there's nothing to comment upon except the rightness of the answer.

The relationship between assessment and grades reflects the relationship between capacity and disposition on the one hand, and performance on the other. Performance is episodic: it results in particular pieces of work that receive grades. Epistemic attitudes and habits aren't graded; we don't give out As or Ds for epistemic modesty, curiosity, or courage and the like. But in grading, the teacher *assesses* not just the performance, but also the characteristics of mind and expression that result in the product.

Education Is Personal

If education is conversation that asks questions and assesses answers, it takes place in a relationship. If the assessment is not just about getting the "right" answers, but about epistemic qualities of the mind, then the relationship has to be personal.

The teacher must know who the student is, not just that there is a student by that name and student number. The student must know the teacher, and know that the teacher knows her or him.

Why this is so is hardly news. It follows from the nature of teaching and assessment as I've just described it. I can assist effectively in the cultivation of epistemic habits when I know, not just how the class is performing, but how the mind of this student is working. Teachers who don't know their students are like fitness instructors who prepare videos to be watched somewhere by somebody; those who do know their students are like coaches and trainers.

Personal knowledge, however, must work both ways. Students need to know that they are known – they learn better when they experience the personal attention and care of the instructor. That attentiveness creates a relationship of trust. If the student can trust the teacher to be fair and supportive, that encourages the quest for knowledge. If the student feels trusted, that engenders confidence. It's much harder to exercise the virtues of epistemic modesty and courage, including the courage to fail, when there is no sense of a trusting and positive relationship.

Furthermore, teaching is much more rewarding when one knows one's students. Judgments about understanding and improvement are better informed. Letters of reference actually mean something. There's lasting satisfaction in having contributed to the maturing of young minds, especially when partnership in conversation becomes, as it sometimes does over time, collegial.

In discussing the convictions of socratic education as relational earlier in this chapter, I referred to the Platonic view of pedagogical relationships in which the teacher is the personification of the object of the student's epistemic desires. His Socrates is, I argued, a more than human representation of the philosophic life; so the attitude of his devoted followers can't be normative when it comes to merely mortal teachers. Still, there's lots of evidence that most people can name a teacher or two who was influential in opening up the world for them. That's often because the teacher cared for the subject and conveyed that love; but it's also because the student felt singled out and cared for, too. Not enough is said about the love of learning these days. Perhaps if we weren't so shy about the language of love in pedagogical relationships, I might have used the concept in talking about curiosity and respect for truth and language. For what better thing might teachers do than instil that love in their students?

Education Is More than a Matter of Degrees

Socrates had no institutional structure, no building, no curriculum for his inquiries into what makes the lives of human beings good.

Undergraduate education that is socratic is carried out in structured interrogative conversation, which can be pursued anywhere as long as there are competent teachers and willing students. The pursuit of philosophical questions in ancient Athens took place outdoors, walking about in open places. Likewise the development of effective habits and attitudes for the pursuit of knowledge in undergraduate programs should not be confined to the classroom. Education is more than a matter of accumulating enough credits for a degree.

In the previous chapter I pointed out that to take students seriously is to situate education within their full lived experience. For each classroom hour, they probably spend five or six waking hours outside formally structured classes. Some of that is lab or library time and, of course, time for the regular necessities of life. But every campus has multiple opportunities for involvement in student societies and government, in plays and concerts and open lectures. The cafeteria has replaced the dining hall, but there is still the possibility of conversation over food.

Now I'm not advocating a regimented campus where most of one's day is programmed in "enriching" activities. Many young people have spent their earlier years with almost all their "free" time planned by adults, which destroys spontaneity and minimizes responsibility for one's own decisions. Nevertheless it's an impoverished view of educational experience that confines it to credit-gaining hours spent in class or completing assignments. It's easy to agree with that; but universities are not usually organized in ways intended to facilitate a more robust education. I remarked earlier on the rarity of interactions between faculty responsible for credit-gaining hours and "student life" staff responsible for non-credit-gaining hours. Each group, I said, goes about its work in untroubled ignorance of the work of the other, though they each create experiences for the same students.

Another indication of this disjunction is revealed in the very language that's used for student experience. Non-credit time is spent on "extracurricular" activities, implying they are inessential to the proper functions of learning. Further, in jurisdictions where government funds at least some costs, there's nothing for these inessentials – students have to pay the freight themselves. Interrogative socratic education challenges this way of looking at undergraduate experience. It claims, instead, that every conversation that includes some knowledgeable participants holds educational potential.

Those sympathetic to the claim that the classroom should extend beyond the formal curriculum will nonetheless respond that their sympathy has to be tempered by the stark realities of life in the twenty-first-century university – especially the anonymity of large urban campuses. True, but curiosity, courage, and persistence can stiffen resolve for change. This isn't a manual about how to effect change, but I will make bold to offer four observations. First, the administrative silos need puncturing. "Student life" professionals and faculty members need to engage in their own interrogative conversations together, to explore how they might support each other's work. I alluded in Chapter Four to the involvement of faculty in advising student societies and clubs – a delicate match making that can't be forced, but that holds potential rewards, especially when younger faculty (or perhaps graduate students) are involved. Second, creative programming can involve students, faculty, administrators, and alumni together in intellectually stimulating events, bringing the resources of the university to bear on topical issues without the burden of assignments and assessment.[35] Third, some course content can be explored in events or activities on or off campus, with varying degrees of organization and formality. That could involve something as simple as encouraging students to see a current film or exhibit on a relevant theme, and setting up an occasion to talk about it. Urban universities have the great advantage of cultural offerings that can enrich the formal curriculum. There are constraints, of course – including costs in money and time for students – and the challenges of organizing more structured events. Voluntary participation means some people won't bother. But these activities do create the conditions for the more personal experience of socratic education outside the classroom. Fourth, food is key. It's not just that students are always hungry; it's also that *conversation needs occasion.* So I don't mean that pizza should be available to be fetched and eaten somewhere in solitude. Instead, since events with food attract participants, they should be structured at least minimally so that people talk to each other. Better, some of the conversations with and among students should involve faculty, graduate students, and alumni.

A university committed to living out the principle that education is more than a matter of degrees will find interest, even thirst, for intellectual and interrogative engagement among its students, staff, and alumni – and even among its faculty, when they are not preoccupied with meeting the requirements for contract renewal, tenure, promotion, or professional advancement. But if they are to teach and assess in accordance with the view of interrogative and personal education I've advocated here, won't that have serious implications for the ways in which they profess their disciplines? What will they teach?

Curriculum and Socratic Education

I've tried to avoid speaking about the curriculum of a properly constructed undergraduate education, and I've acknowledged that each university would have to develop its programs within its own context and resources, but it's impossible to ignore questions about how formal education should be structured in the embrace of socratic education.

It's obvious that socratic education, concerned with knowing how knowledge is gained, does not have the content of disciplinary knowledge. Students are awarded credentials for the study of particular subjects, however, and in granting degrees the university certifies the gaining of specific knowledge. A degree signifies the completion of requirements and courses in disciplines such as history, geoscience, economics, and commerce in a particular subject: Caribbean history, petrology, applied game theory, operations management. Disciplines these days are fluid entities, and a significant number of university programs reflect the intersecting lines of inquiry that focus on fields of study such as the environment, geopolitical areas, or historical periods. But no one receives a degree without having demonstrated knowledge of some particular discipline, field, or area of investigation. Put simply, a degree is *in* something. Socratic education isn't – it's about how one approaches the business of knowing anything. Or to put it differently, it's about self-knowledge. Although there are degrees of self-knowledge, there are no degrees *in* self-knowledge. So, while liberal studies curricula are made up of courses, there's no set curricular content to be advocated in socratic education.

Nevertheless socratic education does have curricular implications for structure, if not for content. From the principles enunciated, it follows that conversation is essential, personal relationships are important, and connections between what happens inside and outside the classroom are desirable.

I've just commented on the possibilities for extending interrogative conversation beyond the walls of the classroom. But how can conversation take place within class time when the pressures of mass education require class sizes in the hundreds? Unless a university is so well financed that it can afford to offer only tutorial and seminar education, the lecture format will have to be the dominant means of education. There are strategies, however, as we saw, to break the one-way flow of information bits in the hydraulics of education: modelling interrogation, including self-interrogation, in the lecture itself; the inverted classroom; tutorials small enough to enable participation by everyone. Moreover, not every course must offer the same format and possibilities. It might be enough to have at least some courses in a program – preferably not restricted to upper years – where conversation is required.

Likewise with personal education. Even if some classes are too large for personal interactions, every student in a program must be known by some faculty, and must know that they are known. It's not good enough that only administrative staff members know who you are, although it's good that they do.

In designing and reviewing the curriculum for a discipline or area of study, then, the university should provoke deliberation among its faculty members about the three principles of socratic education I enunciated above. Even if resources are scarce and the vision of the small collegiate experience of personal education can't be conjured up even in dreams, a resolute commitment to interrogative conversation nevertheless will find ways to educate undergraduates in the fundamental epistemic attitudes and freedoms that constitute human flourishing.

What could be more satisfying than having a part in making possible an education that disturbs prejudice, engenders respect for the limits of knowledge, awakens curiosity, and a thirst for truth, and seasons judgment? And what could have more import for the future of our world than that?

chapter eight

What and Where Are Well-Placed Universities?

In What Place?

Universities are interested in place, but in which sense? The phrase in this chapter's title, "Well-Placed Universities," trades on the complexities of the notion. The expression could describe anyone of high social status, as in the phrase "wealthy, well-placed and handsome" (from the Oxford English Dictionary citation under sense 2a). Universities boast or fret about their status in rankings, and being "well placed" might point to the top tier of universities. As we saw in Chapter Two, reputation is highly important in the university game, with those in the top five, or ten, or twenty (or fifty or one hundred, depending on where one's institution sits this year) unable to remain silent about their standing in the usual league tables. Presidents know too well that those tables are imperfect measures of worth. They are heavily weighted towards research measures such as citations, themselves heavily weighted towards science and engineering; they reflect little of the actual experience of students, itself difficult to assess; and they come up with one score that is supposed to reflect the quality of a spread of disciplines (such as the humanities) that might be of uneven accomplishment within that area. Standing can fluctuate from year to year. Nevertheless, on evidence that would never pass muster within the university itself, presidents cannot help but refer to their institution's standing on international tables when it is well placed. Questioning the evidence happens, naturally, only when standing slips downwards a few notches.

Having been guilty myself of the practice of acclaim-by-association with one of the world's top twenty universities, I understand why forms of legitimization thought to be independent and international are preferable to self-promotion. It's a competitive world, in which it's hard to distinguish the experience offered by one university from that promised by another. It's also a broader world, in which sports league tables make it clear who is gaining rank on whom, providing clear evidence for fans and followers. Anything pointing to relative status in the competitive university world can't be ignored even though there are no rules for winning or losing. Place in the rankings matters.

"Well placed," however, also has another meaning. It's not about relative order, but about fitness. Most often the term refers to being properly situated to achieve a particular purpose: someone is well placed to win the 100-metre dash, to gain a scholarship, or to profit from a rising stock price. University administrators are usually concerned with (if not consumed by) issues of financial sustainability, so being "well placed" might describe those universities that, say, are in a good position to attract enrolment from a particular country or alumni donations from a particular graduating year. No matter where a university ends up in the rankings, it could be well placed to achieve some specific goal.

One more sense of being appropriately placed needs discussion, where place is location. Think back to Helsinki's Senate Square. At the beginning of Chapter Two, I noted the relationships among the university and commerce, government, and religion expressed in the spatial location of their buildings enclosing the square in the centre of the city. The university on the west side of the square is placed to interact with city and society, only a few steps away from the concerns of economic, political, and religious power. In discussing university autonomy I argued that, despite this proximity, the space occupied by the university needs protection from undue influence. Only if there is a shield of integrity around the institution will those in the square be able to trust the university's claims about knowledge.

Although Helsinki's public square marks off the university's place in the city in this striking way, other universities are prominent in their urban locations. Some have large areas with distinct boundaries, such as Peking University or Tsinghua University in Beijing, the University of Toronto, McGill University in Montreal, Emory University in Atlanta. Some occupy buildings scattered throughout a larger urban area with several local sites, such as the University of London or New York University. They might even have campuses in other countries, like Yale-NUS in Singapore. Others, like the University of Cambridge, are visibly present in cities that expand around them. And still others are rural, collegiate universities farther removed from the distractions of swarming city life, such as Grinnell College in Iowa or Bishop's University in Quebec. A list generated as much by whim as by design demonstrates just how diverse are the places in which universities may be found.

But why, it will now be asked, should a university be in any place at all? With the stunning advance in information technology we've seen in recent decades, it can be easily argued that the only "place" required for a university education is a device with Internet access.

Although distance education has been around since the mid-nineteenth century, new technology has greatly enhanced the development of online courses and degrees. A university world without that technology is practically unimaginable any more. Indeed a growing number of established universities have added online education to their on-campus offerings, so that students in online programs need not find their way to campus. The University of Liverpool, for instance, advertises graduate programs in Canada that are entirely online. Eleven Canadian universities have formed the Canadian Virtual University Consortium, offering two thousand courses online leading to degrees. And some institutions, like Athabasca University, require no campus at all apart from some administrative headquarters.

Isn't a *placeless* university an idea whose time has already arrived, even though the university world might be too enamoured of its fabric and real estate to embrace it with enthusiasm? The potential advantages are compelling: reduced costs and increased accessibility – what could be better than that, in an age where the demand for degrees has never been higher? Accessibility is improved when students can study at their own time and pace, and when those not close to a campus can take programs that would not have been available to them. Costs for personnel make up the largest percentage of university expenditures, so if more students can be taught with fewer faculty, that's a saving, especially if universities can share standard courses. And without a campus, facilities and maintenance costs are reduced.

The advantages of placelessness revealed themselves to me when I thought of one of my students who came to retrieve an essay. She was in her first year, and we chatted about her time at university so far. I learned that she lived well north of the city, commuting three hours a day five days a week. We calculated that she spent as much time in transit as she did in class. There was no time left for joining a club or attending a play, concert, or special lecture. As she left the conversation, I began to wonder why one wouldn't give up all this commuting and instead set up a study at home. As long as there's a computer and Internet access, the student could apply to a university online, register, have fees deducted from a bank account, and take online courses. Using digitized library resources, the student could complete work and attain credits sufficient for the degree. The savings in time and money would be significant. With an extra fifteen hours a week, my student would have gained about 225 working days over four years. She would have had no library fines, and saved a few thousand dollars in transit fares.

To push the point even further, the only significant place in a placeless education like this turns out to be wherever the student and the Internet connect through an appropriate device. There is no need to leave home, or even one's bedroom, for the purposes of this education. When enough credits are achieved, the student could even print out the diploma and become an educated person without ever having left the room.

That's too far-fetched, of course – the parchment attesting to the degree has to be signed and sealed – but the thought of a placeless education is in stark contrast to the experience I reported in the Preface. Rounding the corner in that small town so long ago,

I came upon a *presence*: a place, in its collegiate architecture, that spoke the history and meaning of "university." I wanted to be part of that place.

I don't know whether my student had anything approaching that kind of longing when she applied to Victoria College. But sitting for as many hours each week in transit vehicles as in classrooms doesn't permit much immersion in the full meaning of the place that is the university.

Yet, does that matter, if a university education can be made available, efficiently, to many more students by dis-placing the university? What indeed is a well-placed university in the twenty-first century? In repeating this question, I have in mind something more fundamental than *being highly ranked*, or *in an appropriate place to achieve specific goals*, or *in a particular location*. I mean to tease out what it would be for a university to take the notion of place seriously, especially in its understanding of undergraduate education.

The Meanings of Place

The question requires some comment on the notion of *place* itself, and let's begin with noting the difference between *place* and *space*. We needn't worry about philosophical conundrums, however interesting, such as whether space itself has boundaries and if so, what is on the other side of the boundary if not more space. Or the relation of space to time, and whether words such as "before" and "after" can be understood without spatial concepts. For our purposes, it's enough to note that space is a very general notion having to do with extension or area; it doesn't matter what happens to be in that area. For a longer definition there's the Oxford English Dictionary's ninth use (of a total of seventeen): "Continuous, unbounded, or unlimited extent in every direction, without reference to any matter that may be present." If we wish to compare spaces we use measurement: this space is bigger or smaller than that one.

The notion of *place* is more complex and layered. It occurs in a multitude of expressions that have to do with appropriateness, rank or order, relationships, belonging, and ownership. In other words, "place" fills in space with meaning and purpose. A few examples will make the point.

(1) "Place the ball in the upper left corner of the net," or "Place the pan on the middle rack of the oven": such instructions locate their objects in the *appropriate* area of a defined space, where appropriateness is dictated by a purpose or goal. (2) "Save my place in the queue" refers to a spot in relation to others in the line; it's different from the space occupied by a body in a queue, since that space might be identical to any other space. (3) "Know your place, young man" also refers to an order, but also to a social hierarchy that dictates appropriate and inappropriate attitudes and behaviour. (4) If someone takes your seat at a concert, you pull out your ticket and show the seat number, saying, "that's my place, I'm afraid." The seat is yours: it belongs to you. (5) From the claim "we have a place on Amherst Island," the hearer can infer ownership and use; the dwelling is part of the fabric of the owner's life – merely saying that one owns property or a house reveals nothing about actual use or habitation.

Our usage of the word "place," then, is indeed layered with the complexities of purposeful activity and human relationships, especially social relationships and the human experience of belonging and having what's ours. In one particular context, "place" is very closely related to the notion of "home," with "house" relating to the notion of space. ("He left the house this morning" is different from "she left home last night.") One can see why geographers and architects are interested in the relationships between space and place – although a developer advertising "New Homes for Sale!" is promising an experience that can't be delivered by a builder of houses.

But universities as well should be interested in place. I'll argue that place matters a great deal to their successful functioning.

Place and Belonging

To build the case I need to return to the sense of human experience that sets off places from spaces. Since our use of language is neither consistent nor particularly precise, one can't always rely on common expressions to explicate the *experience* of place as distinct from space, but some examples might help. Think of what it's like to visit public spaces such as shopping malls, supermarkets, or fast food restaurants. Those big box stores and mammoth grocery stores are pretty well identical wherever they are located. You could easily imagine yourself walking past the cashier in your town's store, and emerging into a large parking lot in a completely different city. Although this is not a new phenomenon – almost forty years ago I had the same breakfast in Saskatoon as I'd had the previous week in Cincinnati – the commercial disregard of unique places has become increasingly widespread. Despite the efforts of greeters and employees who want to use your first name, the experience of shopping in such locations is impersonal, the relationships merely commercial and therefore humanly shallow.

By contrast, a visit to one's regular barber or bistro can be satisfying on a personal level: human interaction takes place in conversation about past events and future plans. You know and are known; you have a history that somehow matters. You are, of course, a customer, and you don't have to be a friend, exactly; but you have found a place, not just a service.

Place, then, concerns that space in which personal knowledge and identity may be experienced, and an appreciation of something of the uniqueness that makes you who you are. The space inhabited by a family or set of friends is paradigmatic as place; ideally at least there are attempts towards mutual acceptance, understanding, and assistance. Where these fail, one still has a claim on the benefits of belonging. That's the role and purpose of thinking of this location in space and time as *my place*: to enable the conditions of belonging.

Body as Elemental Place

Although the family home might be a paradigm of place as belonging, I'd now like to propose a less intuitive idea: that the human body is the locus of the elemental experience of place. To put it another way: awareness of our body is the basic awareness of what it is to be in a place, to have a place. As an extended object, the body takes up space not occupied by other objects; but it is much more than that. This is *my space*, no one else's. It belongs to me in the most fundamental way. It's mine so profoundly that I cannot trade it or give it away to someone else (though I can donate non-essential parts of it). My body is my very way of being in the world; it constitutes my identity and therefore my place in relation to other persons and things. Just because I am this place in the world, I can enter into relationships, belong to others, own things as mine. Hence we experience fear of bodily disintegration or loss as the fear of losing what is, for us, the entire world.

Understanding one's body as elemental place might help in understanding the way in which we regard possessions, seeing them as the means to preserve and advance our wider place in the world. But rather than continuing with that idea here,[1] I want to ask what this basic idea might have to do with teaching and learning, especially in undergraduate education. I maintain there's something important in an educational experience that respects what might be called our somatic identity: the inescapable fact that we are embodied beings.

Attitudes to Somatic Identity and Place

It's a curious feature of human beings that we are stuck, as the ancients might put it, between earth and heaven. Our embodiment we share with other animals, but in imagination and reason we are godlike, overcoming limitations of space, time, and understanding.[2] Our flesh is frail, subject to all kinds of restraints, and it also behaves in ways we don't choose. Throughout human history, humankind has taken up different attitudes to our embodiment. One is to struggle against our somatic identity. That struggle, for some in the ancient world, was manifested in fear or shame about the body. We can't control its urges, its pains. The body is seen as the distractor of reason, the corrupter of virtue, the last enemy that will do us in at the end. The neoplatonist Plotinus, for instance, seemed ashamed of being in a body, and refused to celebrate his birthday; for him, persons are disembodied intellects. Plato himself wrote about the problems of embodiment, but he didn't go as far as some other thinkers in wanting to deny the body any value.

Radical denial of the body is a minority opinion. What's more characteristic of our kind is a refusal to accept the limits of our embodied powers and abilities. We've found myriad ways to overcome weakness and frailty. In fact you can think of the history of human ingenuity as a massive, determined attempt to push back the limitations and constraints of embodiment. That, in one simple statement, is *the aim of technology*.

Technology and Somatic Place

Among the most striking technological advances of the past few decades has been the series of revolutions in the transmission, storage, manipulation, and display of data that convey bits of information. I don't need to detail how the digital revolution has made the invention of the printing press seem like a childish grunt compared with a Shakespearean sonnet. Interestingly, however, while the massive changes brought about by information technology do not themselves deny our embodiment, nevertheless their collective effect is to ignore as irrelevant the somatic nature of our humanity. Our use of this technology does affect our bodies: the hunched shoulders, bent neck, eye strain, and carpal tunnel syndrome give us trouble. But these are just more problems to be overcome. For the thing that matters is *connectivity to information*. The world of the Internet, with its immediate access to remarkable quantities of information, is *indifferent to place*. It is therefore indifferent to human embodiment, oblivious to the frailties of the flesh. Having already conquered space, it now overcomes time by permitting interaction with information at any time of day or night and in fractions of seconds. Log in; log off; log back in to where you were. Search, click, copy, paste. It is of no concern or interest if you are old, sleep-deprived, depressed, hungry, or recently bereaved – no matter, your byte-bits are purged of any bodily contamination. Whatever it is that is "you" has achieved pure rationality and immateriality: as long as there is two-way connectivity for byte-flows, you might as well be nothing more than a brain in a vat. Perhaps that's too strong a statement, but it lurks deep in the unarticulated assumptions of what we might call info-technocracy: the socio-cultural dominance of a world view in which technology and information exchange structure much of the interactions among human beings.

This brave new world has ancient roots, as I noted in the previous section, in views that denied or denigrated the body in favour of the mind or soul. However, unlike the attitude of some ancient gnostic sects, the human body isn't regarded as evil; it's now simply thought to be irrelevant. Not that the idea of soul is in favour – the common belief these days about human beings is that they are pretty well just complicated bodies, an attitude that sits curiously with the practice of treating embodiment as irrelevant.

Whether info-technocracy has infected the world of education I leave to others to determine. But technology certainly has altered the way the university performs its functions. Vast amounts of knowledge are preserved and made accessible on screens without any need to travel to the physical locations of libraries. Course content likewise: large numbers of students can follow a series of lectures without leaving home. Just as you can now do your banking without ever touching a piece of paper, you can achieve a paper-free university degree, although, as I noted above, at present the diploma is still a physical object for framing. And that returns me to the story of my musing about your becoming educated without ever leaving the house. As noted, this is *placeless education*. Of course my imagined student does have a body occupying space, but it's not an educational place in any recognizable sense. She's in her bedroom in front of a screen. The information being received and returned could be retrieved from anywhere that there's a screen with connectivity. Place is, strictly speaking, irrelevant. It could be an Internet café, a hotel room on another continent – places that have nothing to do with the purposes of education. This student has no somatic presence *as a student*; she knows her instructor or classmates, and is known by them, only by digital representations.

Now I must confess to ambivalent feelings about modes of education that can overcome the limits of time and space that structured my own undergraduate experience. Recalling the advantages of placeless education set out earlier, there's much that can benefit students and institutions in the judicious use of technological innovations. Perhaps one doesn't have to embrace wholeheartedly the mentality of info-technocracy in order to offer education without place. There are certainly educational entrepreneurs who would have us believe so.

But I find myself with another, more guarded, reaction. Critics might attribute its caution to wistfulness or to a reluctance to give up the old way of doing things. But it might have a deeper root – in a conviction about what it is to be human, coupled with a worry about the effect on undergraduate education of educational technology's indifference to the sense of place and embodiment. Is there anything to this worry?

Embodied Education

I want to argue that a well-placed university should embrace *embodied education*, using technology only in its service. Embodied education respects place and somatic presence, rejecting the mentality of info-technocracy. Its stance towards place follows from the view of interrogative education I set out in the previous chapter. Where undergraduate education is conducted as interrogative conversation that is personal and not restricted to the formal curriculum, embodiment is important.

I'll say more about that shortly, but first I want to draw attention to the social significance of *space dedicated to knowledge*. There's a functionally utilitarian attitude to spaces that would reject the notion of dedication – the conviction that certain functions and activities should be carried out only in particular settings reserved for them. That attitude wouldn't care if the same building were used on different days as a place of worship, a casino, a gun store, a courtroom, or a bicycle repair shop. The only question of appropriateness is functionality, whether the activity can be carried out in the space. That's an impoverished view of human society and the ways in which values and beliefs are expressed in the spaces we construct. Judges sit on an elevated bench in courtrooms because the law is above individual interests. There is stability and grandeur in buildings that house legislatures and parliaments, signifying the authority of the state. Temple and cathedral elevate the spirit beyond the quotidian. In like manner, a society's commitment to knowledge is expressed in the space and architecture of its libraries, archives, and universities.

The area of land known as the campus is one geographical expression of space dedicated to education and the conditions of learning. As I noted, not every university has a well-defined parcel of land on which its activities are carried out. But a bounded campus is, quite literally, a protected place proclaiming the autonomy of the university. Public universities usually have been granted land by the state, so although they are regarded as public institutions they sit on private property. They hold authority about who can and cannot access their space. But even where there isn't a clear sense of campus, properly constructed universities carry out their functions in spaces – classrooms, laboratories, libraries, offices – that are dedicated to learning and the essential freedoms required for acquiring, preserving, and transmitting knowledge. The defining characteristics of autonomy and academic freedom, essential to what it is to be a university, require this sense of *protected place*. Where outside influences intrude into the spaces where knowledge functions are carried out, that institution is not a *well-placed* university.

Universities have places, not just spaces. The attitude, attention, and conduct expected in a seminar room differ from what goes on in a coffee shop. The point of going to a classroom isn't the same as the point of sitting in a common room. A council chamber is not a cafeteria. These university places are physical spaces dedicated to the structured conversations of teaching, learning, and deliberation. Not only are there rules for the conduct of these activities; there are also expectations for behaviour in these places that is conducive to good conversation. When you enter such places, you enter as a member of the community with a defined purpose shared with others in the same place. Your surroundings help create that sense of purpose. That's the meaning of dedicated space, in which the dedicated purpose turns space into place. Whereas functionality determines the amount and kind of space, place determines the appropriateness of function.

That said, it's to be lamented that much university architecture in the past many decades has been merely functional, conveying little of the dignity of learning and respect for the search for truth. Towers of commerce, chambers of law and government, galleries, museums, concert and arts halls – there are many examples of impressive architecture and design that provide evidence of what's important to a society. Few university buildings are in that category. In Canada many of those constructed in the twentieth century are now in sad shape; I noted two chapters back the huge liability of deferred maintenance facing universities. Everyone can have their stories about classrooms and halls of painted cement blocks, and desks with chipped arborite arm tablets. Fortunately there are other, better, stories as well. But public funding of university construction has not been adequate to express, in buildings that inspire love for learning, the value of knowledge to society. Where the better stories are about new buildings with architectural merit, it's more than likely they will be named after generous donors.

Financial constraints make it difficult to build places of distinction dedicated to knowledge. But buildings are also an asset, and budgets require revenue that can be generated by renting out university spaces when they're not being used for teaching. That necessary practice , however, does begin on occasion to erode the notion of dedicated space. A well-placed university should not host, in its protected place, activities inimical to its fundamental purposes. The temptation to rearrange some of the institution's usual knowledge activities to increase rental revenue can be the source of friction between administration and the faculty and students.

Of courses, a *placeless* university existing in virtual space has practically none of these problems. It has no dedicated space to protect, maintain or preserve for the sake of knowledge. But what kind of undergraduate experience is available to students in such a university? It's time to provide reasons for my claim that education defined as interrogative conversation is best understood as *embodied* education.

Here's the foundation of the claim: it's about who we are as human beings. We are, quite simply, embodied selves. Any view of the world that is indifferent to our somatic state, denying it or treating it as irrelevant or a nuisance to be overcome, will have a severely reduced understanding of human knowledge, human experience, and human wisdom about right living and flourishing. I suspect that the mindset of info-technocracy leads in that direction, but that's a huge subject that deserves its own careful study. For our purposes here, a couple of observations about embodiment and learning will have to suffice.

Interrogative education has to be relational, between persons – teacher and student, primarily, but also in a community where its members articulate ideas, challenge claims, and learn self-reflection. Although one may read and think in solitude, the process of learning how to know, how to assess knowledge, has to be relational and social. That's especially true in a university: we don't give degrees to autodidacts. Now think about the difference between a solitary and a social experience. You can listen on headphones to a piece of music. You will be able to appreciate without distraction the quality of a recorded performance, since the sound is right there inside your head. Although you can be lost in it, your enjoyment is solitary and placeless. Attending a live performance is different. Extraneous noise might distract you. But your enjoyment is different: it's layered and multiplied. You experience not only your own involvement in the music, but also the involvement of musicians and audience, and their responses to each other. These aesthetic pleasures feed on each other, and the experience is enriched because it is shared. Perhaps it will be said that a high-quality DVD of a performance will convey the experience of audience and musicians. One can be virtually present, immersed in the experience. But it isn't the same. There is no *sharing*; there is only observing. Moreover the experience is entirely in your control: you can decide to stop at any point, without taking into account the wishes, feelings, or needs of anyone else. You are not only sovereign; you are the only person who matters in the moment.

That's not how education works, because (unlike being an auditor at a performance) it requires participation with another.

To engage in interrogative conversation, one must be attentive to the other person. That means attention to embodiment – the twitch of the eyebrow or mouth, the cock of the head, the raised finger, the tensed neck. It's not just that all of our senses come into play in attentive conversation – although they do; it's also that we must *engage* with the other who is present to us. Merely observing won't do.

In some science fiction world, technology might create all the conditions of embodied interaction in a space that is virtual. In that world, embodiment would have to be experienced *as though* it were in an *actual* place. Anyone who has conducted meetings by teleconference knows that we are very, very far away from such a fictional world. A properly constructed undergraduate education needs to happen in a university that takes place and embodiment seriously. That's all the more important for students who are coming to universities these days with increasing hours spent on social media, holding phones in their embrace and staring at screens, rather than looking at others in the eye. They need a full-blooded, human, university experience.

My second observation is about the personal dimension of interrogative conversation and the somatic conditions of effective learning. In Chapter Six I spent some time on the mushrooming of student services that address many conditions that impede successful education. Those conditions almost all arise from our nature as embodied – especially those requiring accommodation and issues related to physical and brain health. Counselling and advising services require personal attention to the individual. These concerns are not going to fade away. A 2015 study of younger students (in grades seven through twelve) predicted, disturbingly, that they will come to universities with ongoing issues. Stress has increased significantly in recent years, with 34 per cent of these young people reporting a moderate to serious level of psychological distress, while more than 25 per cent said they wanted to talk to someone about mental health but didn't know where to turn.[3] Although the social burden on the university is significant, the costs of indifference to the particular problems of embodiment in the twenty-first century are too high to ignore. They have a direct effect on one's ability to participate in the benefits of an undergraduate education. While universities struggle to fund adequate student services, *placeless* education would find it practically impossible to offer the personal attention required, except by reference to other places where embodied human beings – flesh-and-blood people – interact with embodied students.[4]

Given who we are, then, education must take into account all the conditions of our coming to know, including our inhabitation of the personal, intimate place that is our body. As well, since we are social beings, education takes place in relationships and in communities. I remarked in the last chapter on the role of the seminar as the place for multiple conversations, a form of education that has a placeless analogue in chat-groups and online communities. They have their place, so to speak, when participants are unable to meet in one geographical location. But this is a very pale and limp sense of "community," where engagement is not with personal embodied presence. It's even worse: a travesty of community, where participants have been infected by social media's validation of the emotive expression of individual opinion without regard to the other.

One more comment on embodied conversation, and that's about university governance. Universities are protected places, I've argued, and placelessness, without the advantage of dedicated spaces, makes it harder to recognize the autonomy of the university. It also erodes the fundamental idea of the collegium: the problems of placeless interrogative conversation are found, too, in the deliberations among peers necessary to the effective functioning of the university. If there is no campus, it's difficult for the community to get together to debate and decide academic issues. Without senate-like bodies, academic freedom and autonomy are precarious. Even assuming there are such bodies in a virtual institution, meetings in virtual space may convey information but they remain unsatisfactory forms of the deliberative discourse required in a properly constructed university.

Thus far the concern has been with the importance of embodied presence in the classroom and council chamber. As I argued in Chapter Seven, not all learning takes place in formal conversation;

education is more than a matter of degrees. This kind of education takes place in actual rather than virtual university space. In cafeteria and common room, at games and on courts, in study spaces and libraries, in clubs and societies, *unstructured conversation* is carried on. And the subject is more than likely about some form of knowledge or other. The recent guest public lecture, the play or performance just witnessed, the difficult assignment – these are occasions for much informal but nevertheless knowledge-enhancing talk. Often what stays in the mind long after graduation isn't the actual content of a course, but an experience outside the classroom that opened up a new world, that moved a doubting shadow over an unexamined certainty, or that awoke an unexpected taste for new knowledge.

Many of these activities require presence on the campus, and often in unplanned and serendipitous moments. When you share locations in time and space with others, opportunity is created for encounters that, in retrospect, might well turn out to have import for your understanding of the world, and indeed for the conduct of your life.

Dedicated spaces that mark out the protected place of free inquiry and encourage structured and informal conversations about knowledge and how it is best gained: this is what's required for well-placed universities. Placeless education delivers a thin and bloodless experience by comparison.

It must be confessed, however, that, when the experience of students is impersonal and limited to accumulating credits, their education has marks of placelessness, even on a campus. What are the marks, then, of universities that understand the importance of place and use that understanding well?

Universities and Particularities of Place

When discussing reputation, and again when commenting on mission statements in the chapter on governance, I observed that universities are, by and large, all in the same business. That's true at least of undergraduate education, even if some universities offer professional programs – like those dozens of new professional master's degrees – that others don't. It would be difficult to distinguish one from the other by any substantive difference in their mottos and aspirational statements. I pointed out, though, that two features are unique to institutions: their history and their location – their place in time and space. Each university has its own past, especially involving the former members of its community; and each university is located somewhere in the world – except, of course, those placeless virtual institutions. One can refer to the first feature as temporal place, which has to do with the sense of belonging, and to the second feature as locative place, which provides its own conditions for learning.

Temporal Place and Belonging

A few pages back I claimed that one of the fundamental differences between space and place is that "place" can be used to mark out the location where you are known and appreciated, where you experience a sense of belonging. Family and friends inhabit a place that might be a particular spatial location such as a home, or a metaphorical location such as a place in one's heart. (It would be a mistake to read place as space by asking in which ventricle.)

It's no accident that we call the institution from which we graduate our *alma mater*, Latin for "nourishing mother," or that the university calls us *alumni*, from the Latin word for "nursling."[5] No doubt some will think that, in encouraging this language, the administration wants to create a sense of loyalty so that we'll support the institution. But it's not necessary to adopt that cynical view unless your experience was alienating and unhappy – as some family relationships can be. A good education creates not only a thirst for knowledge, but also an ability to discriminate between what will and what won't satisfy that thirst. The university years provide nourishment, forming minds and passions, lives and relationships. So it's not at all inappropriate to claim and celebrate your belonging to this family that welcomed and adopted you as one of its own.

The university's past and present alumni form a notional community that stretches back in time as far as its first graduating class. It's only notional, of course, since, depending on the date of foundation, many members are long past. But even they inform the sense of place that is *this* university, because they are part of *this* family history. Their stories create pride or provide pleasure; their accomplishments inspire or intrigue. If they are well known, there will be markers and monuments on the campus, helping current students as the newest family members to identify with their forebears. That sense of belonging is important, especially at a time of significant change in social and familial relationships and with greater international and cultural diversity on our campuses.[6]

I want to emphasize the continuity of the community through time as an important aspect of place as belonging, for a couple of reasons. The first has to do with how universities change to meet new challenges. In Chapter Five I remarked that changes in programs and personnel take some time to implement, so pace is often slow. Direction, however, is more important than pace. Universities thrive when they grow from their roots, instead of trying to graft on shoots from different species. What works in one place to attract students might not grow as well in a different climate. The identity and reputation of an institution is wrapped up in its history, and the challenge of each new administration is to articulate and shape that historical identity in ways that honour the past while engaging the present. By that effort, the university's place is seen to be both stable and dynamic: reassuring to its long-time alumni and encouraging to the next generation, which wants to identify with and belong to an established community.

The other reason for emphasizing continuity through time is related to the pernicious attitude of presentism discussed in the previous chapter. Students – and indeed faculty and staff – might know alumni who are household names, but they typically understand very little of the history of their university. Recently there's been notable awareness of shameful aspects of institutional history, especially about prejudice and discrimination, and it's important to face up to those issues. (It's unfortunate that, without established institutional ritual and ceremony to mark apology and forgiveness, resolution is sometimes difficult to achieve.) The antidote is not glorification of success, for self-promotion quickly grows tiresome. Nevertheless education does change lives and society, and today's students need stories and models that will give them the determination and courage to persist.

They also value connection with more recent graduates, who have learned to navigate their way in a world where paths to meaningful employment are maze-like. Universities that value place as belonging will attend to alumni, but not just those with established careers and "capacity." Past practice in many institutions has been to invite alumni back to campus after twenty years, when nostalgia is creeping up on them, and when they might have a little more disposable income. But a sense of belonging to the family has to involve more than receiving annual appeals for handouts to keep the *alma mater* in the business of nourishing the young. Of course, that's not a fair way to characterize alumni relations; but it is a concern when appeals for donations for endless worthy causes land daily in the inbox. If alumni are truly to experience continuity of place as continuing to belong to the family, then we have to think about the many ways in which they can participate in the *mater's* family. That might involve putting recent graduates together with current students, and creating opportunities for alumni to participate in the wider unstructured conversations that are part of a good undergraduate education. I should add that interaction between alumni and current faculty is also important for both parties.

The challenge for a well-placed university, then, is to assist in maintaining among its alumni a continuing sense of place. Alumni should value membership in the community, which brought many benefits during their university years, for the intergenerational connections it makes possible. While members of a graduating class might keep up their friendships across the years, introducing them to more recent alumni will bring mutual rewards. A university that can find effective ways to facilitate connections across time for the diverse members of its community will offer its graduates an important benefit.[7]

The Opportunities of Locative Place

Although properly constructed universities occupy a protected social and intellectual place in society, they are located in space as well as time. They have to be somewhere, and the *where* should make its mark on their identity. That is, their location should be a meaningful *place* in relationship to what is around them.

I began this chapter by commenting on how diverse are the places universities are to be found. My general point now is that a successful interrogative education will take advantage of whatever opportunities for conversation its locative place can generate. Since those places are indeed diverse, it is difficult to explore in any detail what those opportunities might look like. But for the sake of illustration, and in order to provoke deliberation on the claim, let me comment on two main types of institution: the collegiate university, usually set in a small town or at some remove from a large centre, and the urban university.

Collegiate universities, when located away from the distractions of the big city, are residential communities or schools where students live very close to campus. With these living arrangements it becomes difficult to avoid interaction with others. Meals bring them together in a form of community as old as the monastery. They have to organize their own social activities. There are enough small classes that students are known by the faculty, who themselves spend time outside the classroom within the precincts of learning. The faculty generally have a strong commitment to teaching, even if some of them also have significant research careers. This kind of education is personal, with structured and serendipitous conversation contributing to the formation of the mind. Friendships are formed for life, along with institutional pride and loyalty. The collegiate university takes the place of learning seriously, as the American novelist Marilynne Robinson recently acknowledged in commenting on collegiate learning: "In the United States, education, especially at the higher levels, is based around powerful models of community. We choose our colleges, if have a choice, in order to be formed by them and supported by them in the identities we have or aspire to. If the graft takes, we consider ourselves ever after to be members of that community. As one consequence, graduates tend to treat the students who come after them as kin and also as heirs. They take pride in the successes of people in classes forty years ahead of or behind their own. They have a familial desire to enhance the experience of generations of students who are, in fact, strangers to them, except in the degree that the ethos and curriculum of the place does indeed form its students over generations."[8]

This description does, however, leave out less positive aspects of the collegiate undergraduate experience, such as cliquishness, limited curricular and program choice, and the difficulties of avoiding teaching that turns out to be ineffectual. Relative isolation means that it takes more effort for collegiate universities to work with other cultural and educational institutions. Their students find education more expensive because of accommodation costs and limited opportunities for part-time work. That poses challenges for economic diversity. The student body can be too uniform, so international students must be recruited not just to meet enrolment and budget targets, but also for the added diversity they bring. Alumni don't live locally, and are not readily available for interaction with the current generation. Nevertheless, and despite such challenges, collegiate education when well done is recognizably a full-blooded experience, in which place and embodiment matter greatly.

Urban universities, by contrast, tend to be large comprehensive institutions with professional faculties, although educating undergraduates forms much of their daily business. Typically only a small percentage of undergraduates live in residence; the vast majority commute, sometimes (as with my student) from considerable distances. Although students might have a greater choice of excellent teachers, an increasing amount of the teaching is done by contract faculty (as we saw in Chapter Four). Since course sections are typically large and require tutorials, graduate students carry out this more personal contact. The permanent faculty members are almost all deeply engaged in research, which might form the main focus of their attention.

Some students are able to find a sense of community and place within the more impersonal institution. It helps if they live in residence, meeting others with whom they share friendship and interests. As they progress in their studies, some will approach or be noticed by senior faculty members, and develop academic ties with them. But for the many others, the sense of a true place for learning is seriously attenuated. I call in evidence my student mentioned earlier, perched every week for as many hours on a bus seat as on a classroom chair. In the experience of those like her, interaction with busy faculty members – or, more likely, their teaching assistants – is usually virtual, through email or a portal. Classes are not just large; they can be massive. For these undergraduates, learning does not have much to do with the university as a distinctive place. Their experience of it as a place for learning might not be all that different from high school, except that they now spend less time in classrooms and more time getting to them. Their education beyond the actual classroom takes place wherever they can find connected space. Their experience bears many marks of similarity to the dis-placed education that I've been calling into question in this chapter. Small wonder that students in these circumstances feel that education is impersonal, that they are known as individuals only as their individual student number.

The differences, then, between collegiate and urban universities can be striking. If you're set on realizing the idea of a "full university experience," as I was, the small institution is highly attractive. Nevertheless urban institutions have some advantages. A large school has a large faculty complement, with more choice for students, which normally means more advanced courses are available. Undergraduates have access to graduate students who can act as models for them. Diversity in the local student population is another advantage; that diversity is economic as well as ethnic, since local students need not pay for accommodation away from home. Off campus, cultural life is richer. Opportunities for part-time employment are greater, although that's a two-edged sword in that it permits increased accessibility but diminishes involvement in campus life.

More significantly, urban universities can structure student experiences that respect urban spaces as places of learning.[9] There is scarcely an old or emerging problem for human beings and societies that cannot be found within a large urban area. The curriculum as structured conversations can, and should, include listening to and interrogating the city and its multiform issues. Beyond that, the unstructured conversation that goes on outside the classroom readily engages the culture, commerce, policies, and politics of the city. The alumni of an urban university are discovered throughout the veins and arteries of the complex body that is the city, and many of them are willing conversationalists with current students. Still, the very size of an urban university makes credible the popular representations of its bureaucratic and impersonal nature. Large institutions must work hard at creating, nurturing, and celebrating smaller communities of undergraduate learning, where faculty, staff, and students meet to discover what each might learn from the other and from the places they inhabit.

In sum the conditions structuring the collegiate university are favourable to education as personal interrogative conversation, and the conditions for the urban university make that education more difficult to offer. But the range of opportunities for education as conversation, both structured and informal, is greater in an urban than in a collegiate locative place.

Well-placed universities understand their particular places in time and space. They celebrate these particularities, building their distinctive identities upon them.

Undistracted and Well-Placed Universities: In Conclusion

We have come to the conclusion of these assertions and questions about the university. Let me, then, roll up into four paragraphs what it means for a university to be properly constructed, undistracted, and well placed.

In the midst of entirely legitimate and timely concerns for engagement with the wider community and society at large, universities must affirm that they are protected places. They must clearly mark off the boundaries of autonomy and academic freedom, explaining and defending the limits of intrusion into free and unfettered investigation and conversation. To be well placed, their physical spaces should inspire respectful and intelligent deliberation – although collegiate architecture needn't imitate the past. Just as it's possible to have a third-rate education in first-rate buildings, so it's possible to have a first-class education in worn-out shabby surroundings. Possible, but not desirable. Respect for knowledge and the knowledge functions of the university should find expression in the physical places defining the university and in its ceremonies and rituals.

Well-placed universities acknowledge the many dimensions of place in student experience, especially for undergraduates. That means understanding the embodied nature of learning by creating a sense of belonging, where one identifies with a community, knows other students and alumni, and is known by members of that community. Education must have a personal dimension, which requires that conversations about knowledge be carried out between student and teacher in both directions, in person and not only in virtual space. The conversations should be unstructured as well as structured, with formal learning and informal learning in overlapping spheres, not segregated spaces. Technology should be placed in the service of more personal education, not replace it. And despite the social burdens placed on the university, the conditions of our students' embodied humanity, including their physical and emotional well-being, must be acknowledged and addressed.

Well-placed universities respect their particular locations. The protected place they inhabit is situated somewhere in a locative place, a geographical location with its own challenges and opportunities. Well-placed universities also respect their own particular histories, carving out their identities by celebrating their past and by welcoming current and future generations into an enduring fellowship. This sense of identity informs a university's *vocation*. Although we use the language of vocation for individuals more than for institutions, it's entirely appropriate to apply it to universities. A vocation is different from a mission statement – as I noted, mission statements for undergraduate education all look very much as though they were produced in the same factory; missions and mottos are highly general and abstract. A vocation, by contrast, attends to the circumstances of the present, which might change at their own unpredictable pace. It's *what is heard* in those circumstances that calls out for response. The deliberative processes for governance in a properly constructed university engage in reflection on the institution's vocation with respect to its members, especially its students, but also to its alumni and to the community in which it is situated.

Finally, the university of the twenty-first century, distracted by demands from every quarter, disappointed by the weak support and growing misunderstanding of the state, and beset by controversies within its walls, needs to be recalled to its own unique place. That is the place for knowledge and for knowing. It is the place where the love of learning flourishes, curiosity is welcomed, and the quest for truthful understanding is carried out with intelligence and humility. It is the place where the freedoms that define our very humanity are cultivated and expressed. Maybe that place is to be imagined only in some other world, not in our present age of cynicism about institutional power, an age in which the full possession of those defining freedoms is still restricted to the privileged few. As with every age, ours is a sorry mess in far too many ways, and our universities have their own share in its messiness. But the world won't fix itself. Power and privilege demand interrogation, wherever they are found. And were the world, or even parts of it, fixed, there would still be more to know. The thirst for what's even more clearly true, and what's better yet, is an ineradicable human longing. Thus far the university is the best institution we've come up with for sanctifying that longing. For the sake of all that is sacred, let us then construct our universities properly, free them from distractions, and place them well. Let us cherish them, as we cherish what is our own.

chapter nine

Epilogue: Apologia pro Vita Sua

One of the most famous books about the university appeared in 1852: *The Idea of the University*, by John Henry Cardinal Newman. It's a larger volume, grander in scope and purpose, than the book before you. My main intention has not been to pronounce on what sort of educated person the university should be developing, although I did say a little about that in Chapter Seven, and since this is indeed about the University, some of the other themes Newman addressed have received some attention.

Although I haven't reflected here specifically on Newman's classic text, another title by him also comes to mind. In 1864, in response to criticisms by Charles Kingsley on his move from the Anglican to the Roman Catholic Church, Newman published *Apologia pro Vita Sua* – a defence of his own life. Given that an *apologia* is not just an account – an intellectual autobiography, for instance – but also a defence, it must arise from contentions and objections to one's ideas and behaviour. The classic instance of this genre is, of course, Plato's *Apology*, in which his Socrates explains his commitment to the practice of philosophy as a duty transcending his duties to the state. He defends himself against the charges of irreligion and corrupting the young.

There are, to my knowledge, no sworn enemies seeking to bring me to account for wrong beliefs and inappropriate actions. But when one takes on an administrative life in the university, there may be muttered comments in the faculty common room about abandoning the real work of the academy in scholarship and teaching. It's not quite like swimming the Tiber to go over to Rome, but there can be a sense that one has left one's colleagues to become, of all things, an administrator, entangled in the nets of bureaucracy, inventing and imposing rules to little purpose.

I must confess, then, straight off: I have been an academic administrator. Not just once. Repeatedly, in various guises. For over three decades. In fact, across my career of too close to half a century I have spent only twelve years as a regular faculty member untainted by administrative responsibilities.

Permit me, nevertheless, to speak in my own defence. To do so, I'll have to confess again, this time to certain passions that have created internal conflict for me across my life. It will emerge that three objects of my interest have vied for attention. The first I met in a Saturday morning class in my first year as an undergraduate at Bishop's University. Unexpectedly I encountered Lady Philosophy – unexpectedly, because I had thought to become a high school teacher of Latin and French. She captured me, and I took as many courses with the word philosophy in them as I could fit in my schedule. While an undergraduate I occasionally wondered what I'd actually do with my life, but I was sufficiently smitten that I took my chances with graduate school. My MA was in philosophy of religion, as a way to carry on thinking about theological concepts that had intrigued me from my youth; and my PhD in Greek philosophy got me more deeply into the ancient world and into close readings of texts. My thesis was supposed to be on Plato's concept of moral and legal responsibility.

I say "supposed to be," because before I could write more than the title of the thesis topic, I was hired at the Scarborough campus of the University of Toronto to teach philosophy. That introduced a second love into my life, but let me stay for a moment with my first passion. By working on the thesis for two summers and staying up till all hours in my third year of teaching, I managed to cobble together a series of studies in Plato's ethics and moral psychology, and ended up with a thesis on Socratic paradox in Plato. With the PhD in hand, I became an assistant professor; two years later I was considered for tenure and promotion just having rolled past age thirty. Policies and procedures on hiring and tenure were poorly developed in those days, to my great advantage. Indeed I later spent a good deal of time as vice-provost ensuring that nobody would get hired or tenured in the lax way that I was.

I am enormously grateful that the University of Toronto has afforded me the privilege of pursuing the philosophical life, giving me security of position and freedom to think and write about my interests and concerns, even when they have been idiosyncratic. I have benefited significantly from membership in an institution that values academic freedom and does not prescribe beliefs or adherence to particular schools of thought. I've been able to bring together my interests in philosophical theology, biblical studies, and the ancient world in a series of publications that might be hard to classify neatly as pure Philosophy, or pure Classics, or pure Biblical Studies, or pure Ethics – or Pure Anything. In trying to flog my first book, I was told that philosophers didn't do biblical studies and that biblical scholars did not do philosophy – so who would read a series of philosophical studies of Paul's letter to the Corinthians? Fortunately someone at the University of Notre Dame Press took the chance on the book. My second book, on Jesus and Socrates, dealt with two iconic figures who were studied by two distinct disciplines that, like Athens and Jerusalem, sometimes had nothing to do with each other. But despite that, and the lack of footnotes in the manuscript, this time it was Yale that took its chances. Along the way there have been articles and papers on Greek philosophy and in philosophical theology or philosophical biblical theology, if there is such a thing. But the time I've had for Lady Philosophy in the past several years was eroded by another competing passion, and I was unable to find sufficient time to write another book.

I've mentioned competing passions, so let me go back now to the second love that got my attention before I finished graduate school: teaching. After my first year of doctoral course work, I was given a section of first-year philosophy to teach on my own – in the pass course, not for specialists. The faculty member in charge of all these sections was Marcus Long, a popular (and populist) professor who'd written a textbook – allegedly sitting on his cottage dock with his lecture notes and a bottle of scotch, according to a high school classmate of mine whose relative had a cottage nearby. Professor Long highly recommended the use of his book, *The Spirit of Philosophy*, in the course, and not having any better idea, I ordered it. I thought at the time that my job was to understand not just the book, but also all the many figures in the history of philosophy to whom Long refers – and then to communicate my ideas to my students. This turned out to be an impossible task. For I had the good fortune to be confronted right away with an elementary truth: teaching is not speaking out loud the thoughts of the teacher, but learning how to connect with the minds and understandings of the students. My students were baffled by my multiform references to other philosophers they had never read. Professor Long's book wasn't a good text for them, so I threw it away and ordered something much more straightforward. (Incidentally, curiosity drove me to see if I could find the book again, but it hasn't survived except in some used copies from independent sellers on Amazon – a sober reminder of the way of all textbooks.)

I took to teaching quite naturally – which means I never had any lessons in pedagogy – no doubt because there's something satisfying about having a captive audience that writes down what you say, regardless of its relationship to anything true. I taught, at the Scarborough campus, courses in Greek philosophy, philosophy of religion, and ethics. Sometimes I was irresponsible: instead of lecturing on Descartes one day, I simply made up a medieval philosopher, Paulinius, whose system was summarized in six propositions. Sometimes I was too dramatic: a student who later became lieutenant governor of Ontario tells the story of my lesson about inductive reasoning and the possibility of "exploding chalk." But I saw at least a few of those early students go on to fulfilled lives in public service and the academy despite me, and some not so fulfilling: a few years ago I had an email from someone who claimed I'd said something about Plato thirty years ago that so upset him he left the university, never to return – sadly, I never would have claimed what he thought I said.

After a sabbatical leave in 1982–83 as Commonwealth Fellow at St John's College in Cambridge, England, I returned to undergraduate teaching at Scarborough, but was enticed to the University of Toronto's St George campus in 1986, and have spent my life in that part of the city for almost three decades. My teaching from 1986 until 2001 was exclusively at the graduate level, in Plato and philosophy of religion. I'm fortunate to have taught, and learned from, some highly accomplished people. Some of them have returned to U of T, at the full-professor level, having spent earlier years at prestigious US institutions. Others have landed positions elsewhere and, of course, some have disappeared into unknown places.

When I came to Victoria University as president in 2001, I decided I should teach undergraduates again, after a lapse of about fifteen years. I gave upper-level courses in Plato and in philosophy of religion – including a course that included both arts and science students and Emmanuel College theological students – but finally decided I should experience first hand what incoming students are like. So I developed a first-year seminar course on Virtue and Vice, which I've taught several times now. It's been a revelation. Some students are excellent, a joy to teach. And a few struggle with writing and thinking at the university level. It's been good to see some with second-class marks go on in succeeding years to do very well and to gain admission to top graduate programs. But a few students had not enjoyed a strong high school education, and they floundered.

There are, then, personal satisfactions in teaching and in seeing students thrive, satisfactions beyond the stroking of the ego that a captive audience permits. It's easy to see why this is a passion that I don't want to surrender. But it is in conflict with my other passions: I have not always done what university professors are supposed to do: give my students the results of my own research in my teaching. I've never taught a course that has made use of either of the books I've written. But I do give my first-year students some manuscripts in draft to read so that they can see how my mind works – if "works" is the right verb. So my own research is usually at the cost of my attention to teaching, and vice versa.

So for the first two of my passions, I dote on Lady Philosophy: philosophical scholarship broadly speaking, and teaching philosophy. But my third passion is rogue and a stranger to the contemplative life of reason. It is, as I've already confessed, academic administration.

It's not thought proper or polite to confess to this love. Academics are supposed to loathe administration, to harbour suspicions about anyone who forsakes the library or lab for the corridors of power. If those who teach do so because they can't do the real thing, then administrators are those who can neither teach nor do research.

I've never quite felt that way. Others must judge whether I've tried to escape research and teaching, or lusted after the power of office. I can only say that I've found academic administration an intellectual challenge, posing all kinds of puzzles requiring careful thought, and yielding satisfactions that have wide institutional reach. It's possible to make a difference in many more lives than those in just one classroom, to enact policies that change experience, to make judgments that improve the lot of individuals and groups. Of course, much administrative work is routine, facilitating the smooth operation of an institution. But some of it can be exciting, and personally rewarding when you manage not to mess up.

I came to administration early in my career, still in my mid-thirties and just a few years after I was tenured. The Scarborough campus had a divisional structure, rather than a departmental one; the Division of Humanities had over a dozen disciplines, and about eighty faculty members. They needed a chair (actually, a chairman in those days) because the incumbent, two years into his term, had been snatched by University College to become its principal. I got asked to be the acting chair(man) in the fall term while a search was conducted, and since they came up with nobody else, the job fell to me. It was a fascinating challenge: to become advocate for the humanities – yes, they were threatened even then – to be a pastoral counsellor to faculty, to sort out disputes, encourage creativity, reward excellence, straighten out the wayward. I ran hiring committees, tenure committees, promotion committees – many, many of them, because the college was expanding at the time. It wasn't always easy: U of T was instituting a merit pay scheme about then, and the members of the division wanted no one to be more meritorious than anyone else since we were all such good friends and colleagues. My first exercise in assessing merit resulted in the most vivid (and patently easy to interpret) dream of pursuit I've ever had, to this day. Yes, I did distinguish the more from the less meritorious, and no, I was not caught.

I suppose those years infected me with a kind of bug. On return from leave over at Cambridge, I was just a little restless teaching the same courses. So when a call came to see the dean of graduate studies, I answered – and found myself being invited to direct the graduate program in religious studies on the St George campus. Since I hadn't applied or been interviewed, I realized they were desperate – but I was ready for something new, so it was a match. I spent a bit of time on the battlefield where the study of religion fought with the study of theology, but was rescued after two years by a request to join the School of Graduate Studies as associate dean for Division I – the humanities. Familiar territory, so I accepted.

I spent six years in the School of Graduate Studies, in every kind of decanal position it could imagine or create. For a while, its assistant dean oversaw prestigious centres and institutes, and I took that on. The position was abolished and folded into that of the vice-dean, so that became the title I wore. Then acting dean for a year. It was a fascinating and rewarding life: sitting on many more tenure committees, working on funding for graduate students, reviewing graduate programs, and participating in the senior administration of U of T. Apart from the smell one autumn in my office (dead squirrels in the attic) and the occasional plagiarism or threat of a teaching assistants' strike, it was a good time.

Inevitably I was called once more to move on. The vice-provost of U of T was stepping down, and no one was willing to attempt to replace him after such a splendid run at solving and resolving problems no one else could handle. Why did I agree? I have no idea, but it was a chance to work with a very talent president and provost. I had great respect for the president's willingness to be challenged by the people around him – he welcomed criticism of his ideas and plans. The provost had a mind like a steel trap, and was rock solid; the deputy provost was smart, analytical, and positive. It was a great team. So I took on a position that was a mess of confused and confusing roles. In addition to receiving grievances from faculty members about chairs and deans (and from deans and chairs about faculty members), I was assessor of tenure files for the president; approver of new positions for the whole university; negotiator of the memorandum of agreement with the federated universities and the colleges; prosecutor of academic offenders; architect and advocate of academic policies. I worked with over a dozen lawyers in human resource and administrative law. The office took on any problem that a dean couldn't solve, and my job was mainly to come to understand how to live with the unsolvable. For the then dean of medicine, I was the university's proctologist; I certainly inspected minutely the soft grey underbelly of the institution. I didn't always operate with precise instruments; I learned that I was known in the president's office as the Velvet Hammer.

There's not space for many stories about academic offences, although in discussing integrity in Chapter Two I did mention examples of misbehaviour of undergraduates (such as the attempt at bribery that resulted in expulsion) and those of graduates (such as the self-confessed plagiarism of a doctoral dissertation undetected by the examining committee), and serious offences by faculty members (such as doctored data in a psychology experiment, detected by undergraduates and ending in termination of employment). I always took a deep breath before picking up the phone, or opening an email. At least there was no time for boredom to set in.

As noted earlier, a commitment to academic administration comes at the cost of one's research. U of T has a good policy to address that concern: a leave after five years of administration in order to recover some lost time. But a good policy requires good practice, and I somehow neglected to take all the entitled leaved, although in 1999–2000 I did take a year to think more carefully about Plato. The following year Victoria University needed to replace its departing president. Vic was founded by Methodists in 1836 and federated with the University of Toronto in 1890. It has two colleges, Victoria, an arts and science college with about 3,300 undergraduates receiving U of T degrees, and Emmanuel, a theological college with United Church of Canada connections, granting Victoria University degrees conjointly with U of T. For some reason the search committee was willing to bet on this non-Vic-grad. In 2001 I moved across to the best position I'd ever had in the large U of T extended family.

It would be tedious to go on about the past fourteen years of my academic administrative life. If I had to characterize my attitude towards this latest period in my career, it would be a passion for cultivation. Much of my earlier administrative life was about problem solving, removing grit from gears, patching up and stitching together, pacifying and cajoling, and other such low and high maintenance jobs. At Vic there came an opportunity to plant, cultivate, nourish, and see growth. Even better, that growth has not been just quantitative, more of the same; it has been a growth in quality – the quality of our community, its members and programs, its space and surroundings. The admission averages of Victoria College students have risen steadily over the past decade, and their accomplishments continue to be stunning – Rhodes Scholars, Gates Scholars, students who gain admission to the top graduate programs in the world. There seems to be a common consensus that a signal accomplishment for Victoria University is the Vic One first-year undergraduate program, begun in 2003 with the invaluable help of the Victoria College principal. It has grown from two streams to eight, offering an enriched and challenging personal experience in small seminars to students across the disciplines. That personal attention has set hundreds of students on the path to accomplishments and careers that continue to give one hope for the future. Much of what I have said in this book about undergraduate education arises out of my own experience in this program.

It's perhaps worth mentioning that, as a university with its own charter and act, Victoria is a member of Universities Canada (formerly known as the Association of Universities and Colleges of Canada). As a member of its (then called) Standing Committee on Acts and Bylaws, I participated in discussions about academic freedom. When the committee needed a new chair, I took on the task of leading discussion about non-discrimination. The organization had not accepted an application for membership from an institution whose stance on same-sex relationships arose out of its religious orientation, but was out of sympathy with human rights as understood by Canadians. The Canadian approach is complicated by its commitment to respect for conscience and freedom of religion. My committee debated long on the issue of respecting both freedom of religion and non-discrimination; it was only after I stepped down as president, and therefore from the committee, that the issue was resolved with a new membership criterion. Its implementation no doubt will be interesting – as they say.

But back to Victoria. Students choose the college not only for its academic programs and federation with U of T, but also for its location and historic buildings. Its spaces make community life not only possible but enjoyable; the newly renovated and expanded student centre hosts clubs and conversations and sessions of another signature program, Ideas for the World, mentioned in Chapter Seven.

Presidents of universities with theological schools or faculties sometimes face challenges in connecting them to the academic life of the arts and sciences. I had long experience with theological schools in the U of T system, having negotiated provisions of academic freedom when I was associate dean of the School of Graduate Studies in the late 1980s. I knew Emmanuel College and was pleased to work with its principal, especially in program development and in hiring the very best faculty as opportunity arose. Over the years Emmanuel's theological studies have deepened and expanded with new graduate degrees, a master of sacred music, and streams in pastoral studies that include Muslim studies and applied Buddhist studies. Emmanuel is a leader in the Toronto School of Theology and is among the best theological schools in North America. At Victoria the connections between the two colleges has never been stronger.

None of this has happened by accident. It's been the dedication and generous support of alumni and friends and the shrewd business sense of the board coupled with a willing understanding of academic mission that have provided the resources for the distinctive that excellence that is the hallmark of the Vic experience.

Come to think of it, the metaphor of cultivation might just be one theme common to my several passions. If I can't quite reconcile them all, or pay sufficient attention to the other two while spending time with one of them, at least I can explain to them an underlying concern with cultivation. My research might scratch around in the soil of scholarship, trying to plant a few bits of philosophical thinking, weeding out the bad ones, helping the promising ones to grow into something that can be taken to the marketplace of ideas. Teaching, of course, is the cultivation of young minds, planting those ideas, pruning, sometimes plucking up the scrawny thoughts that fall on stony ground, and so on. And if Vic has flourished in quality and reputation in this last period of time, it's because the task of administration is the work of many hands in such a fertile field. Such cultivation has been a privilege and a most rewarding labour of love.

There we have it: my confession, rambling on too long and with too much about my stint as president at Victoria University. I make it, begging indulgence, partly to explain my life and whatever constraints on my scholarship and teaching it displays. But more, to defend myself against the assumption naturally arising in the minds of readers of books like this – that the author has lived so much the life of an administrator that the challenges, difficulties, and pleasures of scholarship and teaching are no longer familiar or appreciated. I cannot be both defender and judge of that accusation, however muted. But whatever the verdict, it has been, so far, a wonderfully satisfying life.

It was in response to an invitation to address the Victoria Women's Association in April 2014 that I engaged in the self-reflection recorded here.

Notes

Preface

1 Gary Gutting explains it this way: "Public philosophy draws on academic work to tackle issues of general interest. At the same time, public philosophizing keeps its academic sibling in contact with the concrete human world, which is both the source of all philosophical questions and an important standard for judging answers to them ... [P]ublic engagement both tests and improves philosophical ideas"; *What Philosophy Can Do* (New York: Norton, 2015), xii.

2 Although I've spent time elsewhere on leave, and been active in national and international associations, my career has been within the large University of Toronto family, which explains why so many of the examples and incidents referred to in the notes are drawn from my U of T experience.

Introduction

1 Population has grown in both Canada and the United States over that time by 43 per cent, so with university student increases at around 100 per cent, participation rates have increased significantly. The situation in the United Kingdom is even more dramatic, as its population increase has been only about 18 per cent; the creation of new universities from polytechnics is no doubt a large reason.

2 Doug Lipp, *DISNEY U: How Disney University Develops the World's Most Engaged, Loyal, and Customer-Centric Employees* (New York: McGraw-Hill, 2013).

3 Maggie Berg and Barbara K. Seeber, *The Slow Professor: Challenging the Culture of Speed in the Academy* (Toronto: University of Toronto Press, 2016); see also Jamie Brownlee, *Academia, Inc.: How Corporatization Is Transforming Canadian Universities* (Halifax: Fernwood Publishing, 2015).

4 According to *Inside Higher Education* (2 May 2018), "Liberty University has for some time said that it is the largest Christian university. But Religion News Service recently reported that Grand Canyon University now has more students. The news service also said Liberty had started removing the claim from its website. But after the article ran, Jerry Falwell Jr., Liberty's president, sent a note to the news operation stating that he did not believe Grand Canyon met the definition of a Christian university because it does not require all faculty members to affirm their Christian faith. Grand Canyon asserts that it is indeed a Christian institution."

5 "How Liberty University Built a Billion-Dollar Empire Online," *New York Times Magazine*, 17 April 2018.

6 One example from Ontario experience: in a recent audit, a university presented documentation for the review of some programs that exceeded seven hundred pages each. Most audits involve site visits with interviews of about sixty academic administrators, faculty, and staff over three days.

7 See Jeffrey Herbst and Geoffrey R. Stone, "The New Censorship on Campus," *Chronicle of Higher Education*, 5 June 2017, available online at https://www.chronicle.com/article/The-New-Censorship-on-Campus/240269. Lindsay Shepherd, a graduate student at Wilfrid Laurier University in Waterloo, Ontario, writes in *Maclean's* magazine of the student disruption of an event she organized; see "Why I Invited Faith Goldy to Laurier," *Maclean's*, 22 March 2018, available online at https://www.macleans.ca/opinion/why-i-invited-faith-goldy-to-laurier/.

8 A clear example comes again from Lindsay Shepherd, who reports her student organization was charged $5,473 in security fees to hold an event; she raised the money through crowdfunding. See her tweets for 4 and 5 May 2018: https://twitter.com/newworldhominin?lang=en. See also Christie Blatchford, "Christie Blatchford: Nothing free about Wilfrid Laurier University's free speech policy," *National Post*, 26 April 2018, available online at http://nationalpost.com/opinion/christie-blatchford-nothing-free-about-wilfrid-laurier-universitys-free-speech-policy?utm_campaign.

9 Colleen Flaherty, "Diversifying a Classic Humanities Course," *Inside Higher Ed*, 12 April 2018, available online at https://www.

insidehighered.com/news/2018/04/12/responding-student-criticism-its-foundational-humanities-course-too-white-reed.

10 Quoted in Joshua Philipp, "Jordan Peterson Exposes the Postmodernist Agenda," *Epoch Times*, 21 June 2017, available online at https://www.theepochtimes.com/jordan-peterson-explains-how-communism-came-under-the-guise-of-identity-politics_2259668.html. But see, for instance, Ira Wells, "The Professor of Piffle," *Walrus*, 27 November 2017, available online at https://thewalrus.ca/the-professor-of-piffle/.

11 See Marilynne Robinson, "Year One: Rhetoric & Responsibility," *New York Review of Books*, 14 November 2017, available online at https://www.nybooks.com/daily/2017/11/14/year-one-rhetoric-responsibility/. Reflecting on Donald Trump's first year in office, Robinson diagnoses a deeper problem with American democracy and the education that universities have offered.

12 One authoritative voice speaking to the dangers of attending only to science and technology comes from David Naylor, president emeritus of the University of Toronto and chair of Canada's Fundamental Science Review. *University Affairs* reports that, at the Worldview 2013 conference on higher education and the media, Naylor "said that the current focus in the media and elsewhere on the STEM (science, technology, engineering and mathematics) and business disciplines needs some reflection. 'This zeitgeist worries me … So many of the issues we face are social. So much of what is bedevilling our world is the failure to appreciate our shared humanity. Cross-cultural and inter-faith tensions are a huge issue. And it just seems to me that we are turning away with respect to the social sciences and humanities at exactly the moment in our history when they have never been more relevant'"; see Léo Charbonneau, "Is media coverage biased in favour of universities over colleges?" *University Affairs*, 9 July 2013, available online at https://www.universityaffairs.ca/opinion/margin-notes/is-media-coverage-biased-in-favour-of-universities-over-colleges/. For a personal testimony about the importance of humanistic learning in and out of class, see "Robert E. Rubin: Philosophy prepared me for a career in finance and government," *New York Times*, 30 April 2018, available online at https://mobile.nytimes.com/2018/04/30/opinion/robert-e-rubin-philosophy.html.

13 Peter MacKinnon, in the conclusion to his *University Commons Divided: Exploring Debate and Dissent on Campus* (Toronto: University of Toronto Press, 2018).

14 In May 2018, just before the Ontario Legislature was dissolved for an election, the Ontario government decided to order arbitration and send

striking York University teachers back to work, but the resolution could not pass without the unanimous consent of all parties, and was denied by the New Democratic Party. See Kristem Rushowy, "NDP thwarts government's two attempts to pass back-to-work legislation for striking York University staff," *Toronto Star*, 7 May 2018, available online at https://www.thestar.com/news/queenspark/2018/05/07/ndp-thwarts -government-attempt-to-pass-back-to-work-legislation-for-striking-york -university-staff.html.

15 See Juris Graney, "NDP says new salary rules for Alberta university brass will save $5 million a year," *Edmonton Journal*, 10 April 2018, available online at http://edmontonjournal.com/news/politics/government-to- announce-pay-rules-for-alberta-university-top-brass; see also Chapter Three, note 17, below.

16 Colleen Flaherty, "Uncovering Koch Role in Faculty Hires," *Inside Higher Ed*, 1 May 2018, available online at https://www.insidehighered.com/ news/2018/05/01/koch-agreements-george-mason-gave-foundation- role-faculty-hiring-and-oversight.

17 See Gordon Kent, "U of A honorary doctorate for David Suzuki angers dean of engineering, donors," *Edmonton Journal*, 23 April 2018, available online at http://edmontonjournal.com/news/local-news/furor-erupts -over-honorary-university-of-alberta-degree-for-environmentalist-david -suzuki; and Andrea Ross, "U of A stands by Suzuki honorary degree as donors withdraw, Albertans protest," *CBC News*, 24 April 2018, available online at http://www.cbc.ca/news/canada/edmonton/david-suzuki -honorary-degree-backlash-1.4633770. The report also points out that this would be Suzuki's thirtieth honorary degree (he was awarded one by the University of Calgary).

18 Two examples are the honorary degree the University of Toronto awarded former US president George H.W. Bush in 1997, and the degree the University of Western Ontario (now Western University) awarded Henry Morgentaler in 2005; see Tabitha Marshall and Angus McLaren, "Henry Morgentaler," *Canadian Encyclopedia* (2013), available online at http://www.thecanadianencyclopedia.ca/en/article/ henry-morgentaler/.

19 Much of the research of the Higher Education Quality Council of Ontario is devoted to these concepts. Its president and CEO, Harvey Weingarten, recently promised, however, to stop using the language of learning outcomes and to stick to talking about skills. See Harvey P. Weingarten, "Harvey P. Weingarten – Quality assurance: A simple concept that we overly complicate," *It'sNotAcademic*, 9 January 2018, available online at

http://blog-en.heqco.ca/2018/01/harvey-p-weingarten-quality
-assurance-a-simple-concept-that-we-overly-complicate/.

1. It's All about Knowledge, Period

1 Aristotle made this the opening statement of his *Metaphysics*: "All human beings by nature desire to know."
2 "The truth shall make you free" (John 8.32) is the motto of many institutions. It is carved over the entrance to the Victoria College building erected in 1892 and into the stone face of the original headquarters of the US Central Intelligence Agency, opened in 1959; see Central Intelligence Agency, "CIA observes 50th anniversary of original headquarters building cornerstone laying," *News & Information*, 5 November 2009, available online at https://www.cia.gov/news-information/featured -story-archive/ohb-50th-anniversary.html.
3 In the *Meno*, Plato famously has Socrates point out that, even if you don't know the way to Larissa, you could still get there if you had a belief about the road that happened to be true. One could add that it wouldn't have to be a warranted belief – you might have decided to follow the direction of your dog's tail – as long as it turned out to work.
4 I was once involved in a decision to approve a limited ban on a doctoral thesis the subject of which was deemed so offensive to members of a particular group that they threatened to disrupt the defence, requiring the presence of a security officer in the building. A more common publication delay would be to protect intellectual property while filing for patents.

2. Reputation Requires Integrity

1 See Universities Canada, "Membership Criteria," http://www.univcan .ca/about-us/membership-and-governance/membership-criteria/.
2 See Gallup, "Confidence in Institutions," available online at http://www .gallup.com/poll/1597/confidence-institutions.aspx, accessed 13 April 2018.
3 For example, the University of Toronto framework on research misconduct lists two dozen forms of misconduct; see University of Toronto, "Framework to Address Allegations of Research Misconduct," 1 January 2013, available online at http://www.research.utoronto.ca/ wp-content/uploads/documents/2013/09/Research-Misconduct-Framework-Jan-1-2013.pdf.

4 The most memorable case I had to deal with concerned a junior faculty member who involved a small team of upper-year undergraduates in a research project. I don't need to tell the story exactly as it unfolded to make my point, but something twigged with the students about the results the faculty member wanted recorded. They reported this to the chair, who called me. Since the faculty member was away at a conference, we sealed the office, and two senior faculty members examined the data in the students' possession. One of them figured out the algorithm used to skew data, and when the office was opened after the junior professor returned, files were discovered labeled "good data" or "bad data." The swift end of the story was the end of the relationship between the faculty member and the university and the notification of co-investigators and publications associated with the researcher.

5 My years as vice-provost provide many examples. There was the small group of students who, having removed ceiling tiles from a corridor, crawled through the ceiling space to a secure room where exams were being copied, and retrieved their examination questions ahead of time. That was (among other things) the use of an "unauthorized aid." More blatant was the student who, though he had enough credits to graduate, decided to take one more course but not to do the work. Instead he offered the instructor a sum of money, "twice the going rate" (he said), for an A grade. His fate was expulsion. As I noted to the university lawyer, he "presumed upon the corruptibility of the institution" – my recognition at the time, I suppose, of the importance of institutional integrity. Although malice or desperation motivates some misconduct, sometimes it is the quiet voice of temptation, as with the graduate student who found a manuscript, unidentified, that could easily be turned into a thesis. The examining committee was impressed with the work, and only a guilty conscience eventually led to a confession – and a penalty that revoked the degree but recognized the value of voluntary repentance and disclosure.

6 This sovereignty is often seen as an expression of academic freedom, which I consider in Chapter Four. To anticipate, that freedom does not mean one can assign material and grades arbitrarily. Just as publications are open to peer assessment, so are teaching and grading. However, although universities have appeal procedures for students that provide for second readings and opinions in individual cases, it's difficult for the institution to review the persistent grading habits and practices of a faculty member.

3. Autonomy Is Precarious but Necessary

1 The use of "ivories" to denote piano keys, according to the Oxford English Dictionary, is found in Keats in 1818; its earliest citation for the phrase "tickle the ivories" is 1940, although *The Phrase Finder* has a 1906 citation – see http://www.phrases.org.uk/meanings/382150.html.
2 The beautiful beloved in Song of Solomon 7:4 has a neck like a tower of ivory; the image was later associated with the Virgin Mary.
3 Steven Shapin. "The Ivory Tower: The History of a Figure of Speech and Its Cultural Uses," *British Journal for the History of Science* 45, no. 1 (2012): 1–27, https://doi.org/10.1017/S0007087412000118.
4 As Shapin explains:

> Following the recent history of the Ivory Tower figure is a way of appreciating our connection to the long cultural tradition of debates over the relative merits – moral and intellectual – of the private and public lives. It situates us; it helps us to realize where our present categories and sensibilities have come from; it gives us a sense of belonging. And one thing that this historical sensibility throws into relief is that – I suggest – there has never been a historical moment in which the debate has been so one-sided. The finely poised classical conversation has turned into a monologue, even a rant. In the past, while you might express a preference for the one or the other, practically everyone acknowledged that both engagement and disengagement were necessary moments in human life and in the making of knowledge. It was recognized that neither could be wholly dispensed with, that there was moral and intellectual virtue in both. It could be said that you might, even should, come out of the Tower, but the injunction to leave the Tower at the same time identified its value. The modern monologue finds no worth in the Ivory Tower. The story it tells is historically uninformed and the institutional projects in which the monologue is embedded count as a grand experiment in the production and justification of knowledge which its projectors, and future generations, may come to regret. (Ibid., 26–7)

5 See Organisation for Economic Co-operation and Development, "What Are the Earnings Premiums from Education?" in *Education at a Glance* (Paris: OECD, 2011), available online at https://www.oecd.org/edu/skills-beyond-school/48630790.pdf. The report notes that "[a] person with a tertiary education can expect to earn over 50% more than a person with an upper secondary or postsecondary non-tertiary education" (138).

6 Alan Hughes argues that the Ivory Tower myth should be exploded, as restricting evidence of the relevance to such measures as start-ups and patents masks a great many social interactions between university and society: "Maintaining a strong pattern of knowledge exchange activities is closely connected to what may be termed the 'public space' role of universities: a forum in which a wide variety of individuals and organisations can interact and develop relationships." See Alan Hughes, "Exploding the Ivory Tower Myth," *University of Cambridge Research*, 17 May 2011, available online at http://www.cam.ac.uk/research/news/exploding-the-ivory-tower-myth.

7 In Chapter Seven I'll examine what the undergraduate experience should be.

8 The NSSE website explains what it means by engagement: "Student engagement represents two critical features of collegiate quality. The first is the amount of time and effort students put into their studies and other educationally purposeful activities. The second is how the institution deploys its resources and organizes the curriculum and other learning opportunities to get students to participate in activities that decades of research studies show are linked to student learning." See National Survey of Student Engagement, "About NSSE" (Indiana University, 2018), http://nsse.indiana.edu/html/about.cfm.

9 For comparisons across Ontario universities, see the website of the Council of Ontario Universities, http://cudo.ouac.on.ca/. The data on employment after six months and two years demonstrate high percentages, usually in the mid-90s, over the past many years; retention from year one to year two is also strong.

10 See United Kingdom, House of Commons, Business, Innovation and Skills Committee, "The Teaching Excellence Framework: Assessing Quality in Higher Education," 3rd Report, Session 2015–16 (London: Stationery Office, 2016), 5, available online at https://www.publications.parliament.uk/pa/cm201516/cmselect/cmbis/572/572.pdf. At the University of Cambridge, the template for new-taught course proposals includes a section titled "Graduate Employability and Career Destinations"; see University of Cambridge, "Educational and Student Policy," at http://www.educationalpolicy.admin.cam.ac.uk/quality-assurance/programme-specifications.

11 A sample: New Brunswick: *Post-Secondary Education, Training and Labour*; Nova Scotia: *Labour and Advanced Education*; Northwest Territories: *Education, Culture and Employment*; Ontario: *Advanced Education and Skills Development*, which has the motto, "Helping you get the education and training you need to build a rewarding career"; Prince Edward Island:

Workforce and Advanced Learning; Saskatchewan: *Advanced Education,*
which "is responsible for developing a skilled and educated workforce
that meets the needs of Saskatchewan's labour market."

In the United Kingdom, the current minister of state for universities,
science, research and innovation has responsibilities related to the
Department for Education and the Department for Business, Energy &
Industrial Strategy. And, as another example, the New York State Office
of Higher Education has as its first mandate to "[e]nsure that a high
quality postsecondary education is available to all that provides students
with the knowledge and skills to compete in a rapidly changing economy
and actively contribute to society"; see the website at http://www.
highered.nysed.gov/about.html.

12 Although I'm using glass as a metaphor here, it's worth noting that
much contemporary university construction uses the opaque material of
poured concrete and is merely functional in design. More about this in
Chapter Eight, on well-placed universities.

13 See European University Association, "University Autonomy in Europe,"
at http://www.university-autonomy.eu/. One study argues that these
four categories need to be supplemented by a series of five interfaces –
with government, management/staff, faculty/students, business and
internationalization – to create a holistic understanding of university
autonomy; see Romeo V. Turkan, John E. Reilly, and Larisa Bugaian, eds.
[Re]discovering University Autonomy (New York: Palgrave Macmillan,
2015).

14 Eric Havelock, a faculty member at Victoria University, was developing
a strong academic reputation in Classics and some notoriety for his
active involvement in socialist causes. His political involvement had
been the object of the displeasure of the provincial premier in 1932, but
the president of Victoria had defended his freedoms. In 1937, however,
Havelock spoke out in favour of auto workers, suggesting (falsely) that
the premier and some members of government had a pecuniary interest
in General Motors of Canada. The premier at the time, Mitch Hepburn,
made his displeasure known. After discussion with the president,
Havelock apologized to the premier and volunteered to stay away from
controversial issues. Although the board thought that Havelock had
overstepped the bounds of good judgment and was concerned about
the effects upon freedom of expression, he retained his position, later
moving to Harvard and ending up as the Sterling Professor of Classics at
Yale. See Michiel Horne, *Academic Freedom in Canada: A History* (Toronto:
University of Toronto Press, 1999), 111–14.

The second incident, in March 2017, occurred when the director of the Institute for the Study of Canada at McGill University resigned following the publication of an article critical of Quebec society. The premier of the province complained about the article, and the director apologized, but it seems that did not suffice. There was widespread belief that the university caved in to political pressure and abridged academic freedom; see "Globe editorial: Why did McGill fail to defend Andrew Potter's Academic Freedom?" *Globe and Mail*, 23 March 2017, online at http://www.theglobeandmail.com/opinion/editorials/ globe-editorial-why-did-mcgill-fail-to-defend-andrew-potters-academic-freedom/article34411662/. For further reaction, see Andrew Coyne, "This is not how a liberal society responds to criticism," *National Post*, 24 March 2017, online at http://news.nationalpost.com/full-comment/ andrew-coyne-quebecs-reaction-to-potters-critiques-shows-it-is-no-liberal-society. A contrary voice was that of political scientist Éric Montpetit: "the knowledge it presented was not validated in any way by university research. University professors should sign provocative articles only to the extent that research comes to provocative conclusions"; "After Potter: Media pool or knowledge institution? Universities can't be both," *Globe and Mail*, 29 March 2017, online at http://www.theglobeandmail.com/opinion/after-potter-media-pool-or-knowledge-institution-universities-cant-be-both/article34473173/. Nevertheless the controversy continued, with the *Globe and Mail* reporting the claim that Potter had been asked to resign – see Simona Chiose, "McGill Principal wanted Potter to resign, former trustee says," *Globe and Mail*, 18 May 2017, online at https://www.theglobeandmail. com/news/national/andrew-potter-was-forced-to-resign-from-mcgill-institute-former-director/article35042841/. Peter MacKinnon discusses this incident in *University Commons Divided*, 53–5, 114.

15 Early on, the Crown had a determining hand in university decisions. For instance, the Royal Charter of McGill College (1852) granted by Queen Victoria established a board of governors that elected the principal and professors, but the Crown retained the right to "disapprove of any person so elected," who would cease to hold the position upon being informed of this disapprobation. The language may be of interest:

provided always, that the persons by whom such election shall be made shall notify the same respectively to Us, Our Heirs and Successors, through one of Our or Their principal Secretaries of State, by the first opportunity, and in case that We, Our Heirs, or Successors shall disapprove of any person so elected, and shall cause such disapprobation to be notified to him under the Royal signet and sign manual, or through one of the principal Secretaries of State, the person so elected as aforesaid shall immediately upon such notification, cease to hold the office of Principal or Professor to which he shall have been elected as aforesaid, and the said Governors shall thereupon proceed to the election of another person to fill the office of such Principal or Professor respectively, and so, from time to time, as often as the case shall happen. (McGill University, "The Royal Charter of McGill University," https://www.mcgill.ca/secretariat/charter-statutes/royal.)

To allay any concern, I add that the current Statutes of McGill University do not contain this provision.

The Crown's hand was not always present, however. In the case of my own institution, Victoria University, its charter (as the Upper Canada Academy) from King William IV in 1836 granted the right to appoint trustees, not to the Crown, but to an annual meeting of ministers of the Wesleyan Methodist Church in Upper Canada; and it forbade any religious test for students or teachers. The 1841 provincial act to incorporate the Academy as Victoria College created an academic senate, placing authority to confer degrees with the president and professors. See *The Provincial Statutes of Canada* (Kingston, ON: S. Derbishire & G. Desbarats, Law Printer to the Queen's Most Excellent Majesty, 1841), chap. 37.

16 Glen Jones, "Governments, Governance, and Canadian Universities," in *Higher Education: Handbook of Theory and Research* 11 (New York: Agathon Press, 1966), 363.

17 In April 2018 the Alberta government announced that executive compensation for universities and colleges would be capped – see "Alberta cuts pay, benefits for presidents of colleges and universities," *Calgary Herald*, 10 April 2018, available online at http://calgaryherald. com/pmn/news-pmn/canada-news-pmn/alberta-cuts-pay-benefits- for-presidents-of-colleges-and-universities/wcm/e9e4dd99-825b-4fa6- 915e-f96d1bc9731c, accessed 18 April 2018. A comparison of publicly available information shows that the total compensation for the president of the largest Alberta university was 66 per cent greater than that of the president of Canada's largest university.

18 For Ontario universities, tuition in academic year 2013–14 accounted for 52 per cent of their operating budgets; see Higher Education Quality Council of Ontario, "The Ontario University Funding

Model in Context" (Toronto, June 2015), figure 3, available online at http://www.heqco.ca/SiteCollectionDocuments/Contextual%20 Background%20to%20the%20Ontario%20University%20 Funding%20Formula-English.pdf. According to one source, the US average is about 47 per cent – see Kelly Woodhouse, "Public Colleges' Revenue Shift," *Inside Higher Ed*, 13 April 2015, available online at https://www.insidehighered.com/news/2015/04/13/ report-shows-public-higher-educations-reliance-tuition.

19 This led to a difficult situation when the Privacy Commission ordered the University of Toronto to disclose certain documentation which was the property of Victoria University, documentation over which the U of T had no control. As a federated university, Victoria did not come under the jurisdiction of the Commission at that time, but it took some effort to sort this out.

20 The regulations now specify that the rules for approving and reimbursing expenses for alcohol must be very specific.

21 For the University of Toronto, see the University of Toronto Act, 1978, 2.14 (c), where the governing council has the power to "fix the number, the duties and the salaries and other emoluments of officers and employees of the University and University College."

22 Ontario, Auditor General, *Annual Report 2012* (Toronto: Queen's Printer for Ontario, 2012), chap. 3, sect. 3.12, "University Undergraduate Teaching Quality," available online at http://www.auditor.on.ca/en/ content/annualreports/arreports/en12/312en12.pdf.

23 Ontario, Auditor General, *Annual Report 2014* (Toronto: Queen's Printer for Ontario, 2014), chap. 4, sect. 4.11, "University Undergraduate Teaching Quality," available online at http://www.auditor.on.ca/en/ content/annualreports/arreports/en14/411en14.pdf.

24 The scheme was widely reported in the media; see, for example, Kristen Rushowy, "Ontario universities should offer three-year degrees, classes year-round and more online learning, says provincial report," *Toronto Star*, 22 February 2012, available online at https://www.thestar .com/news/canada/2012/02/22/ontario_universities_should_offer _threeyear_degrees_classes_yearround_and_more_online_learning _says_provincial_report.html.

25 In this case there was a strong response, especially from the president of the University of Toronto; see David Naylor, "Strengthening Ontario's Centres of Creativity, Innovation and Knowledge" (Toronto: University of Toronto, 1 October 2012, available online at https://www.scribd.com/document/109358709/

University-of-Toronto-s-Response-to-MTCU-Discussion-Paper
-October-1-2012.

26 In justifying this extended mandate, the website of the provincial
ombudsman states that it had received a record seventy-two complaints
in the previous year – about student aid, accommodation, program
requirements, policies on marking, sexual harassment, services with
respect to disabilities, staffing issues, and accountability mechanisms. It
also points out that the office has experience with colleges, so it can deal
with universities – ignoring the different legal status of universities as
autonomous entities with their own boards and powers.

27 "In exercising his or her authority under this Act with respect to
universities, the Ombudsman shall consider the application of the
principles of academic freedom within universities" (The Ombudsman
Act, 2014, c. 13, sched. 9, s. 15).

28 It will occur to the reader that, strictly speaking, an ombudsman is
independent of government. But then-treasury board president Deb
Matthews (afterwards minister of advanced education and skills
development) said in introducing the bill that this would "help further
public trust and confidence in government" – not in universities, but in
government. According to the record, her comments went beyond the
actual legislation. She said: "If our bill is passed, the Ombudsman would
be *required to respect* the principles of academic freedom when conducting
investigations. These principles are vital to the mission of universities to
educate and enrich the minds of young people" (emphasis added).

29 In a speech on the bill, the minister of state for universities, science,
research and innovation referred to his count of 215 peers with
university interests; see Jo Johnson, "Higher Education and Research
Bill" (speech to the Universities UK members' conference, 24 February
2017), available online at https://www.gov.uk/government/speeches/
jo-johnson-higher-education-and-research-bill.

30 A statement on the functions of universities, introduced by Lord
Stevenson of Balmacara on 9 January 2017 as an amendment to the
government's Higher Education and Research Bill; see United Kingdom,
Parliament, House of Lords, *Hansard*, 9 January 2017, available online at
https://hansard.parliament.uk/lords/2017-01-09/debates/6293833B
-6057-4EB1-B646-4794DE004A3F/HigherEducationAndResearchBill.
The other four functions in the amendment were:

(2) UK universities must ensure that they promote freedom of thought
and expression, and freedom from discrimination. (3) UK universities

must provide an extensive range of high quality academic subjects delivered by excellent teaching, supported by scholarship and research, through courses which enhance the ability of students to learn throughout their lives. (4) UK universities must make a contribution to society through the pursuit, dissemination, and application of knowledge and expertise locally, nationally and internationally; and through partnerships with business, charitable foundations, and other organisations, including other colleges and universities. (5) UK universities must be free to act as critics of government and the conscience of society.

The third point about an "extensive range" of subjects attracted criticism from those advocating specialist institutions. Since I am considering autonomy here, the discussion concerns only this issue.

31 The whole debate, found in ibid., is worth perusing for its unusual defence of university autonomy.

32 Johnson, "Higher Education and Research Bill."

33 See, for example, University of Toronto, Office of the Vice-President & Provost, "Provost's Guidelines on Donations," rev. 30 April 1998, available online at http://www.provost.utoronto.ca/policy/donations.htm, and the additional documents on advisory committees and naming referred to that memorandum.

34 See Ian Binnie, "Judicial Independence in Canada" (paper submitted to the World Conference on Constitutional Justice on behalf of the Supreme Court of Canada in anticipation of its Second Congress, Rio de Janeiro, 16–18 January 2011), 34, available online at http://www.venice.coe.int/WCCJ/Rio/Papers/CAN_Binnie_E.pdf.

4. Academic Freedom Is Necessary and Messy

1 The declaration was the work of Eleanor Roosevelt and a Canadian lawyer, John Humphrey. The three articles referred to read this way:

(18). Everyone has the right to freedom of thought, conscience and religion; this right includes freedom to change his religion or belief, and freedom, either alone or in community with others and in public or private, to manifest his religion or belief in teaching, practice, worship and observance.

(19). Everyone has the right to freedom of opinion and expression; this right includes freedom to hold opinions without interference and to seek, receive and impart information and ideas through any media and regardless of frontiers.

(20). (1) Everyone has the right to freedom of peaceful assembly and association. (2) No one may be compelled to belong to an association.

2 The ability to form unions and other economic or political groups generates the concern for freedom of association. But surely the issue can be construed more generally: denial of the ability to form social groupings of whatever nature is a restriction on the expression of human need and desire for sociality.

3 In Canada and the United States, the freedoms of research and publication would descend from the constitutional freedom of expression. But in some European countries, the constitutional guarantee of free research is more explicit. For instance, article 5 of the German Constitution states that "Art and science, research and teaching are free," article 33 of the Italian Constitution establishes that "The arts and sciences as well as their teaching are free," and article 59 of the Slovenian Constitution states that "Freedom of scientific research and artistic endeavor shall be guaranteed." See Amedeo Santosuosso, Valentina Sellaroli, and Elisabetta Fabio, "What Constitutional Protection for Freedom of Scientific Research?" *Journal of Medical Ethics* 33, no. 6 (2007): 342–4, available online at https://www.ncbi.nlm.nih.gov/pmc/articles/PMC2598288/?report=classic.

4 The Supreme Court of Canada ruled in 1990 that universities are not agents of government. Eight faculty members and a librarian had appealed to the Court claiming that mandatory retirement had abrogated their Charter rights to equal treatment. In *Mckinney* v. *University of Guelph*, [1990] 3 S.C.R. 229, the Justices wrote:

The wording of s. 32(1) of the *Charter* indicates that the *Charter* is confined to government action. It is essentially an instrument for checking the powers of government over the individual. The exclusion of private activity from *Charter* protection was deliberate. To open up all private and public action to judicial review could strangle the operation of society and impose an impossible burden on the courts. Only government need be constitutionally shackled to preserve the rights of the individual. Private activity, while it might offend individual rights, can either be regulated by government or made subject to human rights commissions and other bodies created to protect these rights. This Court, in limiting the *Charter's*

application to Parliament and the legislatures and the executive and
administrative branches of government in *RWDSU v. Dolphin Delivery
Ltd.*, [1986] 2 S.C.R. 573, relied not only on the general meaning of
government but also on the way in which the words were used in the
Constitution Act, 1867.

5 Hardy E. Jones, "Academic Freedom as a Moral Right," in *The Concept of
Academic Freedom*, ed. Edmund L. Pincoffs (Austin: University of Texas
Press, 1975), 37–51. In the same volume, Judith Jarvis Thompson sets
out the principle that "it is both irrational and unjust to employ a person
to do a thing and then to prevent him from doing it"; see Thompson,
"Academic Freedom and Research," 264. From this it follows that no
university may threaten or sanction a faculty member for teaching,
research and publication in accordance with the truth as the faculty
member sees it.

6 In cases of alleged gross misconduct, the reputation of the university
is sometimes cited as a reason for discipline, but reputation can also
be affected by allegedly outrageous but supportable ideas of a faculty
member. It's not so much the reputation of the university as what that
reputation *is for*. Is it a secure environment? Is it financially sound? Is it
supportive of critical reflection? Those are the issues to be addressed, not
"reputation" by itself.

7 See their respective statements on their websites at https://www.caut.
ca/about-us/caut-policy/lists/caut-policy-statements/policy-statement-
on-tenure and https://www.aaup.org/issues/tenure.

8 See that popular source of wisdom, Wikipedia, under Academic Tenure:
"However, in institutions without tenure systems, academic freedom
and the ability to espouse non-conformist views are afforded no
protections.[citation needed]." The lack of a citation may be telling.

9 For a popular news item, see Ira Basen, "Most university undergraduates
now taught by poorly paid part-timers," *CBC News*, 7 September 2014,
available online at http://www.cbc.ca/news/canada/most-university-
undergrads-now-taught-by-poorly-paid-part-timers-1.2756024.

10 Statistics Canada has announced it will address this lack in the near
future; see Simona Chiose, "Statistics Canada to tally number of contract,
part-time professors," *Globe and Mail*, 15 September 2016, available online
at https://www.theglobeandmail.com/news/national/education/
statistics-canada-to-tally-number-of-contract-part-time-professors/
article31922546/; and Statistics Canada, "UCASS revisited." StatCan

Blog, 18 January 2018, available online at https://www.statcan.gc.ca/eng/blog/cs/ucass-revisited.

11 Personal experience testifies to this. When a faculty member, part-time and untenured, made unwise and provocative comments about his curricular choices (middle-aged male writers) to a young reporter, those comments went viral on social media, and the international press picked up the story. Members of the English department, of which he is not one, issued public condemnations, and there were calls to fire him. Misinformation about the issue was rampant. The immediacy of social media, combined with its inability to communicate effectively in more than a sentence or two, resulted in the widespread belief that students were forced to take his course, that the entire literature curriculum was made up of this one course, and that the instructor, a widely acclaimed novelist whose work was internationally praised, was unqualified to teach undergraduates as a part-time contract lecturer.

As the story unfolded, the most measured responses came, in fact, from students who had studied with him. The facts were that this course was approved by College Council; it was an elective; it was not part of any program requirement; it was typically oversubscribed, with a wait list; and most of the students were women.

Although the instructor's comments to the interviewer were unwise and sensational, I found no reason to suspend or fire him, or to refuse to have him continue his part-time position. The episode reminded me that both internal pressures and external outcries (the story was revived in the press a year later) require effective application of policies and practices concerning academic freedom and integrity. It's also a good example of an issue of academic freedom for non-tenured part-time instructors.

12 This is the case with teaching stream professors at the University of Toronto. In the United Kingdom, academics have not had tenure since 20 November 1987, when it was abolished in the Education Reform Act; see Geraint G. Howells, "Conditions of Employment for Academics," *Northern Ireland Legal Quarterly* 39 (1988): 393–401. Whether academic freedom has been eroded in succeeding decades may be difficult to discern – and whether lack of tenure has had anything to do with particular cases.

13 See University of Toronto Academic Librarians, "Intellectual and Academic Freedom," online at https://utlibrarians.wordpress.com/intellectual-freedom/.

14 "Faculty members and university leaders have an obligation to ensure that students' human rights are respected and that they are

encouraged to pursue their education according to the principles of academic freedom"; see Universities Canada, "Statement on Academic Freedom," 25 October 2011, available online at https://www.univcan.ca/media-room/media-releases/statement-on-academic-freedom/.

In 2010 Cary Nelson, president of the American Association of University Professors, expressed a very expansive view of academic freedom as applied to students: "students and faculty the right to express their views – in speech, writing, and through electronic communication, both on and off campus – without fear of sanction." Again, academic freedom gives "students and faculty the right to study and do research on the topics they choose." And academic freedom, he claimed, "gives faculty members and students the right to seek redress or request a hearing if they believe their rights have been violated." See Cary Nelson, "Defining Academic Freedom," *Inside Higher Ed*, 21 December 2010, available online at https://www.insidehighered.com/views/2010/12/21/defining-academic-freedom.

15 For a long article on the subject in the US context, see American Association of University Professors, "Academic Freedom of Students and Professors, and Political Discrimination" (Washington, DC: AAUP, n.d.), available online at https://www.aaup.org/academic-freedom-students-and-professors-and-political-discrimination. Some of the examples discussed are instances of freedom of speech, rather than of academic freedom.

16 I had to deal with something like this case as vice-provost – mentioned in note 4 of Chapter Two. It turned out that the faculty member had indeed falsified evidence, and was dismissed. The students exercised their own academic judgment about the material and courageously counted upon the integrity of the institution to support them.

17 Sometimes universities mix up an administrative contract and academic tenure, as when a dean is removed for insubordination but also dismissed from an academic position. One such case in a Canadian province in 2014 provoked public discussion of the nature of the freedom of a dean to criticize the administration. On the view developed here, this freedom is conferred upon an individual as a faculty member, not as a dean. The Canadian Association of University Teachers has a statement on academic freedom for administrators that does not separate these roles, but they are indeed different; see Canadian Association of University Teachers (CAUT), "Academic Freedom for Academic Administrators," November 2010, available online at https://

www.caut.ca/about-us/caut-policy/lists/caut-policy-statements/
policy-statement-on-academic-freedom-for-academic-administrators.

Just because administrators don't have the immunity of academic
freedom doesn't mean they can be treated arbitrarily. Any president
who exercises arbitrary power won't be long tolerated in a university.
That brings to mind an exchange witnessed in the youth of my
administrative life, in which the president ordered deans to make certain
budget cuts. One dean demanded discussion and negotiation instead of
commandments, pointing out that even Moses argued with the Lord. If
divine authority is exercised non-arbitrarily, how much more should that
be true of presidential power?

18 The clause in the Universities Canada "Statement on Academic
Freedom," "Academic freedom is constrained by the professional
standards of the relevant discipline," should not be read as constraining
the ability of a faculty member to work beyond a particular discipline
or to question the received views within a discipline. The Statement
adds that "professional standards" refers to the "rigour of the inquiry" –
presumably to what counts as sound evidence and good reasoning
within a particular context.

19 Definitions by several Canadian universities include the freedom
to criticize the institution and society at large, as does the definition
of the CAUT, "Academic Freedom for Academic Administrators."
The Universities Canada "Statement on Academic Freedom" omits –
unfortunately, as I now believe – mention of this aspect of academic
freedom; perhaps the membership, made up of presidents, had too much
experience of criticism that was not always constructive. In the United
States, there is a long history of intramural and extramural freedoms.

20 "Academic staff must not be hindered or impeded in exercising their civil
rights as individuals including the right to contribute to social change
through free expression of opinion on matters of public interest"; CAUT,
"Academic Freedom for Academic Administrators," section 4.

21 The American Association of University Professors (AAUP), "1940
Statement of Principles on Academic Freedom and Tenure," includes
the sentence, with respect to extramural speech, that faculty members
"should make every effort to indicate that they are not speaking for the
institution."

22 That is, the conditions for imposing discipline must be the same as
those for the core academic freedoms discussed above. See Matthew
W. Finkin and Robert C. Post, *For the Common Good: Principles of*

American Academic Freedom (New Haven, CT: Yale University Press, 2009), chap. 6, where they state: "The upshot of this reasoning is that extramural speech cannot be disciplined unless it bears on professional competence" (148).

23 The term "extramural" must not be taken literally. A faculty member could criticize society or government inside the walls, so to speak – at some university event. And it's not simply that the normal provisions of "intramural" academic freedom are extended outside the walls; what's protected, it's claimed, is expression that has little to do with one's academic competence.

24 A fairly expansive statement of responsibilities can be found in the University of Toronto's Memorandum of Agreement between the University and the Faculty Association:

> (a) A faculty member shall carry out his or her responsibility for teaching with all due attention to the establishment of fair and ethical dealings with students, taking care to make himself or herself accessible to students for academic consultation, to inform students adequately regarding course formats, assignments, and methods of evaluation, to maintain teaching schedules in all but exceptional circumstances, to inform students adequately of any necessary cancellation and rescheduling of instructions and to comply with established procedures and deadlines for determining, reporting and reviewing the grades of his or her students.
>
> (b) A faculty member shall be entitled to and be expected to devote a reasonable proportion of his or her time to research and scholarly or creative professional work. He or she shall endeavour to make the results of such work accessible to the scholarly and general public through publications, lectures and other appropriate means. Faculty shall, in published works, indicate any reliance on the work and assistance of academic colleagues and students.
>
> (c) Service to the University of Toronto is performed by faculty members through participation in the decision-making councils of the University of Toronto, and through sharing in the necessary administrative work of their Departments, Faculties, the University of Toronto or the Association. In performance of these collegial and administrative activities, faculty members shall deal fairly and ethically with their colleagues, shall objectively assess the performance of their colleagues, shall avoid discrimination, shall not infringe their colleagues' academic freedom, and shall observe appropriate principles of confidentiality.

25 A sample of statements:

- From the University of Minnesota Board of Regents Policy on
  Academic Freedom and Responsibility: "Academic responsibility
  implies the faithful performance of professional duties and
  obligations, the recognition of the demands of the scholarly
  enterprise, and the candor to make it clear that when one is speaking
  on matters of public interest, one is not speaking for the institution."
- From the Tennessee Board of Regents System statement: "Hence,
  a faculty member should at all times be accurate, should exercise
  appropriate restraint, should show respect for the opinions of others,
  and should make every effort to indicate that he/she does not speak
  for the university/college."
- From the University of Manitoba: those with academic freedom
  "should not state or imply that they speak for the University or any of
  its units unless duly authorized."
- From the Universities Canada statement on academic freedom:
  "Universities must also ensure that the rights and freedoms of others
  are respected, and that academic freedom is exercised in a reasonable
  and responsible manner."

26 In an article in *Maclean's* magazine "correcting" the Statement, a faculty
    member at Cape Breton University edited out this sentence; see Todd
    Pettigrew, "A lesson for presidents on academic freedom," *Maclean's*, 31
    October 2011, available online at https://www.macleans.ca/education/
    uniandcollege/a-lesson-for-university-presidents-on-academic-
    freedom/. CAUT's response to the Statement asked, on this point,
    "by whose definition?" of excess and looseness; see Canadian Association
    of University Teachers, "Open Letter to the Association of Universities
    and Colleges of Canada," 4 November 2011, available online at https://
    www.caut.ca/docs/default-document-library/caut_to_aucc_academic
    _freedom.pdf?sfvrsn=0.
27 To stay with Canadian examples: the University of Ottawa cancelled
    a presentation by a right-wing American speaker; see "Coulter's
    Ottawa speech cancelled," *CBC News*, 23 March 2010, available online
    at http://www.cbc.ca/news/canada/ottawa/coulter-s-ottawa-speech-
    cancelled-1.947821. At the University of Alberta, students protested an
    anti-abortion display; see Maya Gwilliam, "Students protest 'graphic'
    pro-life display at U of Alberta," *Charlatan*, 11 March 2015, available
    online at http://charlatan.ca/2015/03/students-protest-graphic-pro-
    life-display-at-u-of-alberta/. At the University of Prince Edward Island,

the president removed an issue of the student paper that reprinted Danish anti-Muslim cartoons; see "Student paper surrenders edition with cartoons of Prophet Muhammad," *CBC News*, 10 February 2006, available online at http://www.cbc.ca/news/canada/prince-edward-island/student-paper-surrenders-edition-with-cartoons-of-prophet-muhammad-1.594293. Peter MacKinnon explores several Canadian examples of the challenges of free expression in *University Commons Divided*, chap. 3. Other countries will have their own instances, especially the United States since the election of Donald Trump.

28 In one memorable example of silent protest, several University of Toronto faculty members attended, in full academic regalia, a special convocation to award an honorary degree to George H.W. Bush in 1997. Led by the redoubtable Ursula Franklin, twenty-seven of them stood up in protest and walked out silently as the citation was read. "Dr. Franklin exited, waving her cap to a thousand cheering protesters and the world's media. 'It was good television,' she said." The event is recounted at Michael Valpy, "Ursula Franklin was renowned for her devotion to science, pacifism and education," *Globe and Mail*, 26 July 2016, available online at http://www.theglobeandmail.com/news/national/ursula-franklin-canadian-scientist-and-activist-had-a-passion-for-peace/article31123033/, though the venue was the Great Hall at Hart House, not Convocation Hall.

29 A recent disruption at Middlebury College in Vermont is but one example: see "Smothering speech at Middlebury," editorial, *New York Times*, 7 March 2017, available online at https://www.nytimes.com/2017/03/07/opinion/smothering-speech-at-middlebury.html. A University of Chicago committee is proposing ways to deal with disrupters; see Colleen Flaherty, "Dealing with Disruptors," *Inside Higher Ed*, 22 March 2017, available online at https://www.insidehighered.com/news/2017/03/22/u-chicago-committee-proposes-ways-dealing-those-who-shout-down-invited-speakers?utm_source=Inside+Higher+Ed&utm_campaign=30997fcc4d-DNU20170322&utm_medium=email&utm_term=0_1fcbc04421-30997fcc4d-.

30 When an annual student revue long beloved of alumni was about to include nudity, the issue was resolved not by fiat but by dialogue among producers and the office of the dean of students. More generally, I attempted, not very successfully, to encourage student clubs and societies to invite as a mentor or advisor a trusted faculty member who shared their interests. One positive outcome was the inclusion, on the student newspaper board, of an alumna/us in the media business.

31 A defensible reason to remove an issue would be a claim that an article
    had no effect beyond expressing and provoking hatred and prejudice,
    a claim one could make about the republishing of the Danish cartoons
    mentioned in note 29 above.

32 In February 2006, the Victoria University student newspaper, the
    Strand, published a cartoon with two figures in a swan boat entering
    a Tunnel of Tolerance. They were bearded men, one identified with a
    small crescent and the other with a cross. A few months previously,
    those cartoons of the Prophet published by a Danish newspaper,
    mentioned above, had attracted worldwide attention, anger, and
    condemnation. On 4 February the Vatican issued a statement about
    respect for religions and UN Secretary General Kofi Annan appealed
    for calm. (For an exhaustive listing of reactions after the 30 September
    2005 publication of the cartoons, see https://en.wikipedia.org/wiki/
    Timeline_of_the_Jyllands-Posten_Muhammad_cartoons_controversy.)
       The editors of the *Strand* had not consulted with me or any
    administrator, but they had debated this action and written a long
    explanation and justification in the publication – the gist of which was
    the desire to stimulate debate on tolerance. The effect, however fervently
    desired, was very little tolerance and a great deal of outrage and anger.
    The managing editor of the paper found himself in the national media,
    and I was the recipient of scores and scores of emails, many of which were
    anything but polite. There were demands that I remove the issue from
    circulation. Interestingly, the demands within the university came not just
    from the Muslim student society, but also from the central U of T student
    administrative council. (The cartoon itself, and an account of reactions, can
    be found at http://www.wnd.com/2006/02/34902/.) After consulting
    with the president and provost at U of T, I issued a statement in support of
    the *Strand* on the grounds of freedom of expression; it counselled respect
    for differences and the balancing of freedom with responsibility.

33 The claim of a graduate student in "Beyond Posturing," *Bulletin*
    (University of Toronto), 6 March 2006; it arose in the context of the
    incident mentioned in the previous note. The five paragraphs following
    this quotation reflect my response, "Civil Discourse Is Free Discourse,"
    Bulletin, 27 March 2006.

34 An example from my own history is my deciding that there is no duty to
    rent to outside groups a university theatre for a beauty pageant or for the
    screening of a feminist porn film. The wide world provides all sorts of
    material on which students may hone their minds in intelligent analysis
    and critique.

35 This is far too simple a dichotomy, but conservative religion tends to think of this knowledge as propositional dogma, whereas liberal religion is more concerned with knowledge as relational and open.

36 I prefer the phrase "religiously oriented" to a description sometimes employed: "faith based." That expression trades on the faith/reason dichotomy, suggesting that certain convictions are to be "taken on faith," rather than the subject of careful investigation. The implications for academic freedom are obvious. Perhaps some theological colleges are "faith based" in that sense, but that's not true of all religiously oriented schools.

37 Perhaps I'm being too prescriptive here, in arguing that such institutions should be called by other names: theological schools, bible colleges, yeshivas, madrassas, or seminaries. (The root of the word "seminary" is "seed," and one plants seeds in order to get a desired crop.) But note that I am *not at all* suggesting that all theological institutions called by names like this never have autonomy or that they deny their members academic freedom. Institutions are called by their names for historic reasons. Calling an institution a university doesn't make it one; and I stress again that using a term like "seminary" of a school does not entail that it lacks in actual practice autonomy or academic freedom.

38 This view was worked out in practice in 1988 during the University of Toronto negotiations with the member institutions of the Toronto School of Theology for a renewal of the agreement governing, in the main, the conjoint awarding of degrees. Academic freedom was a matter of concern in those negotiations: a couple of faculty members had silently been relocated from one seminary, and it wasn't clear that every member institution had policies that enshrined academic freedom. It was a condition of the agreement, then, that every member institution had to abide by the principles of academic freedom. In particular, each was required to amend its by-laws to include guarantees of dismissal only for adequate cause as defined in the U of T policy, and to act only on the principles and practices of peer adjudication as at U of T. There was agreement that institutions could hire on mission, but once a faculty member was appointed, all the provisions of academic freedom and peer review would come into play. These conditions have safeguarded academic freedom in theology at Toronto for three decades.

39 This isn't the same as John Stuart Mill's critique of voluntary slavery in *On Liberty*, chap. 5, where he claims that the freedom to surrender all freedoms is a contradiction of the very principle of freedom. In the practice I'm referring to, one surrenders only academic freedom. But for an institution to require this surrender from its members and

to claim some residual form of academic freedom would indeed be a contradiction, for it requires acceptance of some authority's decree that a set of beliefs cannot be interrogated. In fact, theology is not different from other disciplines; its history has ample evidence of ideas contested, refined, abandoned, or renewed.

40 AAUP, "1940 Statement," endnote 5. Interestingly, the American Bar Association's 2016–17 statement on academic freedom repeats the 1940 AAUP reference to limitations on academic freedom without mentioning the revision now almost fifty years ago; see American Bar Association, *ABA Standards and Rules of Procedure for Approval of Law Schools 2016-2017* (Chicago: ABA, 2016), appendix 1, available online at http://www.americanbar.org/content/dam/aba/publications/misc/legal_education/Standards/2016_2017_standards_appendices.authcheckdam.pdf.

41 Of course, there can be dismissal for just cause. But cases can be complicated. For a hypothetical example, a faculty member, having initially agreed with an institution's conservative Christian view of marriage, might have struggled with sexual identity and concluded that same-sex marriage was permissible under certain interpretations of Scripture. If that faculty member married a partner, the only "just cause" (assuming academic competence) would be on presumed ethical grounds. It's very difficult to imagine how such a charge could be substantiated without appeal to institutional authority to interpret the issue. That sits ill with academic freedom.

42 Only a little investigation will reveal how Jews were excluded from faculty positions in major universities in the United States and Canada before post–Second World War human rights legislation.

43 There are good theological arguments for the academic freedom I set out in this chapter. One rests on the epistemological humility of the faithful, who constantly must seek divine wisdom without claiming to own it. Another stems, for Christians, from an understanding of work of the Spirit in providing new insights in new circumstances – about which I've written in "Paul, the Mind of Christ and Philosophy," in *Jesus and Philosophy: New Essays*, ed. Paul Moser (Cambridge: Cambridge University Press, 2009), 84–105; and in "Conscience and the Voice of God: Faithful Discernment," in *The Testimony of the Spirit: New Essays*, ed. Doug Geivett and Paul Moser (New York: Oxford University Press, 2016), 66–86.

44 Since this section was written, Peter MacKinnon has discussed this issue directly with respect to Trinity Western University's plans for a law school; see *University Commons Divided*, chap. 5. On 15 June 2018 the Supreme Court of Canada ruled against the university, whose

Community Covenant requires all members to abstain from "sexual intimacy that violates the sacredness of marriage between a man and a woman." On 9 August 2018 Trinity Western University announced that the Covenant will no longer be mandatory for students; see Trinity Western University, "TWU Reviews Community Covenant," *News*, 14 August 2018, available online at https://www.twu.ca/twu-reviews-community-covenant. The requirement continues for faculty and staff.

45 As one example of how this might be done, see Notre Dame Law School's statements:

> Notre Dame Law School is committed to building an inclusive community and welcomes all people, regardless of gender (including identity and expression), religion, race, ethnicity, sexual orientation, social or economic class, nationality, disability, or age …
>
> The Law School welcomes people of all faiths and religions. At the same time, consistent with American Bar Association Standard 205, the Law School reserves its right under the law to make hiring, admission, and other decisions in accord with its Catholic identity and its mission as a Catholic institution. In addition, the Law School reserves all other legal rights as a religious institution.

See https://law.nd.edu/assets/183656/classprofile_2015.pdf. The American Bar Association Standard 205 (c) includes non-discrimination: "These policies may provide a preference for persons adhering to the religious affiliation or purpose of the law school, but may not be applied to use admission policies or take other action to preclude admission of applicants or retention of students on the basis of race, color, religion, national origin, gender, sexual orientation, age, or disability." See ABA, *ABA Standards and Rules of Procedure*, 11, available online at https://www.americanbar.org/content/dam/aba/publications/misc/legal_education/Standards/2017-2018ABAStandardsforApprovalofLaw Schools/2017_2018_standards_chapter2.authcheckdam.pdf.

5. Decision Making Is Complicated: Boards, Colleagues, Presidents, Peers

1 The title of dean is especially confusing to those outside the academy. I've used it of the head of a faculty, as in Dean of Social Sciences, but in North America there are also deans of students, who deal with "student life," with no academic authority per se. Other decanal titles within universities

include deans of chapel, with ecclesiastical and pastoral responsibilities. Oxford has deans of hall and deans of degrees; Edinburgh has international deans for various regions of the globe. The Oxford English Dictionary gives a fuller account of the origin of the term from the Latin *decanus*, the head of a group of ten; the current use descends from eighth-century monastic use, in which a dean had charge of a group of monks and reported to a provost as the bishop's vice-regent. The Oxford English Dictionary makes no reference to deans of students.

2 This was the average age of completion for Canadian students in 2005; see Statistics Canada, "Doctoral Graduates in Canada 2004/2005," *Education Matters* 5, no. 2 (2008), available online at http://www.statcan. gc.ca/pub/81-004-x/2008002/article/10645-eng.htm.

3 As I wrote this, the *Guardian* reported the view of immunologist Bruno Lemaitre that science has been infected by narcissistic personalities who seek out status more than rigorous methods which might result in unspectacular results. Lemaitre is quoted as saying, "[t]he reliance on peer review for publishing papers and awarding grants allows narcissists, characterised by a Machiavellian ability to manipulate others, to network their way to success"; see Hannah Devlin, "Science falling victim to 'crisis of narcissism,'" *Guardian*, 20 January 2017, available online at https://www.theguardian.com/science/2017/jan/20/ science-victim-crisis-narcissism-academia.

4 Who knows, if the figures are taken at face value, what they really signify about quality? High applications to programs might be indications of popularity and accessibility; low retention and graduation rates might arise from student financial constraints; lower cost per student might signal an inferior classroom experience.

5 In some jurisdictions (Alberta, for instance, or the University of Cambridge) what's called a senate has no significant role to play in academic governance; that responsibility belongs to a body of appointed or elected persons the majority of whom are faculty members. Board members may be termed trustees, governors, or regents. The language of senate/board is typical of North American universities; British universities tend to refer to senate and council (although Oxford and Cambridge vest academic and temporal authority in a single council with a minority of lay members). The University of Toronto's unicameral system treats academic matters in an academic board, and general oversight in a governing council (which has delegated final approval of academic matters to the academic board, which has 88 teaching staff, and only 19 of 123 members who are members of the governing council).

6 See Craig Heron, "From Deference to Defiance: The Evolution of Ontario Faculty Associations," *Academic Matters*, Spring–Summer 2015, 15–20, available online at https://academicmatters.ca/2015/06/from-deference-to-defiance-the-evolution-of-ontario-faculty-associations/. Heron argues that there never was a golden age. He also reports that 80 per cent of Canadian faculty associations are unionized. The debate over unionization is not new. Arthur O. Lovejoy argued in 1938 that the similarities in the working conditions of professors and trade workers were superficial, and that trade unions were inappropriate forms of organization for faculty members. See "Professional Association or Trade Union?" *Bulletin of the American Association of University Professors (1915–1955)* 24, no. 5 (1938): 409–17.

7 That is not to say that students are incapable of understanding some academic issues better than do faculty members. When my college council debated a resolution to require all students to include a small seminar course in their first-year course selection, the students carried the day against faculty who preferred not to constrain choice. The students believed from their own experience that a mere recommendation would not work.

8 See Amitai Etzioni, "The Limits of Transparency," *Public Administration Review* 74, no. 6 (2014): 687–8; and idem, "Is Transparency the Best Disinfectant?" *Journal of Political Philosophy* 18, no. 4 (2010): 389–404, available online at https://www2.gwu.edu/~ccps/etzioni/documents/295Transparency.pdf.

9 Ontario requires annual publication of the lists of employees of publicly funded institutions who earn $100,000 or more. The press reports each year the top few salaries, but for universities the main effect of this mandate is to pique curiosity about one's relative standing and to generate peer envy. It's tempting to reflect on the cultural shift about openness and privacy: fifty years ago University of Toronto students discovered their grades – and relative standing in their class – by reading the published examination results in the press. Privacy concerns now protect university student grades even from parents. Toronto was, of course, simply following longstanding Oxbridge tradition – so hoary that Oxford agreed to abolish public posting in 2009, and Cambridge abandoned the practice only in 2016. The protection of personal information is now deeply entrenched in Ontario society, but legislation can override privacy rights of faculty members about salary: these rights disappear once one earns a six-figure salary.

10 As I explain in the Epilogue, under the lax procedures way back then, I was hired by the chair of philosophy into a full-time tenure stream position after a brief conversation with a few people, and nothing but the title of my doctoral dissertation written down. I wrote the dissertation over three summers, and then two years after gaining the PhD was considered for tenure because I had been in place for a total of five years.

11 An interesting early twentieth-century example of presidential academic rhetoric is Robert Falconer, "Academic Freedom" (address in Convocation Hall, University of Toronto, 14 February 1922), available online at http://scans.library.utoronto.ca/pdf/1/4/academicfreedomp00falcuoft/academicfreedomp00falcuoft.pdf. Sir Robert Falconer (1867–1943), president of the University of Toronto from 1907 until 1932, was responsible for implementing the recommendations of the 1906 Royal Commission on the University of Toronto, mentioned in Chapter Three.

12 David H. Turpin, Ludgard De Decker, and Brendan Boyd, "Historical Changes in the Canadian University Presidency: An Empirical Analysis of Changes in Length of Service and Experience since 1840," *Canadian Public Administration* 57, no. 4 (2014): 573–88. Practical advice, along with further information on recent departures, can be found in Rosanna Tamburri, "Why Grooming the Next Line of University Presidents Matters More Than Ever," *University Affairs*, 3 August 2016.

6. Is It Now All about Students?

1 At the University of Toronto, a faculty member may be tenured and promoted through the ranks on the criterion of excellence in teaching as long as there is evidence of competence in scholarship. Excellence in scholarship has always been ascertained through a system of peer review and publication, where one's work is judged by acknowledged experts (as we saw in the previous chapter). To establish teaching excellence requires evidence that goes beyond applauded classroom performance and student praise; see University of Toronto, Governing Council, "Provostial Guidelines for Developing Written Assessments of Effectiveness of Teaching in Promotion and Tenure Decisions," available online at http://www.governingcouncil.utoronto.ca/Assets/Governing+Council+Digital+Assets/Policies/PDF/ppmay142003.pdf. It certainly demands a more rigorous approach than is currently found in the United Kingdom's Teaching Excellence Framework.

2 This has been the case at the University of Toronto, where the rank was initially introduced as tutor/senior tutor. The title was changed when I was vice-provost to lecturer/senior lecturer; and then for January 2016 the professorial teaching stream was introduced.

3 For an analysis of 2008 data in Ontario, see S. Vajoczki, N. Fenton, K. Menard, and D. Pollon, "Teaching-Stream Faculty in Ontario Universities." Toronto: Higher Education Quality Council of Ontario, 2011. http://www.heqco.ca/SiteCollectionDocuments/Teaching-Stream%20Faculty%20in%20Ontario%20Universities.pdf.

4 The University of Waterloo, a comprehensive Ontario university of thirty-one thousand students, devotes extensive resources to educational development, listing thirty-five names on its Centre for Teaching Excellence site; of these nine are Instructional Developers or Senior Instructional Developers. See https://uwaterloo.ca/centre-for-teaching-excellence/about-cte.

5 Educational developers are moving towards becoming a profession of their own: see York University, Teaching Commons @ York, "Who?" available online at https://teachingcommons.yorku.ca/educational-development/developing-the-developer/who/.

6 The University of Toronto student services website lists the following twelve services, in addition to the Registrar's offices for each college and faculty: the Student Success Centre, Accessibility Services, Health and Welfare Centre, First Nations House, Family Care Office, Sexual Gender and Diversity Office, Housing, Academic Services, Centre for Community Relationships, Centre for International Experience, Multi-Faith Centre, Career Exploration and Education. See http://map.utoronto.ca/access/student-services. Graduate students may access these offices, as well as their own services for conflict resolution (mainly over supervisory relationships) and leadership; see http://www.sgs.utoronto.ca/gradlife/Pages/default.aspx. Other listings under Student Services include Mentorship and Peer Programs, Orientation, Transition and Engagement, and Sport and Physical Activity.

7 At the University of Toronto in 2013, 2,012 students were registered with Accessibility Services; the following year, there were 2,248, according to the annual reports of Student Life Programs and Services. Recent reports do not give this figure. The Accessibility Services website, at https://www.studentlife.utoronto.ca/as, lists the documents that are available for those requesting accommodation through accessibility services:

- Attention Deficit Hyperactivity Disorder (ADHD);
- Autism Spectrum Disorder;

- Brain Injury or Concussion;
- Chronic Health Issues (for example, Bowel Diseases, Epilepsy, Migraines);
- Deaf / Hard of Hearing;
- Learning Disability;
- Mental Health – both permanent and temporary (for example, Anxiety, Depression, Schizophrenia, Eating Disorders);
- Mobility / Functional Issues;
- Low Vision / Legally Blind;
- Temporary Issues (for example, broken limbs).

8 For the United States, see Association of American Universities, "AAU Climate Survey on Sexual Assault and Sexual Misconduct (2015)," available online at https://www.aau.edu/Climate-Survey .aspx?id=16525). In Canada and the United Kingdom, newspaper reports, largely reflecting particular cases, are troubling; they demonstrate as well how difficult reporting is. See Brandie Weikle, "Universities face increasing pressure to address campus sexual assault," *CBC News*, 13 September 2016, available online at http://www.cbc.ca/news/canada/ campus-sexual-assault-1.3750355; and David Batty, Sally Weale, and Caroline Bannock, "Sexual harassment 'at epidemic levels' in UK universities," *Guardian*, 5 March 2017, available online at https: //www.theguardian.com/education/2017/mar/05/students -staff-uk-universities-sexual-harassment-epidemic. The difficulties of reporting are experienced by victims in the workplace as well as the university: see Claire Cain Miller, "It's not just Fox: Why women don't report sexual harassment," *New York Times*, 10 April 2017, available online at https://www.nytimes.com/2017/04/10/upshot/its-not -just-fox-why-women-dont-report-sexual-harassment.html?emc=edit _nn_20170412&nl=morning-briefing&nlid=71774938&te=1.

9 "Overall, 11.7 per cent of student respondents across twenty-seven universities reported experiencing non-consensual sexual contact by physical force, threats of physical force, or incapacitation since they enrolled at their university. The incidence among female undergraduate student respondents was 23.1 per cent, including 10.8 per cent who experienced penetration" (AAU, "AAU Climate Survey").

10 The Ontario government's "It's Never Okay" action plan cites this percentage.

11 These policies are complex. They need to address issues of confidentiality, respect for the complainant's decision whether to report, support and accommodation for victims, and appropriate penalties for respondents

within the university's competence; they also need to be cognizant of the possibility of civil or criminal charges and proceedings. As an example, see the University of Toronto's Policy on Sexual Violence and Sexual Harassment, available online at http://www.governingcouncil.lamp4.utoronto.ca/wp-content/uploads/2016/12/p1215-poshsv-2016-2017pol.pdf.

12 The raw figures of visits to health, counselling, and psychological services at the University of Toronto carry a multitude of stories: in 2013 there were 48,416 visits; in 2016, 55,744 visits; and in 2017, 59,212 visits. That's an increase of 22 per cent over four years. Not all of these visits will have arisen from mental health concerns, and anecdotal information should be believed only as anecdote. But I can report testimony of experienced counselors about the use of anti-depressants, self-harm (cutting, for instance, as a significant issue among very bright students), and suicidality. Two-thirds of my own class of talented first-year students volunteered that they had personal experience of suicidality or suicide among friends or family.

13 Another anecdote impressed itself on me, about a residence student from eastern Europe so disturbed that she emptied her wallet and went to a subway station to jump in front of a train. But she paused, remembering the kindness of the dean of students' staff, and went to that office. When contacted by a native speaker, her parents couldn't (or wouldn't) grasp the concept of mental illness.

14 The National College Health Assessment survey, organized by the American College Health Association, is delivered every three years. Over 1.4 million students from the United States and Canada have taken the survey. In 2016, sixteen Canadian universities with enrolments of over twenty thousand, including the University of Toronto, reported these experiences of their students in response to the question, "In the last 12 months, have you felt …": overwhelmed by all you had to do (89%), exhausted (88%), very sad (74%), very lonely (68%), overwhelming anxiety (64%), hopeless (60%), overwhelming anger (45%), so depressed (hard to function) (44%), considered suicide (12%), intentionally injured (8%), attempted suicide (2%). For the report for the University of Toronto, see University of Toronto, "Student Health and Well-being at the University of Toronto: A Report on the Findings of the National College Health Assessment" (Toronto, January 2017, available online at http://www.provost.utoronto.ca/Assets/Provost+Digital+Assets/National+College+Health+Assessment2.pdf.

For a UK perspective, see "Student mental health is suffering as universities burst at the seams," *Guardian*, 11 May 2018, available online at https://amp.theguardian.com/higher-education-network/

2018/may/11/student-mental-health-is-suffering-as-universities-burst-at-the-seams.

15 Two-thirds of Canadian students surveyed for their use of services for mental health said they used psychological and medical services; only 4 per cent received help from a minister, priest, or other clergy (University of Toronto, "Student Health and Well-being").

16 Their professional association is the Canadian Association of College and University Student Services; see the website at https://www.cacuss.ca/index.html.

17 At the University of Toronto, the 2016–17 annual budget for Student Life programs is just over $24 million, of which 70 per cent is paid for by students in incidental fees. The average fee for student services in 2013 was about $700 for the academic year for a full-time student – domestic or international. See University of Toronto, "Compulsory Non-Academic Incidental Fees, 2012–13," 29 January 2013, 8, available online at http://www.viceprovoststudents.utoronto.ca/Assets/Students+Digital+Assets/Vice-Provost$!2c+Students/Fees+Schedules/Compulsory+Non-Academic+Incidental+Fees+2012-13.pdf.

18 See the website at http://www.qaa.ac.uk/en. The body now regulating higher education in the United Kingdom is known as the Office for Students; see the website at https://www.officeforstudents.org.uk/.

19 "Standards and Guidelines for Quality Assurance in the European Higher Education Area (ESG)" (Brussels, 2015), available online at http://www.enqa.eu/wp-content/uploads/2015/11/ESG_2015.pdf.

20 A search of the University of Toronto Library catalogue for "learning outcomes" yields 1,405 book titles and 1,122,307 journal articles. Although some items must be unrelated to teaching philosophy (I didn't examine actual titles), the sheer numbers are evidence of the popularity of this idea.

21 A typical description can be found at Massachusetts Institute of Technology, Teaching + Learning Lab, "Intended Learning Outcomes," available online at http://tll.mit.edu/help/intended-learning-outcomes.

22 In Chapter Four I argued that students may have nascent academic freedom as they learn to exercise the knowledge functions of the university under the guidance of their instructors.

23 Residence is only one way of developing a sense of belonging to a cohort. One small example: students in the Vic One program at Victoria University form about 20 per cent of the undergraduate body, but typically about 80 per cent of what are called leadership positions.

24 In Canada, the University of Toronto is at the lower end, McGill at the higher. A US study of one hundred schools places the mean at under

20 per cent; see Kimberly M. Lewis and Tom W. Rice, "Voter Turnout in Undergraduate Student Government Elections," *PS: Political Science and Politics* 38, no. 4 (2005): 723–9.

25 Holly Moore, "Cheating students punished by the 1000s, but many more go undetected," *CBC News*, 25 February 2014, available online at http://www.cbc.ca/news/canada/manitoba/cheating-students-punished-by-the-1000s-but-many-more-go-undetected-1.2549621.

26 Clemson University, International Center for Academic Integrity, https://academicintegrity.org/statistics/. Similar surveys of high school students put the figure even higher: 95 per cent said they participated in some form of cheating.

27 Sarah Marsh, "Cheating at UK's top universities soars by 40%," *Guardian*, 29 April 2018, available online at https://www.theguardian.com/education/2018/apr/29/cheating-at-top-uk-universities-soars-by-30-per-cent.

28 A University of Toronto website posts the decisions of the University Tribunal dealing with cases of academic misconduct; see https://judicial.governingcouncil.utoronto.ca/Reports/Tribunal.aspx.

29 A 2016 article in the *Atlantic* quotes Don McCabe of the International Center for Academic Integrity as claiming that the only reason students stop cheating is that they are being trusted. I'd add that the trust must be mutual: students must trust the institution to deal fairly with them and to protect the integrity of their degrees. See Margaret Barthel, "How to Stop Cheating in College," *Atlantic*, 20 April 2016, available online at https://www.theatlantic.com/education/archive/2016/04/how-to-stop-cheating-in-college/479037/.

30 Shaul Kuper, "The Student as Customer," *College Planning and Management*, January 2014, available online at https://webcpm.com/articles/2014/01/01/the-student-as-customer.aspx.

31 Bea González, "Students as Customers: The New Normal in Higher Education," *Evolllution*, 28 October 2016, available online at https://evolllution.com/attracting-students/customer_service/students-as-customers-the-new-normal-in-higher-education/.

32 See Stefan Collini, "Higher Purchase: The Student as Consumer," *Speaking of Universities* (London: Verso, 2017), chap. 6. See also Louise Bunce, Amy Baird, and Siân E. Jones. "The Student-as-Consumer Approach in Higher Education and Its Effects on Academic Performance," *Studies in Higher Education* 42, no. 11 (2017): 1958–78, available online at https://www.tandfonline.com/doi/full/10.1080/03075079.2015.1127908.

33 A quick Internet search for students as learners reveals a lot of fuzzy thinking and prescriptive language about the difference. One motivation for using the "L" word is that the "S" word doesn't fit adults who enrol in courses. That would be true of "pupil," which does descend from terms referring to minors. but not of "student." Replacing student with learner doesn't work in idiomatic English in expressions such as "student of human nature," "student government," "student hostel," or "student leader" – to pick out a few phrases from the Oxford English Dictionary.

34 From 100 million students in 2000 to 177.6 million ten years later; see "Summary Report" (International Seminar, "Massification in Higher Education in Large Academic Systems," New Delhi, 10–11 November 2014), available on the website of the British Council at https://www.britishcouncil.org/sites/default/files/massification_seminar_in_delhi_-_a_summary_report.pdf. Another source predicts total global enrolment in 2030 to be 414.2 million; see Angel Calderon, "Massification continues to transform higher education," *University World News*, 2 September 2012, available online at http://www.universityworldnews.com/article.php?story=20120831155341147. This growth will, of course, be spread unevenly across jurisdictions. In Ontario, according to the Council of Ontario Universities, the total increase over fifteen years after 2000 was 65 per cent, from 290,000 students to 480,000.

35 See Sightlines, LLC, and Canadian Association of University Business Officers, "Deferred Maintenance at Canadian Universities: An Update" (Ottawa: CAUBO, May 2014).

36 Philip Lee, "The Curious Life of *In Loco Parentis* in American Universities," *Higher Education in Review* 8 (2011): 65–90.

37 Richard J. Light, at the Harvard Graduate School of Education, has studied the many dimensions of university experience; see his *Making the Most of College: Students Speak Their Minds* (Cambridge, MA: Harvard University Press, 2001).

38 The University of Toronto preface to its Code of Student Conduct is a clear statement of the limits of its reach into the behaviour of students, consistent with the rejection of the *in loco parentis* doctrine:

> The University takes the position that students have an obligation to make legal and responsible decisions concerning their conduct as, or as if they were, adults. The University has no general responsibility for the moral and social behaviour of its students. In the exercise of its disciplinary authority and responsibility, the University treats students as free to organize their own personal lives, behaviour and

associations subject only to the law and to University regulations that are necessary to protect the integrity and safety of University activities, the peaceful and safe enjoyment of University housing by residents and neighbours, or the freedom of members of the University to participate reasonably in the programs of the University and in activities in or on the University's premises. Strict regulation of such activities by the University of Toronto is otherwise neither necessary nor appropriate.

See University of Toronto Governing Council, "Code of Student Conduct," 14 February 2002, available online at http://www. governingcouncil.utoronto.ca/Assets/Governing+Council+Digital+ Assets/Policies/PDF/ppjul012002.pdf.

39 In the current concern about sexual assault among university students, the question of whether law enforcement rather than the university should deal with allegations has caused controversy, partly because of widespread claims of ineffectiveness. See Jeremy Bauer-Wolf, "Who Should Investigate Sexual Assaults?" *Inside Higher Ed*, 11 April 2017, available online at https://www.insidehighered.com/ news/2017/04/11/controversial-georgia-sexual-assault-bill-prompts-debate-reporting#.WOyZ4lX3RRA.mailto. The complications for the university's authority grow more entangled when standards of evidence are challenged, when students from different institutions are involved, when registration has lapsed, when incidents occur in another country in summer sessions in which only one person is registered, and so on.

40 See Bill 132, Sexual Violence and Harassment Action Plan Act (Supporting Survivors and Challenging Sexual Violence and Harassment), 2016, available online at https://www.ontario.ca/laws/ statute/S16002.

41 See Manitoba, Sexual Violence and Awareness and Prevention Act, available online at https://web2.gov.mb.ca/bills/41-1/b015e.php.

Chapter Seven: What Knowledge Should Undergraduates Gain?

1 See Darcy Hango, "Gender Differences in Science, Technology, Engineering, Mathematics and Computer Science (STEM) Programs at University," cat. no. 75-006-X (Ottawa: Statistics Canada, 2013), available online at https://www150.statcan.gc.ca/n1/pub/75-006-x/2013001/ article/11874-eng.pdf. Women were 39 per cent of STEM graduates but 66 per cent of graduates in non-STEM fields. Fewer women study engineering, math, and computer science than science and technology.

2 See Ontario Universities, Council on Quality Assurance, *Annual Report, July 1, 2015–June 30, 2016* (Toronto, 2016), available online at http://oucqa.ca/wp-content/uploads/2016/11/QC-Annual-Report-2015-16-FINAL.pdf.

3 This list of over forty professional degrees at the master's level is from the University of Toronto:

Master of Museum Studies; Master of Music, Performance; Master of Visual Studies; Global Professional Master of Laws; Master of Arts-Child Study and Education; Master of Architecture; Master of Business Administration; Executive Master of Business Administration; Executive Master of Business Administration (Global Option); Master of Education; Master of Education, Counseling Psychology; Master of Finance; Master of Financial Economics; Master of Global Affairs; Master of Information; Master of Industrial Relations and Human Resources; Master of Landscape Architecture; Master of Management and Professional Accounting; Master of Public Policy; Master of Studies in Law; Master of Science, Planning; Master of Science, Sustainability Management; Master of Social Work; Master of Teaching; Master of Urban Design; Master of Urban Design Studies; Master of Engineering; Master of Engineering in Cities Engineering and Management; Master of Engineering Design and Manufacturing; Master of Environmental Science; Master of Health Science, Clinical Engineering; Master of Mathematical Finance; Master of Science in Applied Computing; Master of Biotechnology; Master of Forest Conservation; Master of Health Informatics; Master of Health Science; Master of Health Science, Public Health Sciences; Master of Health Science, Medical Radiation Sciences; Master of Management of Innovation; Master of Nursing; Master of Public Health; Master of Science in Dentistry; Master of Science, Biomedical Communications; Master of Science, Community Health; Master of Science, Occupational Therapy; Master of Science, Physical Therapy. See University of Toronto, *Performance Indicators for Governance 2015* (Toronto, 2015), 47, available online at https://www.utoronto.ca/sites/default/files/PI2015_full.pdf.

This list does not exhaust the names of professional degrees available to students in universities in Canada and the United States. A random search pulls up Master of Military and Strategic Studies, Master of Community Medicine, Master of Disability and Community Studies, Master of Physician Assistant Studies (in which one presumably does not study physician assistants themselves), and the curiously named Master of Pathologists' Assistant (which perhaps inappropriately raises the question of who is mastering whom).

4 The *Times Higher Education* reports ("Smarten up: focusing on student employability from the start," 5 May 2017) that the vice-chancellor of the Technological University Sydney claims "[w]e're not preparing people to be students here, but professionals." That's an interesting distinction, given what I said about students as students in Chapter Six.

5 Sense 6a in the Oxford English Dictionary: "Capability of accomplishing something with precision and certainty; practical knowledge in combination with ability; cleverness, expertness. Also, an ability to perform a function, acquired or learnt with practice."

6 In case you're interested, a skillsaw is so called because it is a circular electrical saw used by hand, and therefore requiring significant manual dexterity.

7 I shan't easily forget a conversation with someone who was a colleague for a time of a German philosopher famous for his distinction between I-Thou and I-It relations. When I asked if my interlocutor was treated as a Thou, the answer was no, with the explanation that the philosopher typically answered a question after a lecture by moving impressively close to the questioner for direct eye contact, but (in my interlocutor's account at least) not actually attending to what was being said. Of course – and this must be acknowledged – even if true, a failure to practise what one preaches doesn't invalidate the truth or importance of what is preached. The lack of a skill or its imperfect use reveals only a failure of technique, not a denial of the value of the activity or relationship it is meant to support.

8 Examples of actual stories that I often tell undergraduates: with an English degree you might become a Supreme Court justice or a minister of finance; with a Philosophy degree, an award-winning playwright or the president of a major environmental organization.

9 Derek Bok, *Our Underachieving Colleges: A Candid Look at How Much Students Learn and Why They Should Be Learning More* (Princeton, NJ: Princeton University Press, 2006), 109.

10 The Higher Education Quality Council of Ontario has been particularly active in research in this area. It reports that the Canadian University Survey Consortium surveyed over eighteen thousand graduating students from thirty-six Canadian universities. "From 29 various skills and characteristics, students were instructed to select the three most important areas for growth and development in university. Thinking

logically and analytically was ranked in the top three by 46% of students." Skills for time management and employment were in the top three of only 21 per cent. See Higher Education Quality Council of Ontario, "EduData – Universities should teach logical and analytical thinking, say students," It'sNotAcademic, 25 August 2015, available online at http://blog-en.heqco.ca/2015/08/edudata-universities-should-teach-logical-and-analytical-thinking-say-students/.

11 From the University of Toronto Library catalogue: twice as many books, but fewer articles, than on learning outcomes.

12 See George Fallis, *Multiversities, Ideas, and Democracy* (Toronto: University of Toronto Press, 2007), chap. 2. Fallis also provides an excellent summary of the concerns of his book in "The Mission of the University," Professional File 26 (Ottawa: Canadian Society for the Study of Higher Education, July 2007), available online at https://csshescees.files.wordpress.com/2014/03/pf_26_fallis.pdf.

13 This example has an added personal advantage for me, since I have spent much of my academic life on Plato's Socrates, explored most extensively in my *Reflections on Jesus and Socrates: Word and Silence* (New Haven, CT: Yale University Press, 1996).

14 Much is made of the "Socratic method" as a pedagogical device to elicit answers from students, rather than simply giving them statements to write down or memorize. Certainly a series of well-constructed questions enables the teacher to identify misunderstandings in the student. As Socrates observes about the slave boy in the *Meno*, continued questioning in different forms might provide answers that give evidence of the student's genuine understanding and insight, rather than mere guessing or parroting the teacher's words. That said, many teachers use the technique of pedagogical interrogation to bring students to a knowledge the teacher already possesses. We must recognize that this device is not the one Socrates customarily employs with his interlocutors, since his profession of ignorance is not (at least in my view) ironical. In fact the slave boy episode in the *Meno* is a rare example of successful interrogation in Plato's Socratic dialogues, no doubt because the truth to be discovered is geometrical. The "Socratic method" as practised by its namesake in Plato is a quest for understanding that approaches (often by negative results) the truth, but never achieves complete satisfaction.

15 A late fellow of a Cambridge college told me some time ago that when he was an undergraduate student of literature he had decided to attend Wittgenstein's lectures, but had given up part way through. Wittgenstein saw him on Trinity Street one day, crossed the road to meet him, and said

that he'd noticed his absence – but excused the undergraduate with the reported words, "I specialize in curing a certain sort of stomach ache. You don't have that ache."

16 Literally, an impasse. Plato's Socrates creates an epistemic impasse in bringing his interlocutor (Meno, for instance) to realize not just ignorance but a paralyzing confusion about how to proceed (*Meno* 80a).

17 Vision, discovery, and silence come together in the well-known poem by Keats, "On First Looking into Chapman's Homer." Keats, not knowing Homer in Greek, had depended upon uninspired English translations until he picked up Chapman's "vigorous and earthy paraphrase" of the *Iliad* and the *Odyssey*. In October 1816 he stayed up late reading them with a friend, then before going to bed wrote his sonnet, which concludes:

Then felt I like some watcher of the skies
When a new planet swims into his ken;
Or like stout Cortez when with eagle eyes
He star'd at the Pacific – and all his men
Look'd at each other with a wild surmise –
Silent, upon a peak in Darien.

No language can quite capture the moment of discovery itself. Keats employs the language of seeing to try to capture this experience – watching, staring with eagle eyes, looking at one another.

(I never did get round to writing my own sonnet, "On First Looking into Arrowsmith's Aristophanes.")

18 It's no accident that the ancients thought much about the connections between the true, the good, and the beautiful. Getting reliable knowledge about what's good for human beings involves a longing and striving for those goods as highly desirable.

19 Less important, though, only in the context of information retrieval. Especially at times of emotional intensity, remembered lines of poetry spring to the assistance of the mind struggling to express the inexpressible. The lamentable lack of memorization in schools is remedied, a very little, by poetry recitation competitions.

20 Plato understood this well. In *Republic* VII, his metaphor of education is *turning the soul around* to see the light, rather than putting ideas into someone's head; in the *Symposium*, Socrates rejects the metaphor of the hydraulics of wisdom, as something that can be siphoned from one mind to another. And in the *Theaetetus*, the vivid image of Socrates as midwife,

assisting at the birth of ideas latently present in the student, reinforces not just the necessity of epistemic autonomy, but also the essential role of interrogation.

21 Plato's Socrates controls the interrogative process and doesn't let himself be questioned in significant ways. My view of socratic education, by contrast, encourages reciprocal questioning.

22 Again, my advocacy of socratic education differs from the stance of Plato's Socrates, whose friends think they don't matter to him – at least according to the accusations of Alcibiades in the *Symposium*.

23 A nicely ironic example of what's just not known with any certainty is the etymology of "paltry": see its entry in the Oxford English Dictionary.

24 Here I'll criticize (with respect, of course) my own institution's current graduation ceremonies. It was appropriate to abandon the practice of kneeling before the chancellor to be admitted to the degree. But to have students process into convocation already having hooded themselves before the degree has been conferred is a misrepresentation of the meaning of the hood. Convocation is meant to be a formal conferral of the degree, representing one's attainment of knowledge that has inherent dignity. It's also a celebration of achievement, although selfies and ceremonial dignity fit awkwardly together.

25 This is the Oxford English Dictionary definition; the term isn't frequent in ordinary speech, but it's been around for a century.

26 Blame depends upon responsible agency, which means the agent knows or should reasonably know that the action is wrong. And, for an *ad hominem* observation, the conviction that a nineteenth-century attitude is morally wrong sits uneasily with some popular forms of moral relativism that are also common these days.

27 Recall that in Chapter Five I referred to the legal concept of judging and the inadequacy of determining the quality of a judge's performance by using numbers as measures.

28 Elementary school report cards graded "conduct," as I remember; I never achieved more than a C, to the disappointment of my parents.

29 See Chapter Two, note 5, where I cite the case of the plagiarized dissertation; the character of the offender mitigated somewhat the penalty.

30 Jessica Lahey comments, in "The Benefits of Character Education: What I Learned from Teaching at a 'Core Virtues' School," *Atlantic*, 6 May 2013: "As Gallup polls show that over ninety percent of American adults support the teaching of honesty, democracy, acceptance of people of different races and ethnic backgrounds, patriotism, caring for friends and

family members, moral courage, and the Golden Rule in public schools, it seems odd that this facet of American education has disappeared from public debate over curriculum and academic content. The core virtues – prudence, temperance, fortitude, and justice – make it into nearly every lesson we teach at our school and every facet of our daily lives on campus."

31 See David Brooks, *The Road to Character* (New York: Random House, 2015), chap. 10. His section on the Humility Code has fifteen propositions that relate to some of the epistemic attitudes I discussed in the previous section, including epistemological modesty. A thoughtful critique of contemporary values, the book advocates a view of character that was partially shaped by a seminar at Yale offered over three years. That's what the university does: it *structures conversations* about ideas and values rather than forming character.

   In my first year Vic One seminar on virtues and vices, we discuss issues such as gluttony, lust, avarice, and lying; the point is not to prescribe behaviour but to provoke self-reflection and deliberation about the attitudes, choices, and commitments that make for human flourishing.

32 In *Idea for a General History with a Cosmopolitan Purpose* (1784), Proposition 6; Brooks makes use of this notion in ibid., chap. 1.

33 Socrates carried out his inquiry in the *agora*, the market place, not to educate *for* the market, but to see what those going about their normal business understood about the value and meaning of human life. A Socrates reborn in our time might well ignore cobblers, cooks, and tanners in his philosophical quest, and visit instead molecular biologists, nanoscientists, macroeconomists, and portfolio managers, acknowledging their expertise (they would all have impeccable degrees and credentials), but questioning their grasp of the fundamentals of human well-being and happiness and what their expertise had to do with that.

34 The responses can't be very sophisticated, making the notion of a conversation rather weak. One is reminded of those Socratic dialogues in which Plato gives very few words to the respondents to Socrates' questioning. They amount to the repetition of "yes" or "no" or "I don't know." (I once tried to write a poem titled "As I said to Socrates the other day" using only those kinds of response. It didn't make much sense.) But at least Socrates interacts with individuals whose epistemic state he can judge, not large groups of relatively anonymous students.

35 One particular example: the Ideas for the World program at Victoria University. In brief, students meet over food with faculty or community

leaders in eight- or twelve-week sessions to discuss current topics. There are several sections, in two of which students act as tutors for community members unable to attend university. The program is well subscribed, and offers learning without extra work. When I asked why students kept turning up even when exams were looming, they explained that they weren't being judged. For information, including media reports, see Victoria College, "Idea for the World, available online at http://www.vic.utoronto.ca/students/I4W.htm.

8. What and Where Are Well-Placed Universities?

1 I explain how I came to this view in reading Plato on avarice, in "Plato on Philosophy and Money," *Philosophy in the Contemporary World* 7, no. 4 (2000): 13–20.

2 Not just the ancients, as Shakespeare's Hamlet demonstrates: "What a piece of work is a man! How noble in reason! how infinite in faculty! in form, in moving, how express and admirable! in action how like an angel! in apprehension how like a god! the beauty of the world! the paragon of animals! And yet, to me, what is this quintessence of dust?" (II.2).

3 See Centre for Addition and Mental Health, *Ontario Student Drug Use and Health Survey 2015* (Toronto), available online at https://www.camh.ca/en/science-and-research/institutes-and-centres/institute-for-mental-health-policy-research/ontario-student-drug-use-and-health-survey---osduhs.

4 Some of whom are troubled enough to cut the flesh that is otherwise ignored: see note 14 in Chapter Six, and Susan Seligson, "Cutting: The Self-Injury Puzzle," *BU Today*, 4 March 2013, available online at https://www.bu.edu/today/2013/cutting-the-self-injury-puzzle/.

5 Julia Cresswell, *Oxford Dictionary of Word Origins* (Oxford: Oxford University Press, 2010), under "alma mater."

6 When we surveyed students on their reasons for choosing Victoria College, half the responses commented on the beauty of the campus with its stone buildings and ivy. I came to believe that, although their architectural judgment might have been superior, the more likely explanation is that the architecture represented a community that has persisted through time with stability and grace. The buildings have endured; the community will endure; and I am becoming part of it.

7 Engaged alumni are all the more willing to support their university financially. As I remarked in Chapter Three on alumni donors, the alumni

relations and fundraising functions should be seamlessly connected in university administration.

8　Marilynne Robinson, "Imagination and Community," in *When I Was a Child I Read Books* (New York: Farrar, Strauss and Giroux, 2012), 23.

9　I am indebted to Professor Robert Gibbs and the Jackman Humanities Institute at the University of Toronto for many discussions (more and less formal) about the place of the university in the city.

Index